D0817693

The Expert Expat

revised edition

Praise for the New Edition

"This comprehensive A-Z guide to international relocation is an easy and interesting read, peppered with relevant anecdotes from real-life experiences. It should be on the shelf of every international corporate HR department and I highly recommend this as required reading for expats and expats-to-be—whether it is the first or the fiftieth international move."

—Faye Barnes, President of the Associates of the
American Foreign Service Worldwide, (AAFSW) and former Director,
Family Liaison Office, US Department of State

"The revised edition is even more comprehensive than the first! Readers will benefit from the newly expanded chapters, especially the one exploring the challenges of relocating third culture kids. The authors offer terrific advice on raising global nomads in the 21st century."

—Robin Pascoe, author of *Raising Global Nomads: Parenting
Abroad in an On-Demand World*, www.expatexpert.com

"Moving abroad to live and work with family in tow is not easy, even when you have done it several times before. Linderman and Hess have covered all corners in this newly updated and revised edition of *Expert Expat*, which now includes invaluable information on safety and security and advice on moving with children that is bang up to the minute."

—Jo Parfitt, author, writer and speaker,
specializing in expatriate living

More Praise . . . from the first edition

"The authors draw on their vast, global experience to give suggestions for dealing with the transition challenges that can so easily overwhelm both the new and the veteran traveler. The information in this book lets the reader follow one of the authors' most fundamental adjustment suggestions: 'Talk to people in a position to know.' These authors know."

—Terri L. Williams, Vice President, Associates of
American Foreign Service Worldwide

"*The Expert Expatriate* weaves practical tips, insightful advice and firsthand experience into an informative guide to living abroad. Melissa Brayer Hess and Patricia Linderman have done a tremendous job addressing both the challenges and rewards expats face during all stages of expatriation and repatriation."

—Betsy Burlingame, President,
www.expatexchange.com

"For anyone considering a move overseas, *The Expert Expatriate* is a must-have. Authors Brayer Hess and Linderman have written the definitive guide to living abroad, filled with practical advice, invaluable tips and rich resources on how to cope with every challenge from learning a new language to helping children and pets adjust. This book won't sit on the bookshelf. It will be consulted often."

—Christine Uber Grosse, Professor of Business
Communication, Thunderbird,
The American Graduate School of
International Management

"I wish that *The Expert Expatriate* had been available when we first joined the U.S. Foreign Service some thirty years ago. This is not yet another dispassionate and footnoted treatise on moving and cultural adaptation. Rather, *The Expert Expatriate* is brimming with wise, compassionate and usable advice from its sensitive and perceptive authors. Because the two authors have either lived or are living this life, their comments all have the ring of authenticity. Anyone who is about to embark on an expatriate existence should read this book before doing so. His or her capacity to adjust and thrive will be all the more enhanced for having done so."

—Metter Beecroft, President, Associates of the
American Foreign Service Worldwide (AAFSW)

"*The Expert Expatriate* is a bible for families facing the simultaneous, peak stresses of moving abroad—changing jobs, homes, schools, neighbors and colleagues, and cultures. It demystifies the adventure and encourages positive coping strategies: from careful planning to reaching out to reconnect in one's new surroundings and to asking often for help."

—William Courtney, former U.S. Ambassador to Georgia and Kazakhstan; Senior VP, National Security Programs, DynCorp

The Expert Expatriate should be required reading for anyone preparing for the adventure of overseas living or contemplating a move abroad. With extensive experience living abroad, the authors provide invaluable, practical advice across a full range of issues—logistics, language, family, employment—involved in creating a successful experience living in a foreign country and in returning to the country of origin."

—Melanie Newhouse, Executive Director, Foreign Service Youth Foundation

The Expert Expatriate? Don't make a move without it! Brayer Hess and Linderman cover the transpatriation cycle from the first whisper of a sojourn through reentry with impressive breadth and depth of detail. Clearly written by two who have lived—and deeply appreciated—life in the global corridor, the book is of particular value to parents guiding their children through experiences likely to enrich and inform the rest of their lives.

—Norma M. McCraig, Founder, Global Nomads International; President, Global Nomads Resources

"A fusion of practical advice and personal experience that will undoubtedly help first-timers come to grips with relocation and even provide experienced expatriates with food for thought. From trailing males to the importance of language learning, Brayer Hess and Linderman write honestly about the expatriation experience, including the problems and frustrations as well as the many joys of living abroad."

—Alex Johnson, Joint Editorial Director, *The Broadsheet*, Spain's Monthly Magazine for English Speakers

"[*The Expert Expatriate*] contains a wealth of advice and ideas for any would-be expat, all of it coming from the best possible source, first-hand experience. Anyone going to work on a foreign assignment or just to live in another country will find this book a valuable resource. It won't make culture shock go away, but it will prepare and equip readers to better cope with it and all the other practical issues and problems such a move involves—before, during and after."

—James Simpson, Former Director of Organizational
Effectiveness, Texas Instruments Europe

"Finally, a hands-on, real-life guide to successful overseas relocation written by women who've been on the move for years. Authors Melissa Brayer Hess and Patricia Linderman demystify everything from the nerve-wracking countdown to moving day to getting settled in a new home halfway around the world with kinds, and more. With *The Expert Expatriate* at your fingertips, you'll get it right the first time. Don't leave home without it."

—Ritta Yee and Vera Nicholas-Gervais, www.expatcoach.com

The *Expert Expat*

revised edition

Your Guide to Successful Relocation Abroad
moving, living, thriving

Melissa Brayer Hess

and

Patricia Linderman

NICHOLAS BREALEY
PUBLISHING

BOSTON · LONDON

First published Nicholas Brealey Publishing in 2007.

20 Park Plaza, Suite 1115A
Boston, MA 02116, USA
Tel: +617-523-3801
Fax: +617-523-3708

3-5 Spafield Street, Clerkenwell
London, EC1R 4QB, UK
Tel: +44-(0)-207-239-0360
Fax: +44-(0)-207-239-0370

www.nicholasbrealey.com

© 2007 by Melissa Brayer Hess and Patricia Linderman

All rights reserved. No part of this publication may be reproduced in any manner whatsoever without written permission from the publisher, except in the case of brief quotations embodied in critical articles or reviews.

Printed in the United States of America

11 10 09 08 07   1 2 3 4 5

ISBN-13: 978-1-85788-384-8
ISBN-10: 1-85788-384-5

Library of Congress Cataloging-in-Publication Data

Hess, Melissa Brayer.
    The expert expat : your guide to successful relocation abroad : moving, living, thriving / Meliss Brayer Hess and Patricia Linderman.— Rev. ed.
        p. cm.
    Rev. ed. of: The expert expatriate : your guide to successful relocation abroad : moving, living, thriving, 2002.
    ISBN 978-1-85788-384-8
    1. Moving, Household.   2. Americans—Foreign countries—Handbooks, manuals, etc.   3. Intercultural communication—Handbooks, manuals, etc.
I. Linderman, Patricia.   II. Hess, Melissa Brayer. Expert expatriate.   III. Title.
TX307. H485 2007
648'.9—dc22

                                                                2007030062

As with the first edition, the authors will continue to donate a portion of their proceeds from the sale of *The Expert Expat: Your Guide to Successful Relocation Abroad* to the Senior Living Foundation, Washington, D.C., an organization that assists elderly members of the American Foreign Service and their spouses.

Visit the authors' website dedicated to this book, *www.expatguide.info*, for updates, links, contact information, and much more.

Dedication

To David, my husband, who made the international experiences possible, and to John and Elizabeth Brayer, my loving and supportive parents, who were always there for me.

—M.B.H

To my husband and sons, who have been the best traveling companions I could wish for, and to my writers' group, the SUNwriters, who have provided nonstop encouragement, help, and support.

—P.L.

Contents

Foreword

As part of a military family, I know firsthand what an enormous undertaking it is to relocate abroad. After weeks of checklists, sorting, and last-minute shopping, you ready the children and ship off the furniture. Then, once all the people, pets, and belongings converge on your new home, you face the daunting task of putting everything back together, settling in, and adjusting to life in a new culture! An international assignment is always exciting, but relocating and successfully adapting to life in a new environment can nonetheless be challenging and exhausting.

It is a pleasure to have the opportunity to introduce this book. The authors, Melissa Hess and Patricia Linderman, have over 30 years of overseas experience between them. They have written this book to share their expertise and hard-learned lessons, hoping to help others deal with the challenges inherent in an overseas relocation. Melissa and Patricia have a talent for bringing the expatriate lifestyle alive, using their own anecdotes and those of others around the world to draw the reader into this rich experience. These are the voices of people who know the reality of living in foreign cultures.

The Expert Expat is more than a simple "how-to" book. You will find plenty of handy tips and good advice on the mechanics of moving. But you will also benefit from the authors' thoughtful reflections on what it means to uproot your family, leave your homeland, and adapt to life in another culture.

The story behind this book's creation is also a remarkable modern-day "cyber event," illustrating how technology has changed expatriate life for the better. The authors collaborated on their concept, sold the idea to the publisher, and wrote this book without ever meeting in person! They first met "virtually" as members of an e-mail group while Melissa was living in Ukraine and Patricia was in Germany. Seeing a need for a book on coping with international relocations, they worked entirely over the Internet to combine their experiences and complete the manuscript! They met in person at the publisher's office only shortly before the book's first edition went to press. I commend this book and its wealth of information to anyone contemplating relocation overseas. It can help simplify, untangle, and enrich what will be one of the greatest experiences of your life.

Alma Powell
Spouse of former U.S. Secretary of State Colin L. Powell
Revised June 2007

Acknowledgments

We would like to express our warmest appreciation to the following people:

For her gracious endorsement of our book: Alma Powell (Mrs. Colin L. Powell).

For ongoing encouragement and invaluable support: Mette Beecroft and Terri Williams, Presidents Emerita, Associates of the American Foreign Service Worldwide; Jan Fischer Bachman; Fritz Galt; Francesca Kelly, Founding Editor, Tales from a Small Planet (*www.talesmag.com*); Kelly Midura, webmaster of *www.aafsw.org* and owner of a web design business; and Pat Olsen. *For inspiration and for being a role model to Melissa:* Dr. Christine Grosse, Thunderbird School of Global Management, Glendale, Arizona.

For going through the entire first edition (!) on her own initiative and offering extremely helpful ideas and personal experiences: Meg Sondey.

For being an always-helpful colleague and a good sport about titles: Robin Pascoe.

For immensely broadening our point of view with their suggestions, experiences, and anecdotes: Renate Alison; Natalie Bennett; Sheri Mestan Bochantin; Suzi Bowles; Fanny Brakchi; Celia Burnett; Janis Foster; Mimi Gabriel; Antonio Graceffo; Nohemí Hartmann; Victoria Hess; Amanda Holmes; Shannon Jamison; Francis Jewell; Alex Johnson; Doug Judge; Katty Kauffman; Colleen and Frank Kothbauer; Dawn, Alexandra and Loic McKeever; Holly Nesbit; Nancy Nolan; Helen Pattison; Kristin Pollock; John Quintus; Steven C. Rice; Martha and João Sanches; Elizabeth, Andrew, Alfred, Charlie, and Eva

Simkin; Isobel Stevenson; Kristi Streiffert; Heike and Dan Terrell; Cheryl Thompson; Michelle Zacharias; and Claudia Zegarra.

For advice on writing and publishing: Mark Taplin, author, *Open Lands: Travels Through Russia's Once Forbidden Places.*

For sharing his veterinary expertise: Robert L. Hatch, D.V.M., Palm Valley Animal Clinic, Goodyear, Arizona.

For advice on shipping pets overseas: Maureen Johnston and the staff of the Overseas Briefing Center, National Foreign Affairs Training Center, Arlington, Virginia.

For patient encouragement, high standards, and steadfast belief in our project: Judy Carl-Hendrick.

And last but not least, to Patricia O'Hare, Erika Heilman, and the rest of the staff of Nicholas Brealey Publishing for their expert guidance and ongoing support of our book.

Introduction

Welcome to the adventure of living abroad! The first step that begins the expatriate* experience is the international move. It is a challenging undertaking to leave a familiar environment behind, confront a new language and culture, and adapt to a very different social and work environment.

The more you do to prepare yourself for this challenge and the more you know about cultural differences and strategies for adjusting to your new country, the more positive your experience will be. This book will show you the way. As two diplomatic spouses with a combined total of 33 years of overseas experience and 21 international moves, we share our own experiences and those of countless other expatriates to help guide you. You will

- learn how to get organized quickly and find the support you need,
- acquire packing and moving tips from people who have moved many times,
- understand the importance of learning the local language and discover ways to maximize the results of language study,

---

*We define an *expatriate*, or *expat*, as anyone who is living outside of his or her home country, either on a permanent or temporary basis. Note that this meaning has nothing to do with the concept of patriotism or being proud of one's country, although the terms are sometimes confused.

- develop strategies to confront a new culture and successfully adapt to your new environment,
- learn ways to support children as they face the challenging but enriching experience of living abroad,
- find out how to take a pet with you as you move,
- learn useful strategies for addressing security, safety, and health concerns,
- find out about employment, volunteer, and creative opportunities for accompanying partners,
- and discover ways to maintain strong ties with family members, friends, and colleagues back home and to lessen the shock of reentry when you return to your home country.

The book you are holding is an expanded and updated version of a guidebook first published in 2002. Since that time, much has changed in the world. The globalization process has continued to advance. Terrorist strikes and the responses to them have increased concerns about security and have made traveling and obtaining visas more of an ordeal. The fear of potentially global health epidemics is rising. At the same time, technology has made it possible for a telecommuter to live on a Mediterranean island while working for a company in New York; for teenage friends to instant-message each other between Taipei and Toronto; and for a grandmother in London to see and talk to her grandchildren in Nairobi on her computer. As we prepared this new edition, we have taken account of these and other developments, adding new insights and fresh points of view from people currently living abroad.

This book is aimed at all expatriates—single and married, employees and accompanying spouses,* with or without children, and moving between any two countries. In this new edition, we have added even more information that we believe will be helpful to the growing categories of

---

*Note: For simplicity—since "partner" can refer to a business partner, and the repeated use of "spouse or partner" can be awkward—we sometimes refer simply to "spouses" in this book, although it is not at all our intention to exclude the many unmarried couples living abroad.

single expatriates and those moving without support from an organization, such as a company, government agency, university, church, or military or diplomatic service.

If you are still undecided about moving overseas, reading about the challenges and opportunities discussed here will help you make an informed decision about whether this experience is right for you. However, to provide a common starting point, we assume throughout this book that you have already made plans to move abroad. If you are still in the decision phase, we recommend that you also review the helpful suggestions in chapter 1 of *GenXpat: The Young Professional's Guide to Making a Successful Life Abroad* by Margaret Malewski (Intercultural Press, 2005). Whether you are still undecided or have already made plans to move abroad, we suggest that you read this entire book before starting your international move. Understanding the process as a whole will help you prepare effectively from the very beginning.

Although the challenges of moving to another country are undeniable, the rewards and opportunities can be even greater. During our years overseas, we have gained in-depth knowledge of other cultures, learned languages, visited exotic and beautiful places far off the tourist track, gotten involved in helping local people in need, and formed close friendships with people from all over the world. We've tested our personal limits (emerging, we think, more flexible and resilient), broadened our view of the world and global affairs, and enjoyed adventures we could never have experienced at home. With this book—along with a bit of flexibility, a sense of humor, and a good dose of curiosity about new people and places—you'll be well equipped for your international adventure. Welcome to the world, and let's get moving!

CHAPTER 1

Getting the Information and Support You Need

Your overseas adventure is about to begin! Along with the excitement of travel and new experiences, you will also need to face all the work of preparing, moving, settling in, and adjusting. Whether this is your first time abroad or you are a seasoned expatriate with several international transitions behind you, every successful move begins in the same way: gathering information about your new location and finding the support that you need.

Preparing adequately for your time overseas will help you avoid mistakes and unpleasant surprises, give you an idea of what to expect and what to bring with you, reduce the early period of helplessness expatriates often experience, and lessen your culture shock. You will feel more confident and will be able to settle in more quickly and easily.

The list of tasks that must be completed before you leave may seem daunting—perhaps selling your car, renting out your house, arranging for others to take care of certain things for you, and completing a stack of projects at work. While you may be tempted to postpone your preparations for daily life abroad so you can finish these tasks at home, don't do it: Save yourself time and aggravation later by *making* time now to prepare for life in your new location.

To make the most of your limited preparatory time, take a moment before you start to consider the ways in which you prefer to receive information. Do you enjoy learning about a new topic from books and websites? Does the idea of a cross-cultural seminar or expatriate orientation appeal to you? Would you rather e-mail questions to a knowledgeable person, or meet face to face for an unstructured question-and-answer session? Taking advantage of all of these options is ideal, but if the date of your move is fast approaching, stick with your preferred resource method and focus on getting the basic information you need. This chapter will provide suggestions about what you can do before you leave and resources that can be of help.

Getting started: the basics

The following list outlines the basics of what you need to do before you leave:

- Gather up-to-date information on passports, visas, work permits, and other requirements
- Identify and contact a moving company as early as possible
- Get a head start on learning the language and culture in your new country (see chapter 2)
- Research specific information you will need to start your new job, as well as the support your employer will provide for your move, if any
- Look into information about and support for obtaining housing
- Learn about living conditions in the host country, including schools for your children and employment opportunities for your spouse, if needed (for advice about a school search, see chapter 5, and for employment considerations for accompanying partners, see chapter 9)
- Solicit tax, financial, and insurance advice
- Explore information about health care and insurance
- Find one or more "sponsors" in the country to help you get settled during the early weeks

If an organization or company is sending you overseas, it will probably provide some level of support. As an employee, you need to know exactly what that support will be. If your organization does not take the lead in explaining what it can do for you and what you should expect to do for yourself, then initiate a meeting with the appropriate person or department. If possible, include your spouse in the meeting to discuss the specifics of your relocation. Will you initially live in a hotel? Will the company help you find an apartment or house, or are you expected to find one on your own? What allowances are offered in areas such as housing, schooling, and home leave?

We suggest you use the preceding list as a basis from which to begin asking questions. It is in your best interest, as well as that of the organization sending you, to have a clear understanding of the kind of support that will be provided and what you will have to handle on your own. This is especially important when a spouse and/or children are involved. Family adjustment problems continue to be the leading reason for failed or prematurely terminated overseas assignments. Of course, every person's experience will be different, and there can be any number of reasons why things go wrong. Unrealistic expectations of what you thought your organization would (or should) do for you do not have to be among them. With some organizations (such as diplomatic missions), expatriate benefits are a fixed package. For many private companies, however, they can be subject to negotiation. For instance, you may negotiate a certain level of benefits in order to accept an assignment in the first place, or you may ask to increase certain allowances (such as schooling) in exchange for others. If you will be working for an organization with little experience sending people abroad—or a local company with few expatriate employees—you may need to do your own research to figure out what kind of benefit package will be fair and adequate in your situation. If you are in this situation, we recommend Margaret Malewski's detailed and helpful advice in chapter 2 of *GenXpat: The Young Professional's Guide to Making a Successful Life Abroad* (Intercultural Press, 2005).

If you are going abroad without a sponsoring organization—or if your employer offers only a salary but no support—you will have to work harder to find what you need. Again, use the list cited earlier as a guide. A good relocation consultant may be able to provide the kind of support an organization would: helping you find a moving company, housing, and schooling as well as providing an orientation to the new country. Look for a relocation service with branches in both the country you are leaving and your new host country. If you can't find one, you still have options. Consider hiring a local person to assist you when you arrive, especially if you don't speak the language. This person can serve as your interpreter, assist you in finding a place to live, show you shopping centers, and help you get other necessary errands done. How do you find such a person? A good place to start is by contacting expatriate groups or real estate agencies in your new host country. Think about what your most immediate needs will be (this book will help) and what the person or agency can do to help. You may only need to hire someone for a day or so each week or on weekends.

Fellow expatriates can be an invaluable source of help, even before you arrive. They will understand many of your needs and can help point you in the right direction. As soon as you know where you are going, start making contact with individual expatriates in your new location—they're usually more than willing to help newcomers. Numerous expatriate websites offer forums, message boards, and e-mail groups where you can start networking. We also update our book's website, *www.expatguide.info*, with a list of the leading resources.

Other sources of information and support

Additional places to find information and support include the following:

The embassy, consulate, or official website of your new host country. Look for updated information on visas, work permits, the tax system, required immunizations and health exams, pet health certificates, importation of personal goods, and other official regulations and requirements. The U.S. State Department's website at *www.state.gov* (click on "Countries") offers a wide range of information that can be useful to travelers and expatriates of other nationalities in addition to U.S. citizens.

Your own country's embassy in your host country. The embassy may provide information about work permit requirements, business opportunities in your host country, security issues, and local expatriate groups from your country. Your embassy may also provide help with overseas voting, lists of doctors and lawyers, and assistance in an emergency.

Colleagues in your host country. Your new co-workers or colleagues in your profession, whether they are fellow expatriates or local employees, may be willing to help fill the gaps where official support from your organization is lacking. They can also provide a very valuable "unofficial" perspective on what conditions are really like in your host country; see if they are willing to answer your questions by phone or e-mail.

Expatriate groups in your host country. In addition to the traditional English-speaking or American women's clubs, a wide range of expatriate groups have sprung up in cities around the world with significant international populations. These may include business networking groups, singles' organizations, charitable groups, sport-based organizations, religious groups, and informal circles such as groups of expatriate parents with young children. Some have websites; otherwise ask your colleagues or embassy in the host country to provide you with contact information. If your new location has no active expatriate groups, look for organizations in a nearby large city or the capital of your host country. Although you may not be able to make face-to-face contact with these group members, they will probably be happy to give you useful practical and cultural advice via e-mail or phone.

People from your host country living in your home country. Immigrants, foreign students, language teachers, and temporary employees may respond with enthusiasm when you express an interest in their country—and they may provide valuable networking opportunities with their friends and colleagues at home. Consider posting a notice at a university foreign student office or language school asking for help and advice about your new host country. You may hire the person for a few hours or exchange some service for the information, such as helping him or her with English.

Cross-cultural trainers and other professionals specializing in expatriates' needs. Look for courses or seminars focusing on the business culture or general culture of your new host country.

Expatriate websites and blogs. New websites and blogs are springing up all the time, offering advice on moving overseas, information about life in specific countries, forums where you can ask questions, and personal accounts of expatriates' lives abroad. Try searching for the word *expat* or *expatriate* and the name of your host country.

Specialized books. Search online bookstores for specialized books on your host country's culture, history, natural environment, travel opportunities, and so on. In addition to travel guides, look for books written specifically for expatriates, such as the Culture Shock! series or books published by Intercultural Press.

One expat notes:

It will make things not seem so "strange" if, when you get to your new residence, you can identify the birds bathing in the street puddles or the bush that blooms so beautifully in the park around the corner. Plus, if you know a little local history, you'll make fewer faux pas like not recognizing a famous local or national hero!

Local publications. Maps of your new city, real estate information, local newspapers (if you can read them), phone books, local expatriate publications, newcomers' guides, tourist information booklets, and local Chamber of Commerce publications can be helpful. Ask a colleague in the country to send you some of these, or stock up during an exploratory visit.

Tax, financial, and insurance advisers. Look for those experienced in working with expatriates in your host country. You will need a tax accountant who has experience dealing with both your home and host countries' tax systems, because you may face complicated issues; for instance, you may have to pay taxes to your home country, the host country, or in some unfortunate situations, both.

Assessing your readiness for a cross-cultural move

In a foreign environment, the single most important source of support you will draw upon may be your own internal resources. Moving into a completely new environment can challenge you in ways you have never been tested before. Life in a foreign country takes you out of the "comfort zone" of your own culture and requires you to rely on yourself as you face new and unfamiliar situations. Though this may not always be easy, the experience provides many valuable opportunities for personal growth.

Cross-cultural researchers have identified numerous personal skills or characteristics that appear to help people successfully face the challenges of expatriate life, including:

- The ability to tolerate frustration, ambiguity, and failure
- Open-mindedness and tolerance of differences
- Flexibility and adaptability
- Curiosity and enjoyment of new experiences
- Good communication and observation skills
- Self-reliance and a strong sense of self

- A sense of humor and the ability to laugh about your own mistakes and misadventures

Of course, individuals fall along a continuum with respect to all of these qualities. No one is absolutely flexible or absolutely inflexible—we all find ourselves somewhere in between. However, those closer to the "flexible" side of the spectrum will probably have an easier time adapting to new living, social, and working conditions.

Some of these traits may be closely related to your natural temperament as well as your past experiences. However, there is evidence that they are also skills that can be developed through training, conscious effort, and/or new experiences. As you read the following sections, consider where you fall on the continuum as you assess your current "readiness" for a cross-cultural move, and think about ways you can enhance your skills in each area.

The ability to tolerate frustration, ambiguity, and failure

In a foreign culture, you can't always get what you want when you want it. In addition, your personal view of how things should be or how they should work may clash with the reality of life in your new country. You may find yourself angry at others and at yourself when things don't work as you think they should.

In a foreign culture, and even in your own, you often have no control over circumstances that may happen. However, you always have the choice of how to react to them. There are certain to be times when your natural reaction is to become frustrated or angry about challenges in a foreign environment. However, you may be able to temper those feelings by educating yourself to better understand the different ways of doing things in your host country. Studying the culture, taking cross-cultural training, or talking with others who have lived in the culture longer than you have are proactive steps to broaden your perspective. You can also prepare yourself with a few anti-stress techniques (such as meditation or exercise) that work for you. Above all, try to develop a more relaxed attitude by taking a wider view of mistakes and frustrations; they will not be permanent, and they may even provide the opportunity for new insights or a fresh start.

A British woman in the U.S. reports:

> *I've always been quite highly strung, but being an expat has definitely made me a much more laid-back person, and people often comment now on how I can just take whatever is thrown at me right in my stride, which wasn't always the case previously.*

Open-mindedness and tolerance of differences

Have you lived, worked, or gone to school alongside large groups of people from different cultures? How did you react? Living in a foreign culture will require you to work and socialize with people whose ways of thinking are quite different from yours. For example, in some cultures, the idea of safety precautions such as putting a baby in a car seat may be rejected because of the belief that God or "fate" will protect the child. Chapter 4 provides suggestions on increasing cross-cultural tolerance and understanding.

Flexibility and adaptability

Whether you are adapting to a new workplace, school, or living arrangement, life is always changing. Some people welcome change, while others are more comfortable with routine. If a new environment tends to be a challenge for you, pay close attention to the suggestions in chapter 7 about easing the transition and reducing stress. Preplanning also becomes more important, so that some aspects of your new environment will be familiar even before you arrive. Taking an exploratory trip, if possible, is also highly recommended.

Curiosity and enjoyment of new experiences

Of course, all people enjoy some kind of a balance between the familiar and the new. But those who are especially eager to learn about and explore the world around them naturally tend to have a more positive experience abroad. If your tastes run more to the familiar, think about the interests you already have—for instance, playing tennis, volunteering at an animal shelter, and collecting antique toys—and figure out how you might be able to pursue them in your new country.

Good communication and observation skills

If you have found yourself unintentionally making social blunders in the past, the good news is that your international experience is likely to raise your social competence (as blunder-prone Patricia was happy to find). Living in another culture tends to sharpen your communication and observation skills. Get an early start by studying the language if you will be in a foreign-language environment (see chapter 2). Practice observation by looking at people (even those from your own culture) with an anthropologist's eye. How do they interact? Do they hold doors to let older people go through first (as in Korea)? When they enter a room, do they shake hands with everyone (as in Germany)? Writing a blog, journal, or series of e-mails home from your new environment can help reinforce your observation skills.

Self-reliance and a strong sense of self

If you are going abroad by yourself, think about your ability to navigate an unfamiliar and sometimes even hostile-seeming environment alone. Build self-reliance by preparing yourself with plenty of advance information. Bring along some stress-busters (e.g., good books, music, or an exercise routine) to fill lonely evenings (see chapter 7 for more advice on singles' adjustment). A strong sense of self is needed as your identity changes abroad, especially among spouses who were formerly employed full-time but now cannot work. The book *A Portable Identity: A Woman's Guide to Maintaining a Sense of Self While Moving Overseas* by Debra Bryson and Charise Hoge (Transition Press, 2005) is particularly helpful—and not just for women.

A sense of humor and the ability to laugh about your own mistakes and misadventures

Having a sense of humor doesn't mean that you are not serious about your life and work—it means being able to step back and see things from a broader perspective. Laughing not only feels good; recent research has shown that it's actually good for your health and stress levels. To cultivate your sense of humor, think often about things that make you smile—amusing memories, funny scenes from movies, or the cute antics of a child or animal. When something goes wrong, think to yourself "How can I find humor in this?" If you can, the inevitable frustrations of expatriate life will seem much more bearable—and you'll come away with hilarious stories to tell.

Living conditions in your new country

To prepare yourself adequately for life in your new country, you will need some specific information on housing and living conditions.

- Typical housing for expatriates and the pros and cons of various locations.
- Goods available locally and items you should bring with you (such as nonperishable foods, personal care items, household needs, and children's supplies).
- Information about electrical appliances (voltage, adapters, appliances provided in typical housing).
- A description of furnishings, if furnished housing is provided, or the types of furnishings you should bring with you.
- The local dress code and the kinds of clothing you will need.
- The local health care system, including the kind of insurance you will need and the supplies you should bring with you.
- Advice about bringing or purchasing a car: host-country restrictions, availability and price of unleaded gasoline, and so on.
- Local employment opportunities, salary ranges, and work permit regulations if you or your spouse will be looking for work.
- Availability and cost of Internet, satellite, cable, cellphone, landline and other services. For instance, can you use your current cell phone in the new country? You may have to have it "unlocked" by your provider, or sell it and purchase a new one abroad.
- Banks, ATMs, and credit or debit cards you can use.
- Information about the international or organizational mail system and customs requirements. Will it be feasible to place orders online and receive packages?
- Information on schooling: What types of schools are available? Are programs in place for children with special needs? Is there a waiting list? What paperwork is required?

- The availability and cost of household help.
- Local recreational opportunities: What equipment and supplies should you bring?
- The expatriate community and typical social events: Do people tend to wear suits and dresses, or shorts and sandals?

This advice and information may come from your colleagues, expatriates in the host country, or other sources such as those mentioned earlier. No matter who advises you, however, keep in mind these three guidelines:

1. *Ask people in a position to know.* For example, if you want to know about employment opportunities for your spouse, ask an accompanying partner who is already working locally. If you are asking about household supplies to bring along, ask the member of the family who does the shopping.
2. *Always ask more than one person.* People may be misinformed, or they may simply have different perspectives. One expatriate may tell you that a particular school is wonderful, for example, while another has nothing but horror stories to relate.
3. *Ask open-ended questions.* Since you are researching an environment that is new to you, find out as much as you can with your questions. For example:

- What do you wish you had known before you arrived?
- What would you suggest I bring with me?
- Where can I go for more information?
- What would you do if you were in my situation?
- Who else should I talk to?

An exploratory trip

An exploratory trip to your new host country can be an extremely valuable part of the information-gathering process. Even if you don't have the benefit of employer-paid exploratory travel, the trip can be worth the money. Most expatriates recommend that both spouses go, unaccompanied by children. (Exceptions would include high school students as well as children with special needs for whom special school arrangements may be necessary.) If you choose to take an exploratory trip, consider the following:

- Arrange to have a colleague or relocation consultant (or at least a knowledgeable real estate agent) show you around.
- Schedule appointments in advance with colleagues (and their spouses, if you are married), representatives of local expatriate groups, and schools, if applicable.
- Look at neighborhoods, possible housing, schools, recreational facilities, and transportation systems. Be sure to include health facilities if you or a family member has a medical concern.
- Ask a colleague or other expatriate to take you to grocery stores and other shops used by expatriates so you can get an idea of what is available and what you may want to bring.
- Seek out sensory impressions; explore as time permits and make lots of notes so that the environment will not seem so strange when you arrive.
- Look especially for positive aspects of the new environment that you can look forward to. Start planning your first outing or adventure.
- Ask the people you meet if they are willing to answer follow-up questions by e-mail.
- Take photos and/or video recordings back to children or extended family.
- Try to look beyond any disturbing elements in the environment (such as beggars, trash, security bars on windows, etc.). Focus on the total quality of life for expatriates in your new country.

Patricia reports:

I moved to Leipzig, in former East Germany, nine years after the Berlin Wall came down. The city was being gradually renovated, but there were still abandoned, soot-blackened buildings everywhere, with their windows broken out. The alley behind our building was full of trash and graffiti. The ugliness was shocking at first. But on the other hand, we could walk from our apartment to the restored downtown area, have coffee and cake at an outdoor café, hear a concert in the church where Johann Sebastian Bach was musical director, and ride our bicycles through a huge city park. The charms of the city definitely outweighed its discomforts.

The importance of a sponsor

When you arrive, you probably won't know how to buy food, find a doctor, get around, or do much of anything else. Having one or more sponsors for your first weeks can make a huge difference in your adjustment and your effectiveness at work or at home.

A *sponsor* is another expat (or sometimes a local person) who has experience "on the ground" and is willing to help you with your transition. This may include providing advance information, getting things ready for you, greeting you as you arrive, and helping you get settled. If you don't work for an organization that automatically assigns sponsors to newcomers, ask if a volunteer would be willing to assist you—perhaps on the condition that you will help another newcomer in the future. Companies and other organizations should be aware that newcomers, and especially family members, without adequate support may have trouble coping with overseas life and may even insist on returning home, wasting the organization's resources, putting the family through great trauma, and negatively affecting the employee's career. An effective sponsorship program can go a long way toward avoiding such disasters. If your organization does not have one, lobby to get one started, for the organization's sake and your own.

If you are moving abroad without organizational support, your need for a sponsor may be even greater—although you may have to get creative to find one. Contact a range of expatriate groups through the channels mentioned earlier and take every opportunity to network. If your religion is represented in your new community, the organization may offer help.

An expat in Mexico advises:

If all else fails, get a phone book for your new location (or check online), look for global companies, and call them and ask if they have expats!

As you find contacts to correspond with by e-mail, ask if they would be willing to provide some support on your arrival. You might offer to pay them, exchange favors, or bring them something special from your home country. A friendly real estate agent or paid local driver or guide can also be extremely helpful during your first days and weeks.

An ideal sponsor should have the same family situation that you do (e.g., with children if you have children—see chapter 5) and live near your new quarters, rather than an hour away across town. He or she must be willing and able to devote some time to helping you, especially on arrival. It is also very useful if your sponsor volunteers well in advance, so you can communicate ahead of time. Of course, you may not find someone who fits this ideal. If this happens, find others in your organization or the expatriate community to provide backup assistance.

If one member of a couple arrives in-country before the other, you will need a sponsor for each of you. One woman we know relied on her husband, who had been in the country for several months, to serve as her sponsor. She sums up the experience in two words: "Big mistake!" Her husband was tied up at work during the day, leaving her to figure out how to get around town, register their son at school, buy food, and take care of other practical details by herself. Ask your sponsor to help you with the following:

- Meet you at the airport, or at least give you clear instructions about taking a taxi (which services are reliable, what to say, and how much it should cost).
- Double-check your housing (whether it is a house, temporary apartment, or hotel) before you arrive, to avoid unpleasant surprises.
- Shop for a few basic foods and necessities to carry you through the first few days (if you are not staying in a full-service hotel). You may want to give your sponsor an idea of the kinds of food items you would like. If there are any special dietary considerations, be sure to mention them.
- Shop, also, for household items such as paper napkins, plastic wrap, aluminum foil, trash bags, and basic cleaning supplies.
- Provide basic information to you on arrival, such as a list of colleagues' phone numbers, numbers for emergency services, taxis,

restaurant delivery, and so forth. A map that includes your neighborhood is also very helpful.

- Lend you things you may need when you arrive or show you where to buy them.
- Take you shopping and help you take care of other immediate errands, such as renting a car or registering a child at school.
- Introduce you to colleagues and local expatriates.
- Be generally available during the early weeks to continue showing you around and answering your questions.

Sponsors assigned to newcomers by their organizations sometimes view the task merely as a formality and do not offer much real help. You may be able to get an idea about your sponsor's level of commitment from phone calls or e-mail contact before arrival. If you suspect that the support offered to you will be inadequate, contact other colleagues or an expatriate group or relocation consultant in your new city before arriving for backup support. If your resources permit, you may want to make reservations at a hotel with concierge services for your first week or so in the country. Insufficient support during the stressful and exhausting arrival period can potentially threaten the entire overseas assignment.

If things start to go wrong and frustration sets in, don't hesitate to speak up, state the problem, and find out what you can do about it. The "stiff upper lip" sometimes has its place overseas, but not during the vulnerable arrival period. In most cases, colleagues or other expatriates will be quite willing to help. Sometimes all it takes is letting others know.

Some thoughts to remember

Don't take for granted what other expatriates or your colleagues do to help you adjust. At the same time, don't feel guilty about "imposing" on people. Pitching in and helping newcomers is considered part of the routine in most expatriate communities, and your sponsor probably benefited from the same kind of help not too long ago. When you get to the point where you start to feel settled and most of the frustrations have passed, go back and thank the people who helped you. Let them know that you appreciated their efforts. Then, when the next new people arrive, it's your turn. Repay your sponsor by being there to help the latest newcomers, in the same way that others were there for you.

With or without support, you will always experience some degree of frustration during the preparation and arrival process. When it hits (and it will), keep telling yourself that you are going to make it through the rough times. Others have done it and so can you. Try to take frustrations with a laugh (or at least a smile) rather than blowing up. A sense of humor is an excellent coping mechanism—particularly useful in getting you through the stresses of an international move and the first weeks in a new country.

CHAPTER 2

Learning the Local Language

We've been in Monterrey for only four weeks, and it is very difficult for me, since I do not speak Spanish. I spoke French when we were posted in Africa and it made a big difference. I know language training is a full-time job and I didn't want to devote that time to it. But now I sure wish I spoke just a little Spanish! By all means, if you have the opportunity, take language training to avoid feeling like a helpless idiot!

—An accompanying spouse in Mexico

Why should you study the local language? The answer is simple: Learning the language will help you make the most of your time abroad. Language skills, even limited ones, open the door to fuller, richer, and more varied experiences. You will meet more people, work more effectively, explore more places, and gain a better understanding of the culture of your host country. Learning a new language also opens you up to new ways of thinking and expressing yourself. Indeed, many people report that they seem to take on a new personality when they speak a foreign language. The ability to communicate in a foreign language also provides an added benefit: it can greatly lower the stress of arrival in a new place. It helps lessen two of the main difficulties affecting newcomers: change overload and a drop in self-confidence (see chapter 7). If you have studied the language, that is one less thing that will be new and confusing in your new environment. And even small successes in the local language will help boost your self-confidence, while the inability to read the label on a carton of milk or say "Excuse me" when you bump into someone will have the opposite effect.

Being plunged into a foreign-language environment without knowing a word of the language is like regressing to the level of a newborn baby: You cannot understand what is going on around you or make your needs known to others. Without the language you will be more isolated, move solely in English-speaking circles, and rely on help from others to get things done. The more proficient you are in the local language, however, the more effective and self-sufficient you will be in the new environment. You can take a local taxi; make a phone call; communicate with sales clerks, maintenance people, and domestic help; ask for directions if you get lost; and so forth. Being able to speak the language helps speed your adjustment to a new place and will help improve your quality of life in a foreign environment. And don't worry about being fluent—even having a beginner's proficiency when you arrive is better than being speechless, and if someone hears you trying to speak the language, in most cases, your efforts will be appreciated.

Melissa reports:

> *During my first week in Kiev, Ukraine, I was on my own during the day to figure things out. I needed groceries, but unfortunately I was in an area of the city where there were only a few "Soviet-style" stores. These were places where you had to tell the lady behind the counter what you wanted and then she would get it for you. Needless to say, I was thankful I spoke Russian. I knew how to ask for what I wanted, and when the lady heard my accent, she became very friendly and started to chat. Without the language, the shopping experience would have been quite a different story. I probably would have looked, turned around, and walked out of the store!*

Speaking Russian enabled Melissa to function independently, buy what she needed, shop by herself without relying on anyone else, converse with a local person, and not feel intimidated by the new culture. Her level of stress was greatly diminished through the use of her language skills.

Of course, there are some cases where language study is not as important as it was for Melissa in Kiev. You may be going to a country where English, or another language you already know, is spoken. Even in that case, however, it is a good idea to familiarize yourself with different words and expressions that are used there while doing your preliminary research on the culture.

In many other countries English is spoken, at least by the well educated, in addition to the local language (or languages). Still, learning at least a few conversational phrases before you arrive will help you make a good first impression. You may be going into a situation where you are isolated from the local society, in a foreigners' compound or military base with its own stores, schools, and other necessities of life. Here, a foundation in the language may give you the ability and confidence to venture out into local society rather than being a "prisoner in the palace."

Getting the language training you need

As just mentioned, language skills are important not only on the job but in every aspect of daily life. Many organizations recognize the importance of language training for accompanying family members as well as for employees. Statistics show that a family's satisfaction is a major factor in the success of overseas assignments, and in turn, language competence has a significant influence on everyone's adjustment.

Accompanying spouses are on the "front lines" of a culture and are often the ones who must do the shopping and other family errands, deal with maintenance workers, and interact with neighbors. Clearly, spouses with language facility will carry out these tasks more effectively, as well as feel less frustrated and isolated. If the accompanying spouse lacks language skills, on the other hand, he or she may be forced to depend on the spouse or someone else from the office to navigate the basic chores of everyday life.

With a happier, more independent spouse and a less stressful home environment, the employee can more readily meet the challenges of an overseas assignment and will be able to put more energy into his or her work instead of dealing with problems at home. Although it may be easier and more cost-effective for the organization to provide training after arrival, at least some preliminary training will reduce the stress of culture shock (see chapter 7) and get the overseas assignment off to a good start.

If you are single and will be living alone, language training is especially useful and important. Besides the demands of work, you will have to take care of all the details of daily life on your own. Even minimal language skills will help you cope with these challenges, communicate within the new culture and reduce the isolation that may accompany culture shock.

Some people mistakenly assume that expatriates can simply "pick up" the language from the environment once they arrive in the country. This is the way children learn, they may argue. However, when parents talk to children, they tend to speak slowly and carefully ("Do you see the doggie?") and wait for the child's response—very much like a language class! Watching hours and hours of local TV won't do the trick, although we've known expatriates who have tried. We recommend some level of preparatory training for everyone in the family aged 10 and above. If younger children will be attending school in the new language, they should have preliminary training as well, at least to the point where they can have a simple conversation and make their needs known (see chapter 5).

Thus, if you work for an organization that does not already offer predeparture language training, try making these two points to the appropriate administrator:

1. Language competence reduces culture shock and raises overall morale, and therefore contributes to the success of the overseas assignment.
2. Language-competent employees are more effective at work, and language-competent family members are more self-sufficient and need less support from the office in their daily lives.

If you are moving overseas on your own—or if your organization refuses to support language training—you still have many options. You may be put off by the high cost of individual language lessons or small-group classes. However, there are many other options for language training, as discussed later in this chapter, and one or more of them will surely suit your schedule and your budget.

How much training is necessary?

An American woman in Kiev, who has an engineering degree from a prestigious university in the United States, complained that she couldn't speak Russian because she "didn't have an ear for languages." When asked how long she had studied Russian, she replied, "I took a six-week survival course."

Misconceptions are common about the time and effort required to gain fluency in a foreign language. Advertisements promise success in "only a few hours a week." Yet many people are disappointed to note that although they studied a language for several years in school, they cannot hold a sensible conversation in that language today. They may conclude, like the woman in Kiev, that they have no aptitude for learning languages.

Learning a language is a lot like mastering a skill such as figure skating or playing the piano: Talent helps, but the main requirements are time, effort, and the willingness to take risks and laugh off mistakes. And just as with those skills, regular practice is necessary to keep up your ability in a language and to make further progress.

Melissa reports:

To prepare for my assignment in Leningrad, U.S.S.R. [now St. Petersburg], I studied Russian for six hours a day over a period of six months. At first it was frustrating and even comical. Each of the class members struggled to mimic sounds and didn't even come close to pronouncing them correctly. Sometimes we were so pathetic, we couldn't help but laugh. It took weeks before we could make sounds comprehensible to our Russian teacher. From there, we started to build vocabulary and grammar. At the end of six months, we weren't fluent, but we were able to make conversation and had enough vocabulary to function in basic, everyday situations. It took six months of full-time study to acquire a base from which we could progress.

The time required for language training varies considerably, depending on the difficulty of the language, the skill level you would like to reach, your knowledge of other languages, and (to a lesser extent) your talent.

For people who speak only English, Russian is a relatively difficult language. Western European languages such as French, Spanish, and Italian may take only half as much time to master. On the other hand, languages such as Chinese, Japanese, and Arabic are even more difficult for most English speakers than Russian.

You may not be able to commit six hours a day to learning your target language, as Melissa did. However, like ice skaters and piano players, you will need regular practice to keep up your skills. In our experience, language learners need *at least three hours a week* of focused study, plus homework, to make any progress at all. With less than that, they find themselves just going over the previous week's vocabulary and learning it all over again.

The good news is that *the first 100 words are the most important.* After all, a few common words and expressions are encountered again and again in daily life: "Hello," "Good-bye," "Thank you," "Excuse me," "Stop," and so forth. Learning how to pronounce the sounds of the language, how to say and respond to basic greetings and simple questions and answers, and how to read common signs, labels, and menu items will take you very far in a new country and give you a foundation on which you can build.

Becoming "fluent" in a language is the ultimate goal—but it may be more than you need. The word *fluent* comes from the root "to flow," and it means that you can speak freely—you may still make mistakes here and there, but you can express nearly everything you want to say in the language. You *can* reach this point with enough time and dedication, but you can also have a perfectly enjoyable overseas experience at the semifluent skill level reached by many expatriates—phrases in the language supplemented by gestures, a few English words thrown in, and hasty searches in a pocket dictionary. In most countries, the local people will be impressed and delighted at your efforts to communicate in their own language and will gladly help you along.

Another piece of good news is that learning languages becomes easier with practice. The more you study and work with languages, the more you begin to understand how they work and develop your own strategies for learning them. If you go through the process of studying and becoming proficient in one language, the next language will not seem as daunting.

You will have a better frame of reference and a higher level of confidence from which to begin your study.

Training options

If you are responsible for your own training (whether reimbursed or not), it is important to consider all available options in order to decide which is best for you. All have advantages and disadvantages. Often, the ideal solution may involve a combination of methods; for example, a short "survival course" provided by your organization may be supplemented through tutoring and self-study. In this section, we will briefly describe the main advantages and disadvantages of each training method as well as other considerations when choosing a program.

Academic courses

Classes in your target language may be offered by a local university or adult education program. Although you will probably receive little specialized attention as a member of a large class, you can probably find other students willing to get together outside of class to practice. The structured environment, with homework and examinations, is highly motivating.

Language schools can be found in most good-sized cities. Compared with university classes, they generally have more flexible schedules and offer a wider range of course options. Small classes or one-on-one tutoring may be offered. Some language schools have developed their own textbooks and teach all students using the same method; others may tailor their programs to the students' requirements. Most schools will allow you to take a sample lesson before signing up for a complete program. A private language school is a relatively expensive option, but the school also has a stake in your success and may make special efforts to accommodate your needs, such as arranging an individualized schedule and changing teachers if necessary.

Working with a tutor

The obvious advantage of tutoring, whether privately or through a language school, is that the program can be tailored to your needs and progress. However, the flexibility of tutoring can also be a disadvantage if you find yourself canceling appointments every time something else comes up. If you work with a tutor, set a schedule and stick to it; paying in advance or paying for missed sessions is one way to maintain this discipline. Also, work out ways for your tutor to monitor your progress using a textbook or self-designed quizzes. Homework and outside practice must also be part of any effective tutoring program. Some tutoring arrangements tend to degenerate into conversation periods, with little progress on the student's part.

Finding the right instructor

Language teachers or tutors may be found through language schools, newspaper ads, university bulletin boards, or by word of mouth among an immigrant or expatriate community. Try to find someone with previous training and experience; *not everyone who speaks a language is able to teach it effectively.* Take a sample lesson before committing to any program.

Many people assume that it is always preferable to learn from a native speaker of the language. However, without special training in language instruction, a native speaker usually has trouble explaining grammar and other rules of the language; after all, he or she learned them as a child and may never have consciously focused on them. A well-trained nonnative speaker, on the other hand, has gone through the same learning process you are facing and may be able to explain things to you more effectively— and more accurately.

If you are learning a language spoken in many countries, such as Spanish, make sure you are learning the version spoken in your target country. The accent and vocabulary can differ greatly; for example, *guagua* (pronounced "wa-wa") means "baby" in Chile but "bus" in Cuba!

Independent study

Self-study options include textbooks, courses on CD, interactive computer programs, correspondence courses, and Internet-based programs. Although these methods can be very effective and inexpensive, they require a high level of discipline and self-motivation. Studying with a partner can help keep you both going.

As Melissa's experience in Russian class shows, learning to pronounce new sounds and speak understandably is a large part of the challenge of beginning a new language. If you are studying on your own, it is very important to make sure you are learning the sounds correctly from the start. Once you learn incorrect pronunciation, you must break that habit—which is not easy to do. Just a few sessions with a tutor may do the trick, depending on the difficulty of the language and your skill at mimicking sounds; people who can imitate others' accents have a head start here.

Taking advantage of your learning style

Melissa reports:

> I had to learn French before going on my first overseas assignment. I was assigned a French-speaking tutor, who worked one-on-one with me, using lessons from a textbook. I had never studied any language previously and found the grammar complicated and the sounds difficult to mimic. I went home discouraged after each lesson. I didn't know it at the time, but my tutor told my husband that I would never speak French. She stated that I was simply incapable of learning the language. When the time came and we moved to France, I enrolled in a class at a language school for foreigners. I spent three hours a day observing and listening to a native speaker of French explain the grammar and lessons. I wasn't forced to speak a lot at first. I could watch, absorb, and then practice what I learned. This method worked for me. In a very short time, I was building my vocabulary, constructing sentences, and using what I learned. It began to make sense. At the end of the year, when we left the country, my proficiency was adequate enough to sell our car to a woman who spoke only French. A few years later, I even earned a college degree in French! How I wish I could track down my first tutor again to show her how wrong she was. I wasn't the problem—the training method was.

With such a wide range of training options, it's important for you to know which study methods work best for your individual learning style. Knowing your preferred style not only will save you time and unnecessary stress, it will also promote more rapid progress.

It is true that aptitudes for language learning differ, and if you have a learning disability, you may find language learning even more difficult. This certainly doesn't mean it is impossible, but you may have to work harder to find the study methods that work best for you.

What is a learning style? The body of literature on learning styles contains many varied ideas and theories about the way we learn. One basic concept, however, is common to all the research: Not all people learn things the same way; there is no one right way to study. For example, some people retain information more easily when they see words or pictures (visual learning), while others prefer to hear spoken words from a teacher or listen to CDs (an auditory style). Still others favor a hands-on (kinesthetic) approach to learning. In addition, some students do their best work alone, while others prefer to learn by interacting in a group. For some a calm, uncluttered environment is important for study; others thrive on a little chaos.

A number of popular books provide questionnaires to help you determine your preferred learning style. More simply, just think back over your past educational experiences. How did you prefer to study? Did you get together with a group of fellow students or work alone? Did you make written lists of facts or ask your friends to quiz you? Did you prefer learning out of books or through hands-on practice?

Once you have an idea of the study environment and methods that work best for you, you can avoid the situation Melissa faced with her French teacher—a learning style that didn't respond to the teaching method. Try to adapt your language program, including supplementary study, to suit your style. For example, visual learners might make extensive use of textbooks, workbooks and computer-based programs; study using word lists, grammar charts, and pictures; and label objects in their homes. Auditory learners might prefer extra hours of classroom time, followed by CDs and movies in the target language. A restless kinesthetic student might especially profit from an interactive computer program or outings with a native speaker. Many people find that they have a mixture of styles, or that their preferred learning methods have changed over the years. If you are still not sure what methods are best for you, try out a few sample lessons before committing to a program, or borrow a CD course, computer program, or textbook from another language student or your local library.

Ways to maximize your success

No matter what method you choose, you can maximize your results by following a few general guidelines. The most important is to take every opportunity to *practice and reinforce* what you are learning. Like the piano playing and ice skating mentioned earlier, language learning requires constant practice. Almost no one can learn vocabulary words or grammar rules just by looking at them or hearing them once. They must be practiced again and again and used in conversation to convince the brain that they are important and worth keeping.

Reinforcing the same material in a number of different ways is especially effective. In a traditional language class, you will probably read your textbook, listen to your teacher, complete some writing exercises, and do some speaking. There are also other ways you might consider to reinforce the material you are learning.

- Read aloud to yourself, a partner, or a recording device.
- Record your teacher in class (with permission) and use the recording for extra practice.
- Listen to audio material on CD or a digital player while commuting, exercising, doing house or yard work, and so on.
- Take advantage of spare moments by carrying language materials wherever you go. Software such as the Rosetta Stone series on a laptop computer offers quick and effective practice.
- Search libraries and online bookstores for books in your target language. Books aimed at children up to about second grade can be helpful to language learners; above that level, they quickly become surprisingly complex, so don't be discouraged if you have trouble with them! Try a romance novel or thriller, or a translation of a book you have already read in English.
- Write or type out key phrases and vocabulary words to help fix them in your memory.
- Test yourself with an interactive computer program or old-fashioned flash cards.
- Post notes, quotations, and even poems around your home. If everyone in the household is learning the language, surprise each other with little notes in the target language.

- Think up associations. It's easy to remember the Czech word for *hello* (*ahoy*) if you think of sailors greeting each other. Ask your teacher about associations other students have used, or make up your own.
- Use physical props. Using senses such as touch and taste will help fix the words in your memory. For example, you might touch something cold and say the word for that sensation in your new language. Consider using props to help you learn the names of colors, foods, articles of clothing, and so forth.
- Rent or go to see a movie in the target language that also has subtitles. Listen to the pronunciation, notice any nonverbal communication patterns, and see if you can find discrepancies between the dialog and the subtitles.

Other strategies

The following additional suggestions may also be helpful.

- Work on pronunciation first. Grammar and vocabulary won't help if people can't understand you.
- Recognize that languages have different structures as well as different words. Resist the temptation to translate word for word from English into your new language. Practice translating whole phrases and sentences instead. For example, if you're speaking German and want to say you're feeling hot, you might be tempted to say *"Ich bin heiss"* (literally "I am hot"). However, that actually means "I am sexually excited." The correct translation is *"Mir ist heiss"* ("to me is hot").
- Consider the cultural context as well as the meaning of the words as you speak your new language. For example, the first thing many English speakers say to each other is "How are you?" Naturally, we look for this expression in other languages and try to use it in polite conversation. However, in some countries, asking strangers about their health is considered excessively personal. And in others, it is rude to ask about the individual's well-being without asking after his or her family at the same time.
- Use the "double-check" method whenever you use a two-language dictionary. For example, you might look up the word *nuts* in an

English-French dictionary, hoping to describe a food you want to buy from a market stall. Cross-check your result in the French-English part of the dictionary, so you won't end up asking to buy eccentric people, those things that fit on bolts, or worse!

- Remember that many languages have varying forms, accents, and dialects, depending on where they are spoken. Iraqi Arabic may not get you far in Morocco, and Castilian Spanish is quite different from the everyday language in the Dominican Republic.

- If possible, study the language during the time of day when your energy levels are highest. Many people find that their ability to absorb new concepts and vocabulary words differs greatly depending on the time of day.

- Find a study partner if that suits your particular learning style. Partners tend to keep each other motivated and on track.

- Set realistic goals and follow through on them. Track your progress in some way: through tests, sections completed in a textbook or computer program, or evaluations by a teacher or tutor.

- No matter what your schedule is, make a commitment to do some homework or extra practice every day. At the very least, learn one new word, phrase, or expression each day.

- Seek out as many ways as possible to expose yourself to the language—and culture—before you arrive in the country. Visit websites and blogs in the language or dedicated to the country, download audio material, or find magazines in the language on a topic that interests you.

- Use the power of rhyme. As ancient storytellers knew, it is much easier to memorize poems and song lyrics than plain text. Look for popular music and children's songs—the lyrics can often be found online—as well as rhyming poems in your target language. Sing along with the songs and read the poems aloud. Also, think of ways to use music and rhyme to help you memorize words and grammar rules. It may sound silly, but once you memorize a list of troublesome verbs set to music, you'll never forget them.

- Take advantage of any opportunities you can find for interaction and conversation. Get together with fellow students for regular conversation sessions. Of course, a patient native speaker willing to converse with you offers the best kind of interaction.

A word about conversation

As children learn language, they are not embarrassed about making mistakes. They may say "he goed" before they learn "he went," and it doesn't bother them at all. Adults and teenagers, though, are often seriously inhibited by the thought of making mistakes and sounding foolish. Many would rather wait until they can speak "perfect" sentences before attempting a conversation. This is unfortunate, because the trial and error of two-way conversation is a great way to learn.

A Canadian woman in Japan reports on what helped her most to learn the language:

> I talked as much as I could, especially to friends who were not Japanese and could not speak English. Their Japanese was easier for me to understand, and we had to use the common language out of necessity.

Many people find that when they converse informally, for example, with fellow students at a university hangout, their foreign-language conversation flows astonishingly well. This has jokingly been called "the beer theory of language learning." Beer, of course, is not necessary—its contribution is simply to make the language student more relaxed and uninhibited. For the same reason, you will probably also find that you speak more easily with friends than with people you want to impress (unfortunately!). Work on overcoming your inhibitions and accepting the fact that you are going to make mistakes. Enjoy the triumph of that first flowing conversation, when you may not have said everything right, but at least you made yourself understood. It's a great feeling.

If you're still not making progress

If your language study is not going well and you are frustrated with your progress, ask yourself these five questions.

1. Are you genuinely making language study a priority? The human brain is extremely practical: it doesn't retain information that

doesn't appear important. If you study only casually, the result can be the proverbial "in one ear and out the other."

2. Are you spending enough time on your language studies? Three hours a week of class, plus daily homework, is an absolute minimum.

3. Are your expectations too high? Remember that studying a language as an adult is extremely challenging. Give yourself credit even for small achievements and celebrate your progress.

4. Have you found the right teacher? As Melissa found while learning French, sometimes the fit between teacher and student makes a big difference.

5. Is the training method you selected right for you, and does it fit your learning style? Another approach may be more effective.

Finally, remember that every word you learn in the local language carries you an important step forward. Even if you end up learning just a little of the language, it may be enough to ease the transition and help you through daily life in your new country.

If you arrive without language skills

If you do arrive in your new country without speaking a word of the language, there are several measures you can take, in addition to those discussed earlier in this chapter, to build your skills quickly.

- Make a list of useful words and phrases and find ways to use them with native speakers of the language. Start with simple greetings and work up from there.
- Make note of the words you commonly see on street signs, billboards, or other advertisements, and find out what they mean. Reading them repeatedly in your daily life will help reinforce them.
- Try to read every written text that comes your way: local newspapers, advertising flyers, even utility bills. Look for words that are similar to those in your own language, and make note of unfamiliar words that crop up again and again.
- Carry a mini-dictionary and notebook (or palmtop computer) with you, and use every opportunity to look up and list new words.

Don't forget to use the cross-checking method described earlier when you use your dictionary, to avoid being like the traveler who asked a porter to carry his "trunk" and used the word for an elephant's nose!

■ Run errands with a local person, if possible, such as a local friend or household employee. Watch and listen carefully to the words and expressions the person uses.

An American expat in Mexico reports:

Attending religious services has been one of the best ways for us to improve our Spanish. First of all, there is always some chitchat at the beginning as people gather. This is a good time to practice greetings, the weather, and so on. In our service, words for songs are projected on the wall, so we can sing along even if we don't exactly know what we are singing about. There are often readings, and we have a bilingual religious text (in our case, a Spanish-English Bible).

■ Ask around for someone who is interested in practicing his or her English in exchange for helping you with the local language.

■ If you begin language lessons in your new country, consider taking as intensive a schedule as possible. This will help you gain needed confidence, and, in addition, being in the foreign-language environment will allow you to use your skills right away and multiply any gains you make.

Like an international move itself, learning a language is undeniably challenging, yet it offers unique opportunities. It gives you the chance to navigate a foreign environment comfortably and competently. It opens up the possibility of meeting people who don't speak English—perhaps including some who have never met anyone from your country before. And it opens up the secrets of another culture—from its daily conversations to its literature—as nothing else can.

CHAPTER 3

Managing Your Move

Patricia reports:

It was late December, a few weeks after we arrived in Trinidad. Our temporary apartment was pretty bare, except for a small potted tree with a red ribbon on it. I had worked overtime up until our departure, and now I was supposed to be doing the creative writing I had always wished I had time for, but I could hardly drag myself out of bed, let alone write. I seemed to spend the whole afternoon each day just trying to make dinner out of the bewildering, limited selection at the neighborhood market. Finally, our small crate of expedited airfreight arrived. It would have been such a celebration to unpack Christmas gifts and decorations, some pleasant music and inviting books, swim masks and snorkels for the nearby beach we hadn't even visited yet, but all the crate contained was our computer and printer, padded with paint-spattered jeans and the other clothes we had worn during the hectic moving days and final housecleaning. Dirty clothes! We threw most of them away in disgust. And the computer—nothing more than a word processor in those days— just sat on the desk for several weeks, unused.

An overseas move is much more complicated than a domestic one. There is more paperwork, more to worry about—and more that can go wrong. At the same time, the psychological stakes are higher. A well-managed move can help ease the transition to a new country, while a poorly planned one can add to your stress, just when you need it least.

The main goal in managing the logistics of your overseas move is not simply to get your possessions from point A to point B, but to *support your adjustment* to your new overseas environment. This means, among other things, you need to do the following:

- Plan ahead to minimize last-minute scrambles or disasters, so you are not already stressed-out when you arrive
- Get financial matters and other paperwork in order, to avoid problems and protect your peace of mind
- Pack in excess baggage or send via airfreight things that will help reduce your stress and provide a sense of home in the early weeks (as Patricia neglected to do in the introductory example)
- Choose items to include in your household shipment that will help you make the most of your stay overseas

Every move has its rough spots—a stomach virus that hits the whole family on moving day or a frantic search for an essential misplaced document. The advice in this chapter will help you minimize the inevitable traumas of the transition so that you can get on with the adventure of living and working in a foreign country. We have included in the Appendix a sample moving plan that provides you with checklists of things to do from the day you make the decision to move abroad.

Planning ahead

As soon as you know when and where you will be moving, create a moving plan. This should include what will you need to do and when will you need to do it. Many of the tasks that need to be accomplished are mentioned in this chapter, but your specific situation may call for others, such as taking a medical exam or making a quarantine reservation for your pet. Consult your relocation consultant, personnel office, or other sources of information (see chapter 1) to be sure you are aware of everything that must be done before you leave.

The list of things to be done may seem long and intimidating—even impossible—especially if you are also making time (as we recommend) for language learning and cross-cultural training. Consider delegating some of these tasks to hired professionals. If you've always wanted to hire a personal assistant, now may be the time!

If you have a family, try to divide up tasks so that everyone feels involved but no one feels unfairly burdened. For example, a teenager might make a video of your belongings for a household inventory. Avoid assigning most of the work to an at-home spouse, with the excuse that the employee spouse is "too busy" at the office. This is unfair (a married employee should at least be allowed enough time off to do everything a single employee would have to do), and the resulting resentment could strain your relationship when it needs to be as strong as possible (see chapter 9).

If you are single, recruit some close friends for support. Extra help is especially valuable as you separate your possessions into various categories (e.g. storage, air and sea shipments) and supervise teams of movers. A bonus: friends who have helped you prepare for your overseas adventure may also be more likely to take the plunge and visit you abroad. Also, if you are employed, try to resist the pressure to work overtime finishing up mountains of projects before you leave. Your colleagues will have to muddle along without you soon anyway. Gradually taper off your activities, and take time off work for necessary moving chores. This can help you avoid stress overload.

Timing your packout

Because your household shipment might take weeks or even months to arrive, you might have to choose between (1) having the movers come early and "camping" for a while in your old location or (2) scheduling your moving day (called "packout" among expatriates) at the last minute and "roughing it" longer in your new country. As tempting as it may be to maintain your normal routine as long as possible, we strongly suggest that you pack out early if possible. Many expatriates move into temporary furnished housing for the days or weeks after packout. Living without your belongings is much easier in your home country, where you already know how to handle the details of life and have a support network in place. If you are shipping a car, sending it early can help minimize the time you spend after arrival without transportation or with an expensive rental car.

Packing out early also offers another advantage: it provides a breathing space between the hectic period of sorting your belongings and the move itself. If you will be renting out your home, packing out early also gives you extra time to clean and otherwise prepare it without your belongings in the way. This is what Patricia and her husband did before leaving for Trinidad. They had the movers pack up their household a month early and moved into a temporary apartment, taking the computer with them to finish up last-minute work and instructing the movers to come to the apartment later for their small airfreight shipment. They congratulated themselves on avoiding a last-minute rush and having time to paint and fix up their home for the new tenants before they left.

Unfortunately, however, they did not think about the importance of their airfreight during the even more stressful arrival period to come. They should at least have taken appropriate airfreight items with them to the temporary apartment, so that they would end up in Trinidad with more than just a computer and useless paint-spattered clothes!

An expatriate in Italy notes:

> I've learned this the hard way: I will never again pack out and leave the country in the same week. You need at least a week in between to say good-bye to friends and places and to wrap up a million little details.

Organizing your finances and paperwork

If you start immediately to get your affairs in order, you can minimize the possibility of last-minute delays and unpleasant surprises. The first step, of course, is to obtain passports for everyone in the family, including babies. Applications for visas and work permits can only be made after you have a valid passport. Have extra passport-sized photos made, in the event your passport is lost or stolen, or in case photos are needed to obtain other documentation required in your new country. Renew your driver's license, if possible, so it won't expire while you're overseas. Apply for an international driver's license (which is basically a translation of your license into a range of languages), if one is necessary in your host country.

A British expatriate in Spain reports:

Every application for anything at all has to be accompanied by at least half a dozen passport-sized photos. It's a standing joke that there is some place where all these photos end up, as no one can actually believe they are needed!

If your bank does not offer online banking, switch to one that does, preferably one active in your new country. Notify your bank that you will be conducting transactions from abroad. Some expats in countries considered to be susceptible to fraud have found access to their accounts blocked when they logged on from a host-country computer.

Arrange a convenient way to handle your regular financial transactions. For example, you may have your salary and other regular income deposited automatically into your bank account, and set up automatic electronic deductions for recurring payments, such as a home mortgage or car loan. Find a way to get cash overseas without excessive fees when you first arrive, such as a bank card that is accepted in your host country. If you are married, make sure that each partner can access an account in either country during regular or emergency travel.

A friend in Taiwan admits:

I am not very computer-savvy (ask my kids). The move has motivated me to go from sending checks to online payment of bills, and to use the Internet to get statements, check balances, and so on.

If you are going abroad as an accompanying spouse without an income of your own, give some thought to your own financial security. Considering the possibility of divorce may be unpleasant, but it is as important as planning for a medical emergency or the loss of your belongings. Your personal "insurance" should at least include a bank account and credit card in your name. Think also about your ownership share in assets such as a house.

Decide how you will handle credit card bills while abroad. Many expatriates have ended up with ruined credit histories or exorbitant late fees because bills did not reach them in time or payments were delayed. Fortunately, most expats now have Internet access and can set up an online billing and payment system. Even if you will not have online access in your new home or office, you will probably be able to find an Internet café to visit on a regular basis. If you are paying off a large balance on your credit card (as is common among expatriates buying things in preparation for the move), you may want to arrange for your bank to pay a set amount to your credit card company each month. As with your bank, notify credit card companies that you will be making purchases abroad, so they don't freeze your cards for "suspicious" transactions from another country.

Organize your essential documents. If you are married, prepare power-of-attorney forms for both you and your spouse, so one of you can make decisions if the other is out of the country. If you are single, recruit a trusted and responsible friend or a sibling to represent you on important matters while you are abroad. Separate your important documents into two groups: those you will hand-carry abroad (see "The Essentials: What to Hand Carry" on page 41) and those to be left behind in a safe place—your lawyer's office or a bank's safe-deposit box. The latter may include adults' birth certificates, marriage certificates, diplomas, naturalization papers, deeds, mortgages, and so forth.

It is also wise to photocopy all of these documents, including the first page of your passport, so you will have records of them both abroad and at home. If you are using a bank's safe-deposit box, it is a good idea to hold it jointly with a trusted relative or friend who also has a key. Leave stocks and bonds with your broker rather than in a safe-deposit box if you think you might sell them while overseas.

Review your health insurance plan to determine if it will cover you while you are overseas, and add extra coverage if necessary. Be sure that the policy includes a provision for medical evacuation to your home country (or a third country if necessary). In some places, expats with international insurance policies are required to make full payment for medical services in advance, which is later reimbursed by the insurance company. Find out if this is the case in your host country, and decide how you will handle the situation (perhaps with a credit card or a large precautionary balance in a local bank account).

Schedule medical and dental checkups before you leave, and schedule any vaccinations recommended for your target country. Ask for copies of your health records and take them with you. Also obtain international vaccination booklets (necessary in some countries), and ask your doctor, dentist, and any specialists you see if they would be willing to answer questions by e-mail if necessary while you are abroad.

If you use prescription medicines on an ongoing basis, ask for a six-month supply. Some physicians are willing to continue writing prescriptions for their patients abroad, which you can fill through reputable online pharmacies. If ordering prescription medicines will not work for you abroad, research the local names or versions of the medicines you use.

Before your belongings disappear into crates, make inventories of them for insurance purposes. This can be done using a checklist (provided by your moving company or insurer) and supplemented by photographs and/or video. Note the purchase date and original or replacement values for important items; attach copies of receipts if you have them.

And just in case the container with your carefully inventoried belongings slides off the ship and disappears into the sea (it does happen!), be sure to purchase adequate insurance. Options include insuring your possessions for transit only or for your entire stay overseas, insuring them for full replacement value or depreciated value, and adding extra coverage for specific high-value items.

Insure your car, if you are shipping or buying one, with a company specializing in international auto insurance. If you plan to rent out your home, choose a property manager who has experience with overseas owners, if possible. Your agent should be able to collect rent, handle emergencies and quick repairs, and find new tenants if necessary.

Find out about the mail situation in your new country. If you have a new mailing address (perhaps through your employer), send out change-of-address forms about a month before you leave. Consider having address labels printed up to make this task easier. Hand-carry your address book in electronic or physical form. Don't forget your magazine subscriptions and professional and alumni associations. If you will not have mail service through your organization or reliable international mail, consider contracting with a mail-forwarding service, which provides a postal address in your home country and periodically packs up your mail and sends it to you overseas by express delivery.

Pack the piano? Store the skis?

As you begin to organize your belongings for the move, you will need answers to four basic questions:

1. Will you ship all of your household furnishings, or are you going to put some in storage?
2. What weight and size restrictions will you face (because of costs, company allowances, or host-country regulations) for your household shipment and stored belongings?
3. Will you be able to send an expedited airfreight shipment in addition to seafreight? What weight limits apply? And what limits will apply to your checked luggage? Baggage limits on international flights are strict—and they are enforced. Contact the airline you will be using, and double-check again close to your departure time, since these rules change quickly. Even more stringent rules and restrictions may apply during periods of heightened security.
4. What items are restricted or prohibited by your moving company or the host country? Commonly prohibited items include live plants, flammable liquids, explosives, and pressurized cans (including seemingly innocent products such as cooking spray). Special permits may be needed for other items, such as alcohol and firearms.

As soon as you know the categories into which you will be separating your belongings (perhaps a carry-on bag, checked luggage, airfreight, seafreight, and storage), start making lists of items to be included in each group. Don't leave this until the last minute; you may be rushed and unable to make thoughtful decisions.

An expatriate in Italy notes:

> We use a three-ring notebook for our inventory, along with some lined paper, plastic document sleeves, and photo pages. It's an easy way to

organize our lists, photos, and receipts. Our older kids don't mind
helping, especially with the photos.

Many expatriates view this organization period as the perfect time to streamline their belongings and get rid of "junk." Some people even hire a professional organizer to help them get their possessions in order before the move. If you are able to do this, great! When deciding what to discard or give away, use what some experienced movers call "the groan factor." Imagine yourself surrounded by a sea of boxes in your new location, unwrapping a wad of packing paper. When you reach the object inside, will you be glad to see it, or will you be more likely to roll your eyes and groan?

Be cautious, however, about purging children's belongings (no matter how "groan-worthy" they may seem to you). As their world turns upside down during the move, they may cling to familiar possessions—even broken toys or tired-looking stuffed animals—more fiercely. Ask for your children's help in choosing items to be sold or given to charity, perhaps in exchange for something new and more desirable (but smaller!). If you feel, over their objections, that some of your children's belongings really must go, try to get rid of them well before the move, so that the two events are not related. Placing the disputed items in storage may also be an acceptable compromise for your children.

If your time is running short and the idea of spending hours sorting and getting rid of years' worth of accumulated belongings before you move pushes you into the red zone, don't panic. As long as you remove prohibited items and are within your weight limit, you may be able to take everything with you (or place it in storage and deal with it later). In fact, if you are moving to an impoverished country, you will probably find eager and deserving takers for your unwanted goods after you arrive.

The following sections include suggestions for items to be included in carry-on luggage, checked baggage, airfreight, a limited household shipment, and seafreight. Of course, your particular choices will depend on your own needs and priorities as well as the living conditions in your new country.

The essentials: what to hand carry

We moved to Pakistan last summer, and though I couldn't leave the
house without getting faint from the heat, I was able to get my Internet

access (call it my "lifeline") set up on my laptop, and it made a world of difference for my morale in those early weeks. Then when we were evacuated, the laptop came with us, together with our folder of disks. This kept me and the kids busy for months.

This observation from a mother of two illustrates some of the advantages of portable computers for expatriates; we highly recommend hand carrying one with you on your move. A laptop is also a good companion on long flights, since you can work, play games, or even watch movies. Some mobile families carry a portable DVD player for each child, as well as portable music players and game systems. Essential paperwork should also be hand carried in an accordion file (choose the kind with a folding cover secured with an elastic band, to ensure that your vital documents won't spill out). You may choose to store and carry some of your documents and records in electronic form.

Your hand-carry items might include the following:

Passports
Visas
Plane tickets
Extra passport-sized pictures for host-country requirements
Children's birth certificates
Adoption papers
Government ID numbers
Mortgage and property management information
Bank and credit card information
Your checkbook
Insurance forms (health, life, home, car, and belongings)
Receipts for expensive belongings
Drug, eyeglass, and contact lens prescriptions
Health and vaccination records
School records
Spouse's résumé and employment documents
Power-of-attorney forms
Paperwork for accompanying pets
Copies of recent tax returns

Salary statements
Information on investments
Your address book

In the rush of departure, don't forget to pack items that will help keep you and your family members comfortable and healthy during the trip. Check current airline restrictions for items that can be carried onboard; for instance, you may have to purchase bottles of water after going through airport security rather than bringing them from home. If you find out that an important item is not allowed in the airline cabin, see if you can include it in your checked luggage rather than surrendering it at airport security. Your carry-on bag should also include a "survival kit" in case your luggage is lost or delayed, including at least one change of clothing, permitted personal care items and essential medicines, your foreign language dictionary (if needed), a travel alarm clock, and a small flashlight. For suggestions on what to carry when traveling with small children, see chapter 5.

Tea bags and teddy bears: what to take in checked baggage

We have both lived for months at a time out of our suitcases alone, and our advice is this: if it really matters, take it with you!

Traveling light is wonderfully liberating, especially if you have a long journey ahead of you with several stops along the way. But in a bewildering new overseas environment where you may not even know how to obtain the simplest necessities, the items in your luggage may take on a new dimension of value. During your first days or weeks in a new country, you are likely to feel stressed, tired, and overwhelmed (see chapter 7). Three general categories of items and suggestions can help reduce your stress and support your transition to the new country.

1. Items that help solve practical problems and make you more self-sufficient: vitamins, shampoo, toothpaste and other personal care items, instant coffee, tea, sugar, paper, pens and pencils, tape, plastic bags for storage and disposal, paper or cloth towels, dish soap,

toilet paper, a few clothes hangers, travel iron, and a dual-voltage hair dryer.

2. Pleasurable items and activities to help reduce stress and soothe your jangled nerves: a portable music system and CDs or electronic files, books you've always meant to read, a camera, a few of your children's treasured possessions, nonperishable packaged foods, swimsuit, exercise clothing, and even supplies for a craft or hobby.

3. Familiar objects that will help you create a sense of home quickly in your new quarters: family pictures in frames, children's decorative items, a favorite coffee mug, and even your own pillow, pillowcase, and towel. (One man we know insisted on filling nearly an entire suitcase with a handmade quilt, saying he wouldn't feel at home without it.)

Bridging the gap: what to take in airfreight

We heard about one couple who each organized their own clothes for their special expedited airfreight shipment. The man put all the clothes he wanted to ship in a particular closet. Through a miscommunication, when the movers arrived, the wife let them pack the contents of the closet in their seafreight instead. The husband went without his entire wardrobe for three months!

If you are able to send an airfreight shipment, these items can be crucial in helping you settle in comfortably. In some parts of the world, your household shipment may take several months to arrive by sea and clear customs—or you may be living in temporary housing for an extended period, as Patricia's family did for six months in Cuba, without access to your household effects.

The considerations for airfreight are similar to those for checked baggage: choose practical items as well as those that will reduce your stress and help you feel at home. The following items can serve as a guide, but we strongly suggest that you get specific advice from a colleague or other expatriate about what basic household goods you will need in your new host country.

- Enough clothing and personal care items (including medicines) for several months (look ahead to changing seasons)
- Computers, TVs, and DVD players (see pages 48–50)
- Digital music, CD players, and radios
- Gifts and decorations for upcoming birthdays and holidays
- A few nonperishable foods that will be welcome treats while you adjust to local food
- A basic set of dishes, cooking utensils, and kitchen equipment if they will not be provided in your new quarters
- Household supplies such as clothes hangers (plastic rather than metal in humid climates) and small dual-voltage appliances
- Sports and hobby equipment (tennis racquet, snorkeling gear, craft supplies, etc.) and toys, games, and activities for children
- Bed linens, pillows, and towels
- Books and magazines

When packing airfreight, remember that it is often handled like luggage (i.e., roughly) by the airlines. Make sure any breakable items are carefully padded, and be sure to purchase adequate insurance for your belongings.

There's no place like home: what to take in a limited household shipment

You may be moving into a furnished house or apartment, especially for a short-term assignment. Of course, "furnished" can mean different things to different people, so find out exactly what is provided and what is not before you organize your belongings. If beds are provided, but you prefer a special type of mattress, find out if you can bring your own. Check on the availability of items such as computer desks, extra bookcases, file cabinets, patio or balcony furniture, and children's furniture. Depending on the country and your shipping budget, it may be best to bring items like this with you or to purchase them after you arrive.

Furnished living quarters can be convenient, but living with anonymous furniture in a rented house or apartment can add to your sense of alienation in a new country. Pack things that will help you personalize your quarters. Your own pictures on the walls, throw pillows, area rugs, photos in frames, and decorative items can help turn a drab corporate apartment into a cheerful, welcoming home.

What if you have no shipment allowance and have to make do with the items in your luggage and a furnished house or apartment? With items such as local textiles (in the form of tablecloths, pillows, wall hangings, or blankets thrown over boring furniture), fresh flowers, a bowl of local fruit, and a few framed posters, you can personalize your place quickly and inexpensively. Look for international stores such as IKEA as well as local outlets. If your host country offers inexpensive folk art or handmade rugs, get out to the markets as soon as you can.

If you are single and caught up in a rush of work, you may neglect "domestic" tasks such as personalizing your living space. However, a study by The Interchange Institute* showed that hanging pictures, arranging furniture, and hosting guests soon after arrival helped reduce expatriates' stress and improve their evaluation of the overseas experience—among singles as well as couples.

The adventure ahead: what to take in seafreight

The following sections cover categories of typical seafreight items that merit special consideration: electrical and electronic equipment and appliances; valuables and family heirlooms; clothing; sport and hobby supplies; holiday supplies and decorations; your car; and "consumables."

Electrical and electronic equipment and appliances. Electrical systems around the world differ both in voltage (the amount of current coming through the wires) and in the number of cycles per second (Hertz or Hz). The United States uses 110 to 115 volts, 60 Hertz. Most of Europe uses from 220 to 240 volts, 50 Hertz. In Japan the electrical system varies from city to city. In some other places, the electrical system can differ from house to house or even within a house, as a friend found in Bolivia!

---

*"Moving Matters: A Study of How to Help International Transferees Relocate," conducted by The Interchange Institute *(www.interchangeinstitute.org)* for Graebel Movers International, 2006.

Get reliable information from your employer or real estate agent about the voltage and Hertz used in your new home. If they are different from those in your home country, many of your electrical appliances will need to be converted or replaced. There are three basic ways to adapt your appliances; most expatriates use a combination of them.

An expatriate family in Prague notes:

> *Our current furnished place came with a pink paisley sofa and high-backed chairs covered with aqua floral damask—not our style at all. Fortunately, we brought our large collection of baskets and textiles from Latin America. They didn't weigh much, but they really helped to personalize the place. As soon as the boxes arrived, we covered our furniture with brightly colored serapes, hung a few Guatemalan textiles on the walls, and lined our baskets up on the shelves. Satisfied, we stood back and admired the miracle—our house looked like home!*

1. *Transformers.* Transformers can be used to convert your appliances to the correct voltage. They can be purchased online or in specialty electronics shops and come in different sizes depending on the voltage (amount of power) they can handle. Note that the small "converters" sold in travel stores are not strong enough for large or heat-producing appliances. Check the back of your appliances to see how many watts of power they require, and make sure the transformers are powerful enough. If you will be running more than one appliance on a transformer at the same time, total the wattages of the appliances. Unfortunately, transformers are relatively expensive and surprisingly heavy. They can also heat up and cause fires or electric shock if not handled properly. In one tragic case, a four-year-old expatriate child was killed while standing on a transformer to wash his hands at a bathroom sink. Be sure to operate transformers on a dry, fire-resistant surface (such as ceramic tile), and keep them unplugged when not in use. By the way, electric clocks and some other devices with internal timers (such as washing machines) *will not* function properly on the "wrong" number of Hertz, even with a transformer. Bring

battery-operated or voltage-switchable clocks, or purchase new ones when you arrive.

2. *Dual-voltage appliances.* Dual-voltage and voltage-switchable appliances can handle either system. Check the appliances you have to see if any are already switchable. For example, most laptop computers are. The voltage and Hertz are usually shown in small print on the back of the appliance. For instance, it might read 115 V/230 V, 50–60 Hz. This means the device can handle both American- and European-type systems. Sometimes there is a small lever or switch that must be moved when converting to the other voltage; double-check this switch carefully to avoid ruining the appliance.

A friend of ours recalls:

> *When I lived in England and shared a house with two French women, I often listened to tapes on a little tape player using a small converter. One day while I was out, one of the Frenchwomen decided to borrow my tape player. She didn't know about the converter issue. When I returned, she knocked on my door and said with a horrified look, "Your tape player, it is smoking!" The power cord connection actually melted.*

3. *New appliances.* If large appliances such as refrigerators and washing machines will require a different voltage, sell or store yours and acquire new ones in your host country, or if they are extremely expensive there, consider ordering ones with the correct voltage from a supplier at home or in a third country.

Aside from the voltage question, there are also different systems for television, videotapes, and DVDs in different parts of the world. A multisystem TV and "code-free" DVD player will allow you to watch movies and recorded television shows from home as well as from your host country. After returning home from the overseas assignment, you can continue to watch the foreign programs and movies you acquired—a nice memento and a great way to keep up your language skills. Several good online companies specialize in multisystem equipment, or look for a specialty store in your home city.

A South African who lived in the United States reports:

Besides my kids' toys and books, the most important thing we took with us—and back home again—was an international VCR that could play NTSC, PAL, and SECAM tapes.

As if all this weren't enough, electrical plugs and telephone jacks differ from country to country. You will need special plug adapters to connect your devices to host-country outlets. These do not change the electricity in any way, just the shape of the plug—as many travelers have found out to their sorrow, such as a friend's visiting grandmother in Prague who plugged in her curling iron and blew out all the lights in the house!

Even if the electrical system is the same in your new country, you will probably need plug adapters. If there are many expatriates from your country in your new city, these adapters will probably be available there. If not, they can be purchased or ordered from specialty international electronics companies. Alternatively, you can hire someone to replace the plugs on your appliances with the local kind, as a friend of ours did in India. Ask a knowledgeable expatriate in your host country to recommend adapters and other electrical supplies that you should bring with you. One piece of good news is that most lamps *will* work in different electrical systems— simply use local bulbs and plug in the lamp with an adapter.

Damaging power surges are common in developing countries. High-quality surge protectors (not just inexpensive power strips) can help protect your valuable electronics. Power outages and "brownouts" can also damage your equipment, not to mention causing serious annoyance when you lose your work because your computer shuts down. An uninterruptible power source (UPS), which compensates for brownouts and short power outages with a battery system, can be a lifesaver in this situation. Although Patricia's home in Cuba had a diesel generator to cope with the near-daily power cuts, there was always a delay of several seconds before the generator kicked in. Connecting her computer to an UPS allowed it to bridge the gap. UPS systems are sold in various strengths; make sure the one you buy can handle the peak wattage of your equipment and is compatible with the electrical system in your host country.

Outside of the most developed countries, electrical outlets may not be properly wired or grounded. An expat in Mexico discovered that although the receptacles in her home had the "third hole," indicating that they should be grounded, none of them actually were. After blowing out two television sets and a Vonage phone, the family hired an electrician to fix the wiring.

In addition to the appliances you currently use at home, you may want to consider bringing along additional equipment to make life easier overseas, especially in a difficult environment. Internet-connected phones, microphones, webcams, air purifiers, water distillers, and bread machines are among the devices that can be extremely helpful overseas.

Patricia reports:

> In heavily polluted Santiago, we had several high-quality air purifiers running all the time. In every country we've had a water distiller—they're slow, but we know we are drinking really pure water. In Cuba, where prepared foods were scarce, we used our bread machine and yogurt maker every day. People were lining up to buy them from us when we left the country.

Valuables and family heirlooms. Deciding what to do with your most treasured possessions can be difficult. Of course, these items can be lost, damaged, or stolen in transit or during your time overseas. However, we have also heard many stories of losses from storage—and even from friends' and relatives' homes—due to insects, water damage, fire, or theft. Since the point of moving your belongings overseas is to support your own adjustment and well-being, ask yourself one basic question while making each decision: where should I send this item so that I feel best about it?

Consider leaving truly irreplaceable family heirlooms with a trusted relative. Small items, such as jewelry, may be stored in a bank's safe-deposit box. However, items that are valuable but not irreplaceable are nice to have with you, as long as they are insured for their full value. You'll probably have more dinner parties overseas than you did at home (especially if you'll have household help), so fancy dishes and glassware will be put to good use. Similarly, decorative objects and collectibles will help you personalize your home.

Antique furniture may be damaged by extreme changes in environment. It may be better off with a relative or in climate-controlled storage. Climate-controlled storage is also a good option for furs and wool rugs. We know of several families whose rugs were destroyed by moths or mildew in regular storage. If controlled storage is not available, leave your rugs with someone who will use them, or take them with you.

Family photographs help provide a sense of home overseas. To safeguard them while continuing to enjoy them, leave the negatives or disks in a safe place in your home country. Some families have scanned or made reprints of their most beloved photos before going overseas, or prepared color photocopies of their albums and left the actual photos at home.

Clothing. Before planning your wardrobe, check with someone in your host country about the dress code at work and in public places. For example, shorts are frowned upon in some tropical countries, even in the hottest weather. Although you may never be mistaken for a native of your host country, it is usually a good idea to approximate the local style so that you do not give offense or call excessive attention to yourself. When researching the local climate, be sure to look at conditions in your specific location, not just averages for the country or its capital city. Variables such as altitude or proximity to the coast can make a big difference. Your housing situation is also a factor. If cold weather is rare in your new location, your home may not have a heating system—as an Argentine expatriate discovered in Australia, wishing she had brought more sweaters and blankets for the few chilly days of winter.

In some countries, locally manufactured clothing is an excellent value; elsewhere, it may not be—or it may only be available in a narrow range of sizes. In many countries you can easily have clothes made, especially for women and children, at a low price. Tailors and seamstresses can usually work from a magazine picture or copy a piece of clothing you already have.

Machine-washable clothes are advantageous in many countries, since dry-cleaning services can be hard to find, unreliable, or quite expensive. In tropical areas, you'll be washing more often as well.

Do take at least some, if not all, of your out-of-season clothes with you, even if your host country has the same climate all year long. You may need them for travel, your next move, or when coming home. Plastic storage bags with one-way valves for pressing out the air are useful for storing and protecting out-of-season clothes.

Sport and hobby supplies. Even if a sport or hobby seems like an obvious activity in your new country, check in advance whether supplies and equipment are readily available at an affordable price. On the tropical island of Trinidad, for example, Patricia found that people enjoyed fishing and cooling off in the sea, but few islanders learned how to swim. They were certainly not equipped with the snorkeling equipment, beach towels, sand toys, inflatable rings, picnic coolers, and so forth that her family expected to pack up for a trip to the beach.

In many places, you may find yourself indoors more than you are accustomed to because of tropical heat, monsoon rains, pollution, security concerns, or simply a lack of public amenities such as museums, parks, and playgrounds in a developing country. Bring lots of indoor activities, and perhaps indoor exercise equipment, if you think this may be the case.

Holiday supplies and decorations. Having a supply of decorations, music, and nonperishable foods (plus family recipes) for your traditional cultural and religious observances can help you maintain a sense of home overseas, especially if a particular holiday is not celebrated in your host country. In general, following your own cultural traditions throughout the year, even if you must adapt them to suit the local environment, can help you maintain your roots in your home culture and feel more comfortable overseas (see chapter 10). You may even consider expanding your observances of home-country traditions, especially if you have children. In addition, holiday celebrations can be an excellent way to share your culture with new friends in the host country, who may be eager to learn about your traditions.

Your car. There is a surprising range of restrictions on the importation of cars from country to country. Vehicles must meet local regulatory standards, of course, along with some rather more confusing rules: for instance, cars shipped to Singapore by expatriates must be less than 3 years old, and a hefty importation fee is imposed.

If you do ship a car, be sure to get good advice and support both before and during the process. We have known expatriates who went many months without their vehicles because the local authorities insisted on a particular change to a car, while the mechanics said they didn't have the part or making the change was impossible. If the make and model you ship is not commonly sold in your new country, it's a good idea to bring extra parts and supplies (such as windshield wipers and signal bulbs) with you. No loose items can be shipped inside the car itself; send these with your household effects.

"Consumables." The availability and prices of "consumables" (personal care items, household supplies, and nonperishable foods) vary widely all over the world. What you might consider a basic product—such as orange marmalade, popcorn, or fabric softener—may not be sold at all in your host country. If you are going to a country where consumer goods are scarce or very expensive, you may want to add some to your household shipment if this is allowed.

Some countries do not allow shipments of food, or certain items may be restricted or subject to an agricultural inspection; be sure to check in advance. Your shipper or moving company may not be aware of these rules, so do your own homework by checking with the appropriate customs office or website of your new country. It's also important to consider the conditions your goods will experience in transit. When leaving Santiago, Patricia was able to include several cases of wonderful, inexpensive Chilean wine in her household shipment—but the wine didn't taste the same after sitting several months in a hot warehouse.

Find out if you will have a way to receive packages overseas; if so, you may be able to place orders later online or from specialty catalogs (a number of companies specialize in shipping consumables to expatriates). Before you begin ordering, though, find out what restrictions and prohibitions apply, whether you will have to pay duty on these items, and what the shipping costs will be. If international package mail is unreliable in your host country (as it has been in many of the countries where we have lived) and you have no mail service through your employer, you will have to rely on express delivery services such as UPS or DHL, which can be quite costly.

As always, check with a colleague or other expatriate in the country to find out what is available and at what price. This should ideally be someone from your home country, so that he or she knows the kinds of products you expect. Also, the person should be the family shopper—we've talked to office-bound employees who really had no clue what was out there in the stores. Expatriates who have lived in your host country in the past can also be good sources of advice, but keep in mind that market conditions can change very quickly. Also, as we pointed out in chapter 1, it's always good to get a balanced view by asking more than one source for advice.

Patricia reports:

> *I enjoy stocking up for a new country. I go to a wholesale buyers' club and buy things like restaurant-sized boxes of plastic wrap and aluminum foil. I then don't have to worry about buying the stuff for the next two or three years! But I've gotten carried away. Once I noticed that the expiration date had passed on two large bottles of painkiller tablets I had purchased long ago. They contained 500 tablets each! How many headaches did I really think we were going to have?*

Once you know what products you are looking for, try to be more careful with quantities than Patricia was with her headache tablets! One method is to keep track of how much of the product you use during a typical month, then multiply by the number of months you plan to spend abroad. One couple had the clever idea of marking dates with permanent ink on the side of shampoo bottles and other containers several months prior to their departure to keep track of the quantities they used. Remember, unlike Patricia, to check expiration dates: it's no use shipping a two-year supply of vitamins that expire in six months. Take into account, as well, that your habits may change in a new country. If fewer convenience foods are available, for example, you may be doing more cooking at home.

The following are some of the typical consumables taken abroad by expatriates.

- Foods typical of your home country (such as maple syrup from Canada, peanut butter from the United States, Marmite from Britain, and Nutella from Germany), traditional holiday foods, convenience mixes, baking needs, and favorite sauces and spices (such as salsa, curry, and pesto). Flour-based products such as cake mixes can be stored in the freezer to extend their expiration dates.
- Breakfast cereals, chips, cookies, and crackers. These go stale quickly, but consider taking a small supply as a treat.

- Children's favorite foods, along with supplies such as disposable diapers, baby foods, and so forth. Keep in mind, however, that your shipment may take months to arrive. It is best to find a local source for baby food and formula (or breast-feed and make your own baby food at home).
- Personal care items: favorite brands of shampoo, deodorant, non-prescription medicines, cosmetics, and so forth.
- Paper and plastic products such as food storage bags, plastic wrap, paper towels, paper napkins, bathroom tissue, and so on.
- Household cleaning and laundry products. However, if you will have household help, they may prefer to use familiar local products; get advice on this. If you do ship cleaning products, be sure they are packed separately from foods! They can pass on a soapy taste and smell.

Plastic boxes to the rescue!

In many of the places we've lived, we have been seriously plagued with dust, mold, and bugs. We've discovered scorpions in the children's toys, cockroaches munching the glue from envelopes, and mildew in our clothes. High-quality plastic boxes with tight-fitting lids are an excellent defense against these pests. Various categories of loose items—craft and hobby supplies, gift-wrapping materials, small toys, office supplies, collections, extra packaged foods, stored clothes, and even the contents of "junk drawers"—can easily be organized and protected in their own plastic boxes. An added bonus is the fact that self-contained boxes are much easier to move and store than the miscellaneous contents of a drawer or shelf. Just be sure that your packers fill up any empty space in the box with crumpled paper, so that the contents don't rattle around and break. Plastic boxes are very expensive in some places; if this is the case in your host country, consider bringing a generous supply. Plastic bags—especially the high-quality zipping kind and those with a valve to remove air—are also good for this purpose.

Have you found this discussion of consumables a bit frustrating, because you are concerned that you won't be able to ship or pack supplies for your move abroad? Don't worry—we've been there too. Soft bathroom tissue is nice, but the coarse kind works just as well. You will certainly find food, soap, and other basic supplies in your new country, no matter its level of economic development. It can be culturally enlightening and part of the adventure to use only local products. And meanwhile, as trade barriers are reduced in many parts of the world, more and more products are becoming available to consumers. Here are just a few suggestions that might be helpful if you will be "living off the land."

- Be sure to include food- and pharmacy-related vocabulary in your language studies, to help you read labels and ask for what you need.
- Ask local contacts or colleagues to take you shopping. They'll know where to find quality local products at the best prices.
- Research local recipes—online, in recipe books, or among local contacts—so you will know what to do with unfamiliar vegetables and cuts of meat. Ask for food preparation advice from market vendors, who may speak a bit of English and will be happy to help a foreigner (perhaps while overcharging you—but that's part of the "tax" you pay for living abroad!).
- If household help is affordable, hire a cook, find a housekeeper with kitchen skills, or pay a chef to come in once a week for a few hours and prepare foods to be frozen, as Patricia did in Cuba.
- If you are wistful for a taste of home as a special treat, see if you can find an international food market, perhaps in a neighborhood of immigrants or expats from your home country, or in an upscale shopping mall—and don't pay attention to the price tag or expiration date on your prize!
- When all else fails, ask visiting friends, family, or colleagues to bring a few items you crave. A German friend calls these "suitcase foods"—and their special status often makes them taste better than they ever did at home.

An American family in Taiwan reports:

You can get a fake designer bag at a street market for about $15, while you have to pay almost $10 for a box of Rice Krispies, my son's only accepted breakfast food, in a store that imports American products.

"Honey, they packed the passports!"—preparing for packout day

In your advance planning with your moving company, find out exactly what is expected of you, what the movers are responsible for, and how long the process will take. Build in a few extra days for delays. If you have any choice in the matter, try to strike a balance between the number of workers and the length of time taken: enough movers so that the work moves along quickly, but not so many that you cannot supervise them. A few volunteer friends or relatives can be a big help.

A British man in Spain reports:

> *Before we'd cleaned it, the movers in London packed our soup dish in which we'd had our last English meal. When we opened up that box, it was pretty stinky!*

A few other important considerations:

- When the packers begin their work, things can disappear quickly. We know of several cases where movers boxed up passports, plane tickets, and other essential items by mistake. Before the movers arrive, pack your luggage and carry-on bags, including your children's backpacks or suitcases, and put them somewhere else: in your car, in your hotel room if you are sleeping away from the house, or even at a neighbor's home. At the same time, remove things that belong with the house and shouldn't be shipped, such as extra keys, appliance manuals, library books, and so forth.
- If you are sending an expedited shipment (such as airfreight), have it packed and weighed first. For some reason, moving companies seem to prefer to pack up smaller shipments last. However, it is in your interest to pack and weigh your expedited shipment first, so that if you have any weight left over, you can still add things. To make this easier, clear out a room or corner before the movers come, put your airfreight items in a pile, then designate an extra pile of things to be added if weight permits.
- Make sure there is no doubt about what is to be shipped and what goes into storage.

Melissa recalls:

> *We finished our packout and moved to Kaduna, Nigeria, an isolated city 800 miles north of Lagos. Once there, we eagerly anticipated the arrival of our household effects, because Kaduna is a small place with very little available locally. Three months later, our shipment arrived. Our excitement soon turned to shock, however, when we saw that all of our items to be stored had been shipped! The belongings we really needed were now sitting in storage. To resolve the problem, we had to ship our unwanted household effects back and then wait an additional three months for the correct belongings to arrive. We lived with the bare essentials and what we had brought in airfreight for a full six months.*

Consider using color-coded stickers or stick-on notes to label furniture and other items being shipped, going into storage, or being left in the house. Another option is to physically separate the items, if possible, so that everything in one room is to be shipped and everything in another room to be stored. Willing friends or relatives who understand your "system" can be a great help. Once packed and boxed, your goods will probably be loaded into large wooden crates for shipping or storage. Be sure to double-check what is written on these; they should be clearly labeled with your name and destination.

One family notes:

> *We always have one small room that the movers may not take anything from. We find that over the course of moving day, we keep finding things and tossing them into that room!*

Recruit your movers as allies. Treating your moving team well usually pays off in better handling of your possessions. Consider offering food or snacks as well as coffee and other nonalcoholic drinks. Even if you have objections about the way something is being packed, phrase them as positive requests: "Could you put an extra layer of paper on that, please?" rather than "That's going to break if you pack it that way!" If you are available, alert, and friendly throughout the moving process, the packers are more likely to feel they can approach you with questions, allowing you to solve problems on the spot rather than facing unpleasant surprises later. At the same time, it is only sensible to take precautions against possible theft. Hand carry small, valuable items, or pack them yourself. We have also known cases where entire boxes disappeared, so recruit friends to help make sure every box goes onto the truck and to supervise your shipping crate until it is nailed shut.

An expat in Mexico relates:

> *My husband sprang for a feast of roasted chicken for the movers here and they did a superb job. For the money it will cost to feed the crew, you will reap it back one hundred times over in great service.*

Saying a proper good-bye

Your friends and extended family may show a wide range of reactions to the news of your overseas assignment. Some may worry about you; others may secretly envy you; some may make immediate plans to visit you abroad. If members of your extended family have been used to seeing you often, the idea of your being so far away may be quite painful.

It is important to address the concerns of the people close to you before you leave, especially to reassure them that you will still be part of their lives. Here are some ideas that may help.

Emphasize your availability. Explain how you plan to keep in touch and how often you plan to come home to visit. Make it clear that your loved ones are invited to visit you; if possible, describe something in your new country you would love to show them.

Acknowledge and calm their fears. People who care about you may have an unrealistic image about your lifestyle overseas, especially the potential dangers you may face. Listen to their concerns, and try to reassure them with specific, positive information.

Work out family commitments and emergency plans. Many expatriates find themselves torn between family responsibilities, such as assisting elderly relatives, and their overseas commitments. Each family must work out solutions to these dilemmas that seem fair and minimize discord.

Perhaps, for example, if others in your family who are close by must contribute more time to helping an ailing parent, you can offer to bear more of the financial burden. You might also consider hiring a professional (such as a geriatric nurse) back home to check up on an elderly relative regularly, for example, and alert you to any problems or emergencies.

Work out in advance what you and other family members will do if a crisis occurs. Some employers will pay for emergency travel to assist family members. Let your family know about your contingency plans for an emergency and keep them informed about how to reach you at all times.

Show that you care. Parents in particular may feel abandoned when you move overseas. Specific actions on your part to stay in touch demonstrate that you care. If they do not use the Internet, you may want to purchase and set up a computer system for them, along with a Web-based phone service. You might even offer to help pay for their plane tickets so they can visit you.

Ignore unusual predeparture behavior. What does it mean when people who are close to you seem to become distant and unfriendly as the date of your departure approaches? This may simply be their way of protecting themselves from the pain of saying good-bye. In some ways, the separation may feel worse for them than for you. After all, you are going off on a big adventure, while they can only look ahead to missing you in their daily lives. Although getting the "cold shoulder" may upset you, try to understand it, and make an effort to résumé contact once you are overseas. You may find that they are relieved and happy to hear from you.

Amid the rush of moving, it's easy to forget the importance of saying good-bye in your own way to the familiar environment you are leaving behind. Saying good-bye and acknowledging your feelings about leaving will help you bring this chapter of your life to a close and begin the process of moving on. Even if you plan to return to the same location after your time abroad, it is important to recognize that things will not be the same when you come back: neighborhoods change, coworkers leave for new jobs, families grow or break apart, neighbors move away.

Farewell parties, of course, are an excellent way to say good-bye to a large number of people at the same time. If nobody organizes one for you, do it yourself. In addition to relatives, friends, neighbors, and colleagues, don't forget to say good-bye to service people you deal with often, such as your grocer and mail carrier. Take photos of things and people you'll miss. Make note of things you *won't* miss as well.

As you say good-bye, plan ways to keep in touch. Consider preparing postcards or announcements with your e-mail and postal address for your friends (including children's friends). If you will be dropping an e-mail account associated with a local provider, sign up for at least one Web-based account well in advance. Also consider signing up for an Internet phone service that will give you a local telephone number in your old location, or giving friends and family members calling cards with inexpensive phone minutes for your new country.

A stopover trip

If you can manage it, a stopover trip on the way to your new home, even just for a weekend or a few days, can be a welcome interlude. It can help break up the journey to your destination, let you get some sleep, and give you a head start at overcoming jet lag. Furthermore, an enjoyable stopover trip (for example, in an interesting new city or at a beach resort) can give you valuable "breathing space" after the stress of the move and before the hassle of settling in. If you have family members along, a stopover provides an opportunity to take time for each other, look forward to your new adventures, and listen to each other's concerns. The right short vacation along the way can help you arrive in your new country with a positive attitude—rested and ready for the challenges that lie ahead.

On the other hand, you may not have the time, budget, or patience for a vacation. If you are moving with a cranky toddler or two large dogs (or both!), if you have already spent several weeks in temporary housing, or if you are simply eager to get settled, a stopover trip may be an unwelcome distraction. Decide what is best for you.

CHAPTER 4

Crossing Cultures Successfully

Moving into a new culture can be an exciting adventure, but it has also been compared to suddenly finding yourself playing a game without knowing the rules. The moves the other players are making don't seem to make any sense. And worse still, everyone clearly expects you to make certain moves—but you have no idea what they are or when and how to make them.

The wife of a Saudi diplomat recalls:

> It was my first evening in the United States. I was so tired, unpacking my suitcases in our new apartment. Then the doorbell rang. When I opened the door, I saw monsters with bloody teeth and terrible faces! They shouted something I didn't understand, and I screamed and slammed the door. A few minutes later, the bell rang again. I looked through the peephole. There were more horrible demons at my door, different ones! I phoned my husband at the embassy; I was ready to go back to Saudi Arabia that minute. But he just started laughing, and then he explained to me about a holiday called Halloween...

There is no substitute for learning about the culture of the new host country before arriving to ensure a smooth international relocation. Although it might seem easier to wait and learn about your new country once you're there, preparing ahead of time—while still in the comfort of your own culture—will give you the tools to make local friends, work with host-country colleagues, avoid common pitfalls, and enjoy your new country from the start. The more you know and understand about your new host culture, the more confident and competent you will feel in those challenging early weeks (see our tips in chapter 7 on how to cope with transition shock after arrival).

This chapter is designed to guide you through the preparation process. First, it describes effective cross-cultural communication— learning to deal with people across cultures with a true understanding of their cultural differences. Next, it suggests specific ways to build your cross-cultural skills. It also discusses common cultural differences encountered around the world, to help you identify the challenges you may face as you confront the unique culture of your new host country. Finally, this chapter explores cross-cultural issues to consider when hiring and working with domestic help in your new country.

Cross-cultural communication: bridging the gap

Cultures include assumptions, values, expectations, and attitudes that have developed among groups of people over time. No matter where in the world you are going, and no matter how open-minded you are as a person, there will inevitably be times when your own values, expectations, and habits clash with those of the local people. Even if you already speak the same language as your new hosts or share cultural roots, you will still need to bridge the gap between your own culture and theirs.

An Australian woman who has lived in Thailand and the United Kingdom notes:

> In a place as "foreign" as Thailand I expected everything to be different and often difficult, but in Britain things looked superficially the same, so the differences came as more of a shock.

Unfortunately, you can't assume that people in your host country will meet you halfway and show understanding for your cultural differences because you are a foreigner. Unlike you, they may never have traveled out of their country before and found themselves forced to adjust to another culture. They may not even realize that people in other countries have different ways of doing the things they accept as "normal." As a guest in their country, you have the responsibility for reaching out as best you can and trying to accommodate to the culture around you.

Four general stages are involved in bridging the gap between your own culture and another. You may find that you work through them in a different order from the one given here, or you may find yourself moving back and forth among the different stages as your knowledge increases.

1. Realizing that people in other places have developed different ways of dealing with the greater and lesser questions of life.
2. Familiarizing yourself with your own culturally based values, expectations, and attitudes, rather than taking them for granted.
3. Studying the specific attitudes, expectations, and values of your target culture.
4. Learning how to interact with people in another culture based on an understanding of their point of view, whether or not you agree with it or adopt it yourself.

Building cross-cultural skills

The following sections present some specific measures to help you move as effectively as possible through the four stages just outlined.

Putting common sense in context

One of the first requirements for cross-cultural communication is simply realizing that people in other places have very different ways of going about their daily lives, including different attitudes and values. What is considered "common sense" in one culture may make no sense at all to people who grew up somewhere else.

Even if you have never lived overseas before, you have probably become aware of some of these differences in encounters with people from different countries, ethnic groups, or even regions within your own country. Perhaps you once suddenly realized in a language class that an expression you were learning couldn't be translated adequately into your own language. Or perhaps you politely admired a decorative object in a foreign friend's home one day, and she promptly insisted that you accept it as a gift—which wasn't what you had in mind at all!

To boost your skills in this area, first think back over your experiences with people from other backgrounds. Or immerse yourself in another culture by spending time in an immigrant neighborhood, watching a foreign movie, or reading a novel written by someone from a different culture. Try to identify ways in which the values, attitudes, and expectations you encounter differ from your own. As you read the "Common Cultural Differences" section later in this chapter, think about the cultural differences you have observed while traveling or in personal encounters.

Especially if you have not had many cross-cultural experiences, read more about the subject (look under "cross-cultural communication"). Even better, take a cross-cultural communication seminar. If you don't have an employer that offers this kind of training, it may be provided by a language school or employee relocation service in your area.

Cultural self-awareness

Before you can succeed in understanding another culture, you must become aware of your own. As you begin to realize how your own values, attitudes, and expectations have been shaped by your home culture, you will be in a better position to see things from the point of view of people in other cultures.

The following are some tips for increasing your awareness of your own culture.

- As you read the "Common Cultural Differences" section later in this chapter, think about your own values, habits, and attitudes.
- Seek out opportunities to talk to immigrants or foreign visitors to your country. Ask them about things they found strange or difficult to adjust to when they first arrived.
- Read books that describe your own culture. See if you can find guidebooks or websites for people moving to or visiting your home country. You may be surprised (and perhaps even insulted!) by what you find—and it will help you understand what people in other countries might find surprising and unusual about *you*.

- Think about your parents' and grandparents' values, expectations, and attitudes. Which ones have changed through the generations? Which have remained the same? The ones that have stayed the same will represent some of your deepest cultural assumptions. Haul these out into the open and examine them. Think about how you will feel if you encounter people who don't share them.

Information about the new country

Information is the key to success in a specific culture. Learning about your new host culture before you arrive will give you a head start on your own adjustment, help you make a favorable impression on the local people—and, of course, prevent embarrassing cultural errors!

- Look for information that specifically addresses your new culture: on websites and in books and manuals (such as those published by Intercultural Press and the Culture Shock! series of books on specific countries).
- Read literature, popular books and magazines, fables, and even children's stories from your new country, in translation if necessary. Watch movies set in your target country (especially those by local filmmakers) or films about immigrants from that culture. Pay close attention to the cultural attributes they reveal.
- Study the language if at all possible. (See chapter 2 for specific recommendations about language study.) Not only will it open doors for you once you arrive, but the language itself also provides valuable insights into the culture. Pay special attention to common sayings and expressions—but make sure they're up-to-date; some books of sayings would have you saying the local equivalent of "Groovy, man!" Have a native speaker check over your list, if possible.
- Take a seminar that focuses on the culture of your host country. If you will be doing business in the country, a specific business culture seminar will pay for itself many times over.
- Try to meet people from your new country—or at least other expatriates who have lived there—before you go. Ask specific but

open-ended questions, like "What should I watch out for when I arrive?" and "What mistakes do newcomers often make?"

- After you arrive, simply interacting with ordinary people may be your best source of information. The fruit seller at the market, your next-door neighbor, local employees at the office, local business-people, and your household help, if any—all have something to teach you about the new culture. All you need is a willingness to reach out and to observe.

Sensitivity

Cross-cultural communication takes a sensitive touch. Once you become aware of the depth of cultural differences as well as the specific differences between your own culture and that of your host country, you can take the final step in cross-cultural communication: learning to interact with the local people based on an understanding of their point of view, whether or not you agree with it or adopt it yourself.

This can be a very delicate task, requiring you to suppress many of your own reactions and to hold back criticism of things that appear nonsensical or "wrong." But like you, the local people have been raised to think that their way of doing things is the best way. They will rarely respond favorably when a foreigner insists that his or her way is even better. Showing respect for the local culture is not only the polite thing to do; it will help you make friends and interact successfully with the local people.

People from small nations, especially in the developing world, are often very sensitive about outsiders' impressions of their country. Even your airport taxi driver might ask, "How do you like our country?" Think up an all-purpose, positive answer as soon as you can. The people are very friendly; the landscape is beautiful; the food is delicious—something you can say with conviction.

Expatriates from wealthy and powerful countries sometimes assume that citizens of less-developed nations will naturally recognize and admit their own countries' weaknesses. Yet this is rarely what happens. People don't like to think of their homeland as impoverished and lacking power. They may not even believe it is true; school systems all over the world tend to emphasize—even exaggerate—the positive in order to build national pride. Instead of being grateful for advice and aid from more-developed countries, poorer nations tend to resent such intrusions, often viewing them as unwelcome and patronizing interference. If you are a citizen of a rich country moving to a poorer one, remember this psychological element as you deal with the local people. An attitude of superiority will get you nowhere fast.

It can come as a shock to realize that what you do overseas doesn't just reflect on you personally; it also reflects on your home country and your fellow citizens. This awareness can add a bit to the strain of living abroad—you may feel as if you always have to be on your best behavior. However, you may find, like many expatriates, that your efforts to make a good impression overseas can ultimately lead to personal growth.

In spite of all this, you will sometimes feel the urge to vent complaints about the host country and culture. This is only natural. Just don't do it with local citizens or even at a club where expatriates gather; save it for discreet and sympathetic friends. And try to make sure that you don't make griping an ongoing habit, or you will risk slowing down your own adjustment and turning overseas life into a bitter, unpleasant experience.

Of course, there are things going on in some parts of the world that few outsiders would condone: oppression of women, persecution of ethnic groups, political repression, and so forth. Yet no matter how concerned you are by events in your host country, be careful about becoming involved in political movements for change. Since you are a foreigner, your interference may be resented, and you might even end up making things worse. However, some expatriates we know have managed to follow their consciences by helping individuals, working for nongovernmental organizations, or writing about events in the country for an international audience. Get good advice before you act; alienating a repressive government is a good way to find yourself an ex-expatriate with a permanently cancelled visa.

Common cultural differences

Cultures are living, changing entities that emerge from a wide range of influences. History, climate, geography, religion, economic factors, and neighboring cultures all help determine the foods people eat, the way they dress, the homes they live in, and the patterns of their daily lives. Even more subtly, these factors combine with others to affect how people view issues such as time, work, the family, and interpersonal relationships.

Cultures are not uniform throughout a country—instead, many variations and gradients can be seen among regions, ethnic groups, generations, and particular individuals. Americans who arrive in Germany expecting most people to be wearing lederhosen and feathered caps are just as disappointed as Germans who think most Americans sport ten-gallon hats and cowboy boots. It is incorrect, and even offensive, to expect every individual to fit some sort of national stereotype. However, generalizations about the culture of a particular place can be useful as long as they are viewed merely as guidelines to help the foreign visitor understand and adapt.

As you set out to understand your new host culture, you will encounter external differences; expectations, expressed in the form of written and unwritten rules; and underlying attitudes or beliefs.

External differences

Unique and obvious external attributes are what spring to mind when most people think of a different culture: Indian curries, classical music in Austria, Haitian paintings, Indonesian batiks, Carnival in Brazil, African wood carvings, onion-dome churches in Russia, and so forth.

Although differences in local foods, dress, and similar customs may pose a challenge at first, these cultural traits also provide some of the most colorful, exotic, and enjoyable experiences of overseas life. Even better, by living in the country you will gain opportunities to experience these phenomena more fully than any tourist. Local friends, colleagues, and even household employees will likely be pleased to help you gain an "insider's" view of their culture. With a Ukrainian friend, for example, Melissa visited an icon painter's studio, attended a Christmas pageant at a Ukrainian kindergarten, and had her home blessed by an Orthodox priest, among many other unique experiences. The external attributes of your host culture are likely to provide more pleasures than pitfalls. However, you will also confront other cultural traits that can present much more of a problem: the not-so-obvious values and attitudes of the people around you.

Written and unwritten rules

The written and unwritten rules of another culture are harder to identify than the colorful, more obvious phenomena just described. And if you break the rules, you may face social embarrassment, legal trouble, or even physical danger. Before you arrive in your new country, or as soon as possible afterward, ask a local contact, experienced expatriate, or cross-cultural trainer to explain the following rules of your host culture.

Traffic laws and customs. What are the basic traffic laws, and what do the various signs mean? How does one call a taxi or use public transportation? When do pedestrians have the right of way, and when don't they? If two vehicles are approaching an unmarked intersection, what should the drivers do?

Dress. What is considered appropriate dress for men and women? What is not acceptable? Some travelers find this question offensive, believing that the way they dress is their own business. However, clothing sends signals to the people around you—about your wealth, your level of formality, perhaps even your sexual availability—signals that vary greatly from culture to culture.

Melissa reports:

> *Visiting Cairo once, I saw a young American girl walking briskly on the street by herself, nervously looking over her shoulder at every turn. The girl had good reason to feel uneasy. Every man on the street was staring at her thin, spaghetti-strap top, miniskirt, and high heels! Though this type of fashion may have been suitable at home, in Egypt, a Muslim country, such inappropriate dress attracted unwelcome attention.*

Greetings and forms of address. What are the usual greetings between strangers, friends, men, and women? When are first names used, and when are they not? An overly informal greeting or form of address may be seen as rude, derailing a relationship before it even starts. Greetings may take the form of questions which one is not expected to answer.

Handshakes, hugs, or kisses on the cheek may also accompany greetings. Find out when these are expected and who should initiate them (see also "Personal space and the body," page 76).

An expatriate from South Africa recalls:

> *It took me a while to realize that when an Indonesian friend asked me "What are you doing?" it was actually a greeting, not a request for information or a prelude to a request for a favor.*

Gestures. What gestures are typically used in your host country? What gestures or body language are considered rude or sexually suggestive? Everyday gestures can be a cultural minefield because they are used so often, yet they vary greatly from country to country. For example, nodding the head up and down means "no" in Bulgaria but "yes" in most other places. The thumb-and-forefinger circle that means "okay" among Americans and scuba divers has a very insulting meaning in France. And a gesture of fingers pinched together, pointing upward, means "Wait a minute" to people in the Middle East, but "Up yours" in the Latin world.

In Europe and North America, opening and closing the hand with the palm up means "Come here" but "Good-bye" with the palm down. In many other countries, however, people gesture others to come with the palm down. A female professor in the United States once had a brief conversation with a male student from the Middle East and then waved good-bye with her palm down. He thought she was gesturing for him to follow her, so he did . . . right into the ladies' rest room!

Patricia reports:

> *I was walking across a university campus with a male Saudi Arabian student, when he suddenly took my hand in his, swinging it happily as we walked along. Since we were both married, I was a bit shocked—in my culture, hand-holding is an intimate, often sexual gesture. However, I remembered that Arab men often hold hands with each other while walking, and I hoped that my student's gesture was intended in this spirit. It turned out that he never made any other sort of sexual advance to me, and we remained friends.*

Taboos. Are there any cultural or religious taboos? For example, some religions do not allow nonbelievers to enter a place of worship. Devout

Muslims do not eat, drink, or smoke during daylight hours during the month of Ramadan, and it is rude or even illegal in some places to break this fast in public. As an expat in Thailand was surprised to discover, "You have to remember never to step on a coin or put a bill in your shoe. The money is adorned with images of the king and you have to be respectful."

Shopping. What are the usual procedures for shopping? Is haggling over prices expected? When is tipping expected (or not allowed), and how is it handled? Is touching the merchandise considered offensive? Melissa was once very embarrassed when a vendor in France shouted at her for attempting to select her own pieces of fruit, a common practice in her home culture.

Etiquette. What rules of etiquette should guests and hosts follow? How are gift giving and thank-yous handled, and what gifts (if any) are appropriate for particular occasions, such as being invited to dinner? In some countries a gift of flowers must always have an odd number of blooms— an even number is reserved for funerals!

A Canadian expatriate in Japan notes:

> *"Omiyage" (souvenirs)* must *be bought for everyone you work with when you travel, no matter where. I remember some people buying hundreds of magnets as presents when they were on their honeymoon!*

Neighbors. What responsibilities do people have toward their neighbors? What rules apply to noise, pets, trash disposal, parking, and so forth? What level of friendliness is expected among neighbors? When a new resident moves in, which side usually takes the initiative in getting acquainted—the newcomers or the established residents? Or is friendliness not expected or even welcome?

Daily schedules. What daily schedule do most people generally follow? In Spain, Argentina, and Chile, for example, restaurants don't even open for dinner until 8:00 P.M., and dinner parties may start at 10:00 or 11:00. In Germany, *Ruhezeit* (quiet time) is enforced after working hours, on Sunday, and even during the lunch break; even throwing glass into recycling bins during this time is *verboten!*

An Austrian-American expat in Taiwan reports:

> *There seems to be no public restriction about fireworks or noise restrictions at night. The month before and after Chinese New Year, fireworks go off almost every night, all night long. The temple below our apartment building performs chants, drumming with cymbals, etc. at various festivals for many days, preferably starting at 10 P.M. until around 2 or 3 A.M.*

Smoking. Tolerance of smoking in restaurants, offices, and public facilities varies widely around the world. If you are a smoker moving to the cigarette-unfriendly United States, or a nonsmoker moving to smoker-friendly Turkey, you may have to adjust your habits significantly. Although the situation may be uncomfortable for you, complaining or breaking the rules is not likely to have much effect.

Alcohol and drugs. What are the local customs and laws concerning alcohol and drug use? Many Europeans are surprised by the strict laws in the United States related to alcohol. Travelers may also be unaware of the severity of drug laws in other countries. Unless you have a special dispensation, such as diplomatic status, you are fully subject to the laws of the host country and can be arrested and imprisoned for breaking them, whether you are aware of them or not.

A consular officer in the U.S. diplomatic service reports:

> *I've seen numerous tragic cases where young adults were talked into carrying drugs into a country for a dealer. They may have been assured that the laws were lenient, that customs officials had been paid off to look the other way, or that their embassy could get them out of any trouble. In the course of my work, I've visited many of these unfortunate people in foreign prisons where they were serving sentences of 10 or 15 years.*

Attitudes and values

The attitudes of your new hosts may present the greatest challenge of all. Why? First, they are not easy to uncover. Natives of your host country will readily tell you about their customs and rules (i.e., external differences and written and unwritten rules), but they may not be able to explain the attitudes and values that guide their behavior—mostly because these are taken for granted and accepted as common sense.

Second, some values and attitudes of the host-country locals may clash strongly with your own. Some things they do may appear senseless, wrong, or unfair, according to *your* value system. As you get to know the country and its people better, you may find that actions that offended you at first really do make sense in the context of the local culture. However, you may confront some local attitudes and practices that you continue to find truly misguided, no matter how well you come to understand the culture.

One expatriate reports from her time in Zambia:

> *When the husband of my live-in housekeeper died, her in-laws came to the house and demanded to take away everything from her quarters, even the children, because it all "belonged" to him, not to her, and they were traditionally entitled to it. We simply couldn't respect this aspect of their culture, and we stationed a guard at the gate to keep them out.*

Nevertheless, a respectful, good-faith attempt to understand the following types of values and attitudes prevalent in your host culture will reward you in several ways. You will better understand why the people around you do the things they do. You'll learn how to accept them and interact with them on their own terms, thus avoiding offense. And last but not least, your own way of thinking will be broadened by your exposure to different points of view, whether or not you ultimately find them convincing.

Time

Some cultures, especially in the West, view time as linear, rigid, and scarce. "Time is money," they say, as they rush from appointment to appointment, feeling stressed if they are behind schedule. Other cultures see time as more flexible and abundant—there is always enough to go around.

Patricia reports:

> *I faced this kind of culture for the first time in Trinidad. When I arrived,*
> *strangers would call out after me as I strode down the sidewalk: "Slow*
> *down! What's the hurry?" If I invited people for dinner at 6:00, they might*
> *show up at 8:00, or not at all. Another day they might drop in on me*
> *without notice and stay for hours. Being from the East Coast in the U.S., I*
> *found this attitude quite frustrating at first. However, I eventually learned*
> *to adjust my expectations, and I came to appreciate running into Trini*
> *friends—at home, out in public, or in their offices—and having them drop*
> *whatever they were doing for the simple pleasure of my company.*
>
> *I had to adjust my expectations in the other direction, however,*
> *when I moved to Germany. Once I was having coffee with a German*
> *friend and told her I had to be at an appointment in 45 minutes. "You'd*
> *better get going," she said with concern. My impulse would have been to*
> *take another 15 minutes to enjoy our conversation, accepting the risk*
> *that I might be delayed by traffic. But my friend was right within the*
> *German cultural context, where being even 5 minutes late to an*
> *appointment is considered unprofessional and rude.*

Personal space and the body

Researchers have documented the curious fact that people in every culture
have a typical "personal space envelope"—people who are waiting in line
or having a conversation feel comfortable at a highly specific distance
from each other. If you move to a culture with a larger personal space
envelope than yours, you may perceive the people as distant and cold.
However, if the typical personal space envelope in your new host country
is smaller than yours, you may have the uncomfortable feeling that people
are crowding in on you and even find yourself constantly backing up during conversations, as the other people keep inching toward you!

Eye contact also varies from culture to culture. In Europe and North
America, direct eye contact is valued as a sign of honesty and openness. In
some Asian cultures, however, it is considered rude for subordinates to
look directly into their employer's eyes. In many parts of the Middle East,
eye contact between men and women is interpreted as flirtation.

Similarly, cultures vary greatly in the amount of interpersonal touching they consider normal. In many places women greeting each other touch cheeks for an "air kiss"—one, two, or even three times, depending on the country. Russian and Middle Eastern men hug each other in greeting. As mentioned earlier, hand-holding between friends is common in Asia, the Middle East, and many other places.

A British man in Spain notes:

Spain is a far more tactile country than Britain—kissing on cheeks, touching arms, and so on. Everybody shakes hands, even close friends. What older men do is kind of grab each other's heads and rub them a bit. Not the kind of thing you see in the U.K.! I haven't had any difficulties with these customs; the problem is more the reverse. When I go back to London, I end up kissing almost total strangers.

Living in eastern Germany, Patricia was surprised to find that mixed-sex public nudity is perfectly acceptable, and even expected, on some occasions—at swimming pools, beaches and saunas, and even in some parks. At the same time, the German culture adheres to a strict sense of privacy. Strangers rarely speak to each other without a good reason, there is little touching between friends and acquaintances, and men don't call out suggestive comments to passing women. Thus, even if they are stark naked in public, individuals and family groups are surrounded by a cultural envelope of privacy.

In many Middle Eastern cultures, women wear long sleeves and long skirts, cover their hair, and in some places even their faces. These barriers are seen as demonstrations of religious piety and measures to avoid sexual temptation. In many other cultures, extremely revealing bathing suits are quite acceptable in the right context, while complete nudity would be considered offensive and provocative.

You will probably find yourself adjusting to the host country's standards of personal space, touching, and dress after the first six months or so in your new country, although they may never feel completely comfortable to you. Remember, of course, that it is safer to err on the conservative side. We have known of more than one case where the natural cultural behavior of an expatriate was interpreted as sexual willingness, with very unfortunate results.

Gender roles, relationships, and the family

Some cultures still maintain the view that males and females should occupy separate dominions, and role differentiation is rigidly adhered to. Females' educational, occupational, sexual, and marital choices may be more limited than those of males. Acceptance of homosexuality also differs greatly across cultures.

If you are a woman moving to a traditional society, you may be worried about receiving inferior treatment there. In our experience, however, this is rarely the case. As a foreigner, you will be viewed as standing outside the traditional cultural pattern. You may have to dress modestly in public and perhaps endure some sexist remarks, but there are also advantages to being a foreign woman in a traditional society. For example, you may be able to make friends among both local men and women, while a foreign man would find himself restricted to the men. Also, men in "macho" societies with a chivalrous tradition may turn out to be more helpful and cooperative with women than with men.

If you are a single man moving to a traditional society, be aware of the possible consequences of any type of relationship with a local woman. For example, what seems like quite innocent behavior to you may place a local woman in dishonor or appear to her family as a promise of marriage.

A male expatriate in Taiwan notes:

> I've noticed that a Western man's idea of a casual date or even "going steady" is an open-ended arrangement, whereas most women in Taiwan would interpret dating as leading to marriage. I heard of one such woman staying home night after night by the phone waiting for "her guy" to call her back.

The family plays a much larger role in some societies than others. In many countries, children remain with their parents until they are married. Extended families may live together or count on each other for support. In numerous countries, if a person makes money, he or she is expected to share the wealth with the entire extended family. Hiring a domestic worker in some African countries may mean supporting a family of 12.

Social classes and ethnic groups

Many relatively poor countries are highly stratified, with a rich elite, a small middle class, and a large number of impoverished peasants. These social classes often correspond to ethnic groups—in some Latin American societies, for example, wealthy landowners tend to be of European descent, while indigenous people and those of mixed ethnicity are over-represented among the poor.

Depending on your relative wealth in the host country—and perhaps even your ethnic group—you may suddenly find yourself categorized with the elite. An expatriate earning a European-level salary may automatically be among the richest people in a small, less-developed country. If you happen to physically resemble the country's upper class, you may find yourself an involuntary beneficiary of local prejudice. On the other hand, if you look different from the majority of local citizens, you may find yourself enduring stares, rude remarks, or even active discrimination. Find out if either of these situations occurs in your host country, and prepare yourself mentally before you go.

Likewise, prepare yourself for the possibility of prejudice and overt discrimination against ethnic groups that may be prevalent in your host society. Deciding when to speak up in protest or remain silent out of politeness is a touchy question that most expatriates must deal with eventually. However, serving as a good example of tolerance and understanding is one of the best roles we expatriates can play in the world.

Rules, authority, and doing business

Attitudes toward rules also vary from country to country. In some places, you must follow the rules whether they make sense to you or not; for example, if bathing caps are required at a pool, even bald men must wear them.

In other societies rules may be flexible, depending on the situation. In still other countries, rules may be "on the books" but ignored in actual practice—unless the person in charge feels like harassing someone that day.

A South African expatriate was surprised by rigid school rules in the United States:

> *When my son forgot about a dental appointment and boarded the school bus, I couldn't get him off it myself without official sanction from the teacher!*

An Australian moving to Britain complained that:

> *The rules for opening a bank account when you first arrive are almost impossible. The magic key for opening an account is a utility bill, but you can't get a bill until you rent a house, which is difficult to do without a bank account, and 'round it goes!*

A British accompanying husband in Spain reports:

> *Spaniards may keep saying no, can't do this, can't do that, but then if you keep on (politely but firmly), they quite often say "Podemos hacer una cosa" ("We can do a thing," literally), which means they're going to bend or break some rule.*

Cultures also vary in their approach to authority. In many societies, authority isn't earned primarily through competence but comes with age, social status, or seniority within a company. Great respect may be shown to people in positions of authority. In dealing with host-country colleagues, it is crucial to understand the local concept of authority and to work with it, not against it.

An Australian woman in the U.K. reports:

> *I have come to recognize, after some time, that even in a relatively informal industry, there is an expected level of deference to high-level managers (in terms of the words and tone used rather than what is actually said) that does not exist in Australia.*

Business interactions and negotiations may be handled in a very different manner in your host country from what you expect. Negotiations may depend more on the development of a relationship of trust or the exchange of favors than on the presentation of an attractive business proposal. In many societies, it is considered rude to say "no" outright. If you come from a more direct culture, you may find yourself exasperated by endless postponements and evasions, while the other party just wishes you would take the hint and drop the whole matter!

A cultural unwillingness to say "no" can also quickly lead to factual misunderstandings. When Patricia taught English to Japanese students, she had to remind herself not to ask them whether they understood the lesson—they would invariably say "yes" to be polite. The only way to find out if they really understood was to have them demonstrate what they had learned.

Melissa reports:

> In Algeria, I would sometimes ask a local person directions to find a place, follow the instructions, and learn later that what the person said was completely wrong. I only succeeded in getting more lost. When I asked Algerian friends about this, I learned that when a foreigner asks for directions, local people want to help. They are so eager to help, in fact, that they will not admit when they don't know the directions! Rather than say, "Sorry, I can't help you," they will take a guess and give you some sort of information when they honestly don't know the right answer.

An expat in Thailand explains what he has learned about "saving face" in Asia:

> I have lived in six Asian countries. In Asia, you always have to remember the importance of saving face. I have seen a school reschedule exams that had been planned for months, because the principal accidentally said the wrong date in a public speech. When the exams were suddenly rescheduled, I asked the Asian co-workers why the schedule had changed. They all dutifully said, "The schedule didn't change; it was always scheduled for this day." So I took a copy of the school calendar and showed them that the exam dates had been moved. The answer was simply, "Yes, exams are very important."

When something goes wrong at your office or in your personal life, you will probably ask "why?" This is a question that isn't normally asked in Asia. As a result, in most instances the question won't be answered to your satisfaction. If you ask again, you are being impolite. Often when the explanation makes no sense at all, it is because someone made a mistake. But no one is allowed to say that person made a mistake, because they would lose face.

In a weird way, it does make sense and does reduce stress because all you care about is that there has been a mistake. Since you can't go back in time and change it, why worry about how or why? Just solve the problem and move on.

Business culture and practices can differ from industry to industry as well as from country to country, and even regionally within a country. If you will be doing business with the local people, we strongly suggest the following measures.

- Purchase guidebooks on cross-cultural business dealings, especially those focused on your new country or region. Take them with you to the country for ongoing reference.
- If you are not with an organization that provides specific training in the business culture of your host country, take a seminar on the subject, perhaps at a cross-cultural training institute.
- Talk with home-country colleagues in your field who have experience doing business in your host country, paying them as consultants if necessary.

Religious beliefs, beliefs about fate, and superstitions

The religion or religions of your host country will inevitably affect the local people's outlook on life. Learning about local religious practices can give you deep insight into the cultural and social life of the people, as well as being a fascinating experience. Once Patricia was lucky enough to be invited by a friend to a traditional early-morning service at a Hindu *mandir*. The rituals with incense and flowers and the sermon emphasizing peace and serenity helped her to better understand her friend as well as Hindu traditions.

A belief in and acceptance of fate is prevalent in many parts of the world, especially in less-developed countries where early death and other calamities are common occurrences. Many cultures, for instance in the Middle East and Latin America, also place great emphasis on divine power, believing it futile, even arrogant, for humans to speculate about the future. Every plan may be accompanied by the admonition "God willing"—*Insh'allah* in Arabic, *Dios quiere* in Spanish.

Superstitions about actions that seem to "tempt fate" are also common in many places. In many Arab societies, for instance, it is considered unlucky to comment on how strong and healthy a child looks. In numerous countries, baby gifts are not given until the baby is born or even much later, when the baby is named. In Germany, it is unlucky to give birthday gifts or wishes before the actual date. The fact that many buildings in New York City, for instance, have numbering that skips the thirteenth floor shows the power of superstitions even among highly educated people.

In some countries you may encounter beliefs in witchcraft and similar supernatural powers. These conceptions are not likely to affect you as an expatriate. However, it is worth learning at least a little about them, so that you don't break a taboo without realizing it. In addition, just as you would not make fun of another religion, be sure not to ridicule local beliefs, even if they appear absurd to you.

Crossing cultures at home: managing domestic employees

Though friends back home may envy you when they hear you have domestic help, the reality of an individual working or even living in your home creates the potential for problems you may not have considered. When this person is from another culture, the potential for misunderstandings is far greater. If you have never had a housekeeper, cook, or nanny from another culture work in your home, there are important considerations to take into account to ensure that the working relationship is positive for all involved.

This section will provide you with the essential information you need when hiring, living with, and firing (if necessary) domestic help in cultures where it is common (and sometimes even expected). It will also help you to avoid cross-cultural misunderstandings by identifying the problems that may arise.

A luxury or a necessity?

If you are from a country where employing full-time help is rare, you may feel uncomfortable at first with the idea of having people working in your home. You may see it as an unnecessary luxury or an unwanted invasion of your privacy. The large gap between your income level and that of domestic workers can also cause discomfort. However, you will likely find that household help is a necessity, not a luxury, in countries where it is common. Household chores may take the entire day in the absence of labor-saving devices, convenience foods, or supermarkets.

In addition—and this may seem odd—if you decide not to employ help, instead of being admired by the local people for your self-sufficiency, you may be resented for denying a job opportunity to needy workers. Because expatriates usually offer above-average pay and working conditions, jobs in their households are usually considered highly desirable. What seems like a very low salary to you may be enough to support your staff and his or her family, and even their extended families.

If you have never had full-time help in your home, you will have some adjustments ahead of you. Your privacy will surely be reduced, and you will have to play the role of employer—and a cross-cultural employer at that—in your own home. On the other hand, the benefits of having reliable, compatible help in your home are undeniable: coming home to a clean house and a freshly cooked meal after work or running errands; having a "built-in" babysitter; and spending your weekends enjoying the host country rather than vacuuming and scrubbing bathrooms. Finding the right people to make this attractive scenario come true is the subject of the following sections.

Melissa reports:

> *My African housekeeper in Kaduna, Nigeria, gave me a Christmas memory I have never forgotten. I had been cooking all day for a large dinner party and was looking forward to sharing one of my favorite holiday recipes with my guests—a hot spiced fruit punch. The aroma of cinnamon sticks and whole cloves, simmering in a fruit mixture for hours, filled my home with a lovely holiday fragrance. "This is wonderful," I thought. "Now*

that everything is finished, I can clean up and get ready for the party." I had half an hour before the guests were to arrive. I changed quickly, and as I walked back into the kitchen, I noticed my housekeeper drying the clean, empty pot the punch had been in on the top of the stove. "Where's the punch?" I asked. "Oh, Madame!" he replied in a nervous voice. "I throw out!" To my housekeeper, the punch looked like a useless, leftover liquid.

What to consider before hiring

Start by finding out what kind of domestic help is available where you are living. You will also need to know about standard local hiring practices. People who have lived in-country for some time, such as colleagues, friends, or acquaintances in the expatriate community, can usually provide you with the necessary information. Asking questions is the best way to start.

- What kind of employees do people have?
- What are they usually paid?
- What hours do they work?
- What types of benefits are usually provided? Transportation costs? Uniforms? Time off? Sick days? Health benefits? Holiday bonuses? Severance pay? Contracts?

Also important are cultural issues that relate to the work situation in your country. For example, you may want someone who cooks and does child care, but these may be considered completely separate jobs in your host country. When Melissa lived in Nigeria, she would have preferred a female housekeeper, but in that culture, only men were available for that job. In Chile, female housekeepers don't wash windows. You are supposed to contract for a male housecleaner, a *mozo*, to come in to do them. Every culture will have its own unique set of customs relating to domestic work. Once you know what kind of help is available, what is expected of you as an employer, and any important cultural considerations to keep in mind, you are ready to begin your search.

Finding and hiring reliable domestic help

First, where do you even find the applicants? As usual, we suggest that you network through the international community in your area. It is almost always better to hire someone who has previously worked for expatriates. He or she will have previous training and experience working with foreigners and meeting the demands of an expat household. The person who held your job before you, if applicable, may have employed domestic help whom you can interview. In addition, English-language newsletters and newspapers (which may also be posted online) might include classified ads with experienced domestics looking for work. Check expatriate groups, international schools, missionary communities, and embassies or consulates in your city. In some countries, like the United States, you can contract with specialized housecleaning businesses.

Once you have identified a few candidates, you will want to set up interviews. Although there is no single interview method that works in all countries and cultures, we offer some suggestions that can be applied or adapted to most situations. First, be clear about your needs and expectations prior to the interview. As a general guideline, before interviewing anyone, you should have already decided the following:

- What your needs are
- How much you are willing to pay
- Working hours
- Work requirements (the job description)
- Your expectations of your employee (honesty, punctuality, confidentiality, etc.)
- What benefits you will offer (vacation, sick leave, overtime, etc.,)
- Whether you will have an initial probation period
- When you are likely to make a decision and how you will notify the person you decide to hire

After you have clarified your needs and expectations, you are ready to set up interviews. If the person you are interviewing does not speak your language very well and you don't speak more than a smattering of the local language, find someone to help you: a local employee from your organization, a friend or acquaintance, a local student, or a paid interpreter.

Once you have located someone who can help, write down your expectations as well as questions you would like to ask the prospective employee. Have this sheet with you during the interview. Remember, if you are using an interpreter, an interview will take twice as long, so save time by preparing the information you want to convey and the questions you want to ask in advance.

When working with an interpreter, keep your sentences concise. If sentences are long or rambling, the interpreter may not be able to remember everything you said and might leave out important details.

The interview format will vary with each country and culture. In Nigeria, Melissa informally interviewed her housekeeper in a casual conversation while he was in the backyard of his employer at the time. In Ukraine, she scheduled appointments and asked applicants previously prepared questions while they sat at her dining room table.

The rapport you establish during the interview will be the first indicator whether this is the right person for you. In addition to specifics about the job, ask questions that help give you a general impression of the individual's character, personality, and approach to work. Be sure to ask for letters of recommendation.

Your gut feeling counts for a lot here. The person you decide to hire will be working in your home. You will want someone who is trustworthy and reliable and who has a good work ethic. The personality of the individual is equally important. Remember, though, that body language and other cultural signals common in the host country may differ from what you would expect at home. For example, looking directly at an interviewer may signify honesty and self-confidence in your home country, while in another country this behavior may be considered rude. Being direct and praising one's own strengths may be admired in some countries but may be considered arrogant in your host country. If you have already learned some of the cultural ground rules of your host country, you may be able to adjust your expectations accordingly. If not, having a person familiar with the local culture (such as a colleague) present at the interview may be helpful.

It is also important to consider the educational level of the person you are interviewing. Melissa's interview with her uneducated cook in Algeria differed from her approach to a college-educated housekeeper in Ukraine. With the Algerian cook, she discussed simple, basic issues such as hours, salary, and job requirements. With the Ukrainian employee, she was able to discuss more detailed issues such as a benefits package and a written contract.

Managing household help successfully

So you have interviewed and found the right person to work in your home. He or she looks like a good match for your needs. What could go wrong? If you have never had a person from another culture working in your home, you might be surprised. In most cases, when problems arise, they usually stem from either a language barrier or cultural differences. We will look at each in turn. (For a discussion of working with caregivers for your children, see chapter 5.)

The language barrier. Problems inevitably occur if you and your household help cannot understand each other. You are frustrated because you are not getting what you want, and your household employees become nervous because they can't understand you but know you are unhappy with their work.

Although a language barrier takes time to overcome, you can make a sincere effort in that direction. You may opt to learn some basic vocabulary relating to the home or, better yet, make a greater commitment to learning the new language. The employee may speak a few words of English and be willing to work at learning more. Having a bilingual dictionary handy will be a necessity for both of you. For some languages, picture dictionaries are available that include pictures of the rooms in a house, accompanied with the names of items in each room. These can be very helpful.

What if neither you nor your help speaks the other's language at all? A friend of Melissa's in Ukraine experienced this situation. To deal with the problem, she asked Melissa to come to her home the first day and tell the housekeeper in Russian what she would like her to do. From this, the employee had a clear idea of what was expected of her. Each time she came, she did basically the same type of cleaning, so after the first time, getting the job done was never a problem.

When the friend needed to ask questions, clarify information, or make other requests, she would give Melissa a call, and Melissa would translate over the phone. She couldn't rely on Melissa all the time, of course, so sometimes she resorted to pantomime to get her point across. It wasn't long before she and her housekeeper developed their own means of communicating. In this case, finding someone available who could speak the language, explain what to do the first day, and fill in the occasional gaps when necessary was a highly effective way to cope with a language barrier.

Cultural expectations and the working relationship. Cultural differences can make themselves evident from the very beginning, when you are establishing your working relationship with your employee. Expatriates from countries such as the U.S., Canada, and Australia tend to prefer a casual, egalitarian management style. It may feel natural for them to ask household staff to call them by their first names and to eat at the family table. What is intended as a gesture of kindness, however, will probably just make the employees uncomfortable. They have their own cultural expectations of the working relationship: perhaps wearing a uniform, calling employers "Sir" and "Madam," and eating in a separate room. It is best to recognize and respect these expectations. Expats from other countries may prefer a strictly hierarchical arrangement with their staff. If the employees are used to a casual relationship with their employers but are treated as lower class, tension will result.

Even in a culture where a huge gap in social status separates employers from household staff, however, there are still many ways to show respect and consideration for the people working in your home.

- Keep the relationship professional at all times, and insist that your children also treat your staff with respect.
- Show that you respect your employees' culture. Allow time off for important local holidays and events, for example.
- Ask your employees for their advice. The way things were done in your home country may not work in your host-country environment. Your employees may suggest more effective methods.

In most cases, treating your employees fairly and professionally will result in a good working relationship. However, there are times when the balance swings the other way. Some expatriates, especially at-home spouses living abroad for the first time, report being intimidated by bossy staff who take over the household, ignoring their employer's requests. This may be a result of limited cross-cultural skills on the part of the household employee. Consider that an expatriate may arrive in a country with limited language skills and be obviously bewildered by some of the customs and practices around him or her. Especially if a household employee has never tried to learn another language and doesn't know how much of a challenge it is, he or she may interpret your fumblings with the language as a sign that you're not very bright or unable to cope with everyday life.

Patricia reports:

> *Once, when talking in Spanish to my Chilean gardener, I couldn't remember the word for "bucket." From the expression on his face, it was clear that he assumed I didn't even know what a bucket was. Perhaps he thought I was so rich and spoiled that I had never encountered one before.*

In addition, if an expatriate employer tries to be extremely friendly and generous at the beginning of a working relationship, some employees may interpret this "inappropriate" behavior as a license to take advantage of the situation. What to do?

- Try to hire employees with some cross-cultural experience in the first place, such as previous jobs with foreigners or knowledge of a foreign language.
- Be assertive and professional from the beginning of the relationship, making it clear that you are in charge and that the employee's job depends on his or her cooperation.
- Show your competence, not just your helplessness, to your employee. This is good for your self-confidence as well.

Patricia recalls:

> *I know that my nearly illiterate housekeeper in Chile thought I was a little soft in the head, because my habits were so different from hers. But when she saw me typing away at the computer, or hooking up the wiring for the cable TV, I could sense how impressed she was. Once I heard her say to a repairman, with obvious pride, "The Señora can do that."*

Melissa reports:

> *I had an expensive, beautiful royal-blue velvet dress that had been specially made for me when I lived in North Africa. Gold threads, hand-embroidered in a filigree pattern, made it the most unique dress I owned. Intending to wear it for a very formal occasion in Kiev, I asked my Ukrainian housekeeper to iron it. I explained what was needed and also showed her exactly how I wanted the dress turned inside out and ironed from the inside. My housekeeper answered, "Yes, yes, I understand." My language skills were adequate, so I felt confident that all would be well. Later, I was shocked to find the dress hanging in my closet with a permanent outline of the iron burned on the front. My housekeeper had ironed the dress from the outside, using an iron so hot that it singed the fabric!*

Avoiding accidents and misunderstandings. As Melissa's story illustrates, *yes* can mean different things in different situations, depending on the culture. It may mean "Yes, I really did understand and know exactly what you want." Or it can mean "I really didn't completely understand, but I'll give it my best shot and hope what I do comes close to what you want." In some cultures, people will say *yes* even if they don't understand, since it would be impolite or disrespectful to say *no* to a request from a person of authority or high status.

In all of our homes abroad in developing countries, there have been occasions when domestic help inadvertently damaged or ruined personal property. Many times this happened because they were using household items which were unfamiliar to them. In some cases these products or devices did not exist in their own culture, so they had no experience with them. In addition, sometimes they were not able to read the instructions or settings on our appliances.

If you want to be sure that your household help understands your directions, you will most likely have to spend considerable time working with them. Even if you "inherit" employees from your predecessor, don't forgo your own training. If your employees can read labels and instructions in the local language, you may consider using them in your home, posting laundry instructions on the washing machine, for instance.

If a household object, utensil, or appliance is so important to you that you would be upset if it were ruined or stolen, don't let your domestic employees use it. Substitute something in its place or designate yourself as the only authorized user. In addition, there is no reason to subject your household staff, who may have an extended family in great financial need, to unnecessary temptations. Unfortunate situations can also occur when household help is accused of stealing objects that have merely been misplaced. For everyone's sake, keep your valuable belongings, such as cash and expensive jewelry, secure.

Some expatriates complain of the theft of low-value items—food, cleaning products, T-shirts, even underwear—by household help. In some countries, employees may view this practice as harmless, the equivalent of taking a pen or notepad home from the office. Encouraging your employees to ask you for things they need—while making it clear that stealing will result in the loss of their jobs—may help prevent this problem.

Health and safety issues. Especially if your employees have had little schooling, training may also be necessary in matters of health, hygiene, and safety. If measures such as filtering drinking water and disinfecting vegetables are necessary in your host country, make sure your employees do this consistently and correctly. Since bacteria and viruses cannot be seen, an employee who never had science training in school may not understand how they are spread, as an expatriate in Zambia found when she saw her housekeeper wiping the kitchen counters with the same dirty rag she had used to clean the bathrooms!

If your employee cares for your children, make sure that he or she has basic knowledge of first aid and knows what to do in an emergency. Some expatriate groups have organized health and safety courses in the local language for household help, with excellent results.

If you have to terminate an employee

Firing someone is never easy, and doing so abroad can be more traumatic than firing someone at home. Many times the job you have provided is not only the person's livelihood, but also that of his or her immediate and often extended family. Such situations make terminating the employee even more difficult.

In some countries, especially developing ones, local people may view an employer as another part of the extended family. Often, their perception is that you have a lot of resources and they don't. Since you have more, they assume that you will help them. They may not understand the straightforward approach of signing a contract, then terminating an employee when their contractual obligations have not been met. In these situations, try to help them find another job or help in some other way; this will lessen the blow. It will appear to them that you have met your obligation as an employer.

In Nigeria, it became necessary for Melissa to fire her housekeeper due to cultural differences she was never able to resolve. Her appliances and kitchen equipment were so unfamiliar to him that he often inadvertently damaged or even destroyed things. She dismissed the mishaps at first; however, after several months she decided that her only choice was to let him go. He, his wife, and five children lived behind her house in a small building, so this was not a situation where she could fire him and never see him again. In addition, the building had become the family's home, so they would have nowhere to go when he no longer worked for Melissa.

To resolve the problem in a way that worked for both sides, Melissa's husband explained the specific problems with his work. Her husband then told him that he and his family could remain in the house until he was able to find another job. On occasion, Melissa and her husband helped the housekeeper's family with food and other necessities. Although losing his job was difficult, this situation was ultimately beneficial to both sides. The damage to Melissa's household equipment stopped (and her level of stress diminished), and he and his family had a place to live in the interim period between jobs. He ended up staying an additional six months before finding another job and moving on. Melissa and her husband didn't mind. They knew they had helped the family and fulfilled their obligation to them.

If you have to terminate an employee, remember to first check if there are local labor laws that apply and consider the cultural issues specific to employment in your host country. If you can release an employee in a manner that leaves his or her dignity intact and fulfills your obligation as an employer, you have achieved the optimal solution to a difficult situation.

Household employees as a cultural resource

Sometimes household employees may be from a third country (such as Patricia's Guyanese housekeeper in Trinidad). This can add even more cultural interest (and potential for misunderstandings) to the mix.

If your household employees grew up in your host country, they can potentially serve as a fascinating "bridge" to the local culture, if they are willing and you develop a good relationship.

A U.S. expat recently returned from Venezuela recalls:

> *My chauffeur was like a bodyguard. He was very well educated and we invited him and his family to our home for dinner. We knew he was doing the job for the excellent money it paid. His wife was a school teacher, his kids brilliant and beautiful. He certainly helped me understand some aspects of the Venezuelan culture I would not have known about. Speaking Spanish was key to having these insightful conversations with our conductor.*

In Chile, Patricia's housekeeper cooked traditional Chilean dishes such as a meat pie with hand-grated corn. For Chile's national holiday, she presented Patricia's young son Alex with a colorful traditional horseman's costume she'd knitted herself—which Alex proudly wore to the celebratory parade.

In Cuba, contact between local people and foreigners was restricted. Household employees (although hired through government offices and presumably required to file reports on their employers' activities) were among Patricia's most valuable windows into the host culture. Her housekeeper—a grandmother who arrived for work sitting sidesaddle on the back of her husband's bicycle—was always willing to explain Cuban customs and expressions that Patricia found puzzling. (In exchange, Patricia always carried necessities such as shoes and underwear in her housekeeper's petite size back from home leave in the United States!)

The retired woman who came once a week to clean Patricia's apartment in eastern Germany was perhaps the most active "bridge" of all. She and her husband invited Patricia's family to their apartment on numerous occasions, where they told fascinating stories of the ravages of the war and their experiences under communism. It's been four years since Patricia left the country, and the couple still sends her children chocolate and other German treats on holidays, and phones every member of her family on their birthdays!

The rewards of navigating a new culture

Tourists pay thousands of dollars for a brief glimpse of the exotic sights, traditions, and customs of a foreign country. Expatriates' experiences—which can be so much richer, broader, and deeper—should therefore be priceless.

A long-time expat advises:

> *Some aspects of your new culture will be endearing and you will adopt them; some you will miss when you leave. In Europe, I love ordering beer at the movies. In Taiwan, I like taking off my shoes at school. And in Japan, I like the carpeted subway. I appreciate that people in Korea bow to one another as a sign of respect.*

In this chapter, we have focused on the challenges commonly faced by expatriates in confronting a new culture, because we believe preparedness is the key to a smooth international move. We also believe, however, that the rewards of cross-cultural encounters outweigh the challenges. Your appreciation for the arts, crafts, music, and cuisine of another country; the memories of the unique places and events you have witnessed; your friendships with local people; the extensive knowledge you have gained of your host culture; your cross-cultural communication skills—all of these will stay with you long after you leave the country. They may also permanently change the way you view the world.

Children raised abroad have been called "third-culture kids"—they don't quite belong to the host culture, but they are also different from typical kids in their "passport" country. The more you come to understand about your host culture, and the more time you spend overseas, the more you will find yourself becoming a "global nomad" or "third-culture adult." Gradually, you may find yourself adopting some of the habits and ways of thinking prevalent in your host country. Furthermore, you may begin to advance in the skills we discussed in chapter 1 (such as adaptability and communication skills) and to take on the characteristics that many experienced expatriates seem to share, no matter what country they come from.

- A strong interest in world affairs
- A global perspective on the problems facing humanity
- Cross-cultural curiosity, sensitivity, and understanding
- A love of travel and discovery
- A determination to maintain friendships across great distances

Of course, some of these traits may be what lead people to become expatriates in the first place. Still, experiences abroad tend to strengthen all of these tendencies.

As you spend more time abroad, you may find yourself seeking out other expatriates without regard to their nationality. In Germany, Patricia joined a Spanish conversation group to help maintain her skills in the language. Although each member of the small group was from a different country—Mexico, Switzerland, Holland, Ecuador, Cuba, Peru, and the United States—they found what they had in common to be more important than their differences. Above all, they shared the experience of being temporary sojourners in their host country.

Confronting a new culture and learning to live in a strange new environment may be one of the greatest challenges you will ever face. As you rise to this challenge, you will find yourself changing, adapting, and growing. Before you realize it, you will become a seasoned expatriate, a third-culture adult . . . a citizen of the world.

CHAPTER 5

Moving Children Overseas

Some parents moving overseas don't give much thought to their children's adjustment process. "Children are resilient," they tell themselves. Yes, fortunately, children are quite resilient, but there is much you can do to make the adjustment process go more smoothly for them.

Other parents moving overseas may ask themselves, "What am I doing to my children?" Children tend to prefer the familiar and hate to be uprooted. They don't want to leave their friends and adjust to a new school. Learning a new language and seeing the sights of a new country sounds more like a chore than an adventure to most kids. In addition, concerns may arise about raising children in another country. Patricia's in-laws used to worry that their grandchildren would learn to speak only Spanish and wouldn't be able to communicate with them!

The good news is that for most families, living overseas offers many more advantages than disadvantages. It exposes children to different cultures, languages, and ways of looking at the world. It makes them more flexible and more understanding of other people's differences. It can also bring families closer together as they learn to depend on each other in a strange new environment.

As mentioned earlier in the book, children who have lived abroad for significant periods are often called *third-culture kids (TCKs)*. They learn to switch back and forth between their home-country and host-country cultures as needed and often develop a unique "bicultural" identity. Third-culture kids also tend to be more knowledgeable than average about geography and world affairs. If they are exposed to another language abroad, they may speak it fluently, without an accent.

In addition, because of their experience with cross-cultural moves, TCKs are often able to adapt well to new social situations, make friends quickly, and deal well with adults. They tend to be kind to newcomers and outsiders because they have experienced those roles themselves. Their roots are tied more to people than places, and they may think that having friends scattered around the world is natural.

Patricia reports:

> In Leipzig, Germany, I volunteered to accompany the second graders from the English-speaking international school on the streetcar to their swimming lesson each week. There were only eight children in the class. Just for fun, I counted them in English and asked who could count in another language. Hands went up, and students happily counted in German, French, Ukrainian, Czech, and Dutch. The next week, a Chilean girl, who had just moved to town and spoke only Spanish, joined the class. Her classmates handled the situation with ease, taking her hands and showing her what to do in the swimming class when she didn't understand the instructions.

The effects of living abroad are not all positive, of course. Third-culture kids face sadness at leaving friends, the difficulties of adjustment to a new culture, and feelings of not quite fitting in, even when they return home. However, most adults looking back on mobile childhoods view their experiences in a positive light. Studies show that TCKs are above average in university attendance and that they gravitate toward professions in which they can use their language and cross-cultural skills.

Informing children about the move

Your child should find out about the move from you. Children can feel a betrayal of trust if they first hear about such an important event in their lives from someone else.

When should you tell your children about the move? There are advantages in keeping life "normal" as long as possible, especially for the youngest children. A toddler need not be told about the move until a week or two before packout. Elementary school-aged children should have at least a few months to prepare and say a proper good-bye, if possible.

It is probably best to inform children aged 11 or 12 and up from the beginning and to include them to some extent in your own planning and deliberations. "Be honest. Don't sugarcoat," advises one experienced mother of teens.

If you have more than one child, choose a time frame appropriate for the oldest child and then inform everyone at once.

When you decide to tell your children about the move, prepare yourself a little beforehand. This is an important moment; it can set the tone for the rest of the move. It is best to discuss the move with your children at a time when you are relaxed, when you have plenty of time to answer their questions, when there are no distractions, and when they are in reasonably good moods.

Here are some objectives to keep in mind as you discuss the move with your child or children.

- Present the move in a matter-of-fact, positive way.
- "Universalize" the move by mentioning other families you know who have moved abroad. Children's books about moving can be helpful for younger children; there are also specialized books and workbooks for kids moving abroad, such as those available from Intercultural Press and BR Anchor Publishing.
- Answer questions calmly, patiently, in an upbeat manner, and truthfully to the extent of your children's ability to understand.
- Provide emotional support by acknowledging your children's feelings of anger, fear, or sadness. Reassure them that this is normal and that others feel the same way when their families move.

Coordinate with your spouse about what you are telling the children, or inform the children in a "family meeting" with both of you present. Be careful not to contradict each other on any major point, which could lead to confusion, mistrust, or unnecessary fears. Younger siblings should be encouraged to direct their questions to you, not to older siblings, who are likely to provide an inaccurate or frightening perspective on the event.

Similarly, children may develop an inaccurate perception from over-hearing parental discussions about the move. Try to monitor your own discussions from a child's point of view. When you express your personal fears and worries to your spouse, try to ensure that your children cannot overhear. This does not mean that you should avoid discussing any nega-tive aspects of the move with your children. You can—and should—talk about people and things you will miss, for example. But try not to raise undue fears about questions such as whether your family will have enough money, find acceptable housing, and so on. Children need a feel-ing of security about such basic issues, especially during a period of tran-sition such as a move.

However, this does not mean that you should insist on turning every conversation about the move around to the positive with oversimplified responses like, "You'll make plenty of new friends and everything will be fine!" Try, instead, to acknowledge and validate children's concerns, while reassuring them in a conversation such as this: "I know it's not easy to go to a new school where you don't know anyone. I've already e-mailed the school for some names of families with kids your age, and we'll all try to help each other make new friends."

Your children's negative feelings and worries about the upcoming move may be expressed in behavioral changes such as trouble sleeping, problems in school, or aggressiveness toward parents or siblings. Offer extra support when you see this happening. One mom was discussing the family's upcoming move with her 13-year-old daughter when the girl suddenly shouted, "I hate you!" Instead of becoming angry, the mother wisely chose to reflect her daughter's feelings, saying "You are really angry that we have to leave our house in Ohio, leave your friends, and move to a place you have never seen." "Yes, I am," the daughter replied, and the conversation continued.

Timing the move

Many families recommend moving a few weeks before the beginning of the school year in the new country—that is, if you have any choice in the matter. If you arrive at the beginning of summer vacation, it may be diffi-cult for your children to find friends (many expatriate families take an extended home leave during the summer). Arriving two weeks or so before the school year begins (or, as a second choice, during a midyear school vacation) gives children a chance to get settled in the new environment but not enough time to become bored or lonely. Then they will probably be eager to start school and to make new friends.

If you must arrive abroad at the beginning of the summer break, you may need to be more creative. Look for homeschooling and missionary families in the new country, who may not follow the typical schedule for travel and vacations. If resources permit, an at-home parent might have the chance to travel and explore the new country with the kids during the summer—perhaps renting a beach house in Turkey or staying in a family hostel in Sweden. Some families have one parent remain in the home country with the kids for part of the summer, so that they can attend summer camps and visit relatives while the employee sets up the new household.

Information and involvement—keys to children's morale

Especially if this is your children's first move, they may not know what to expect. Fear of the unknown may be strong. Many families report that young children worry about being left behind. Reassure them that this cannot happen. Older children's worries may center on adjusting to a new school and finding friends. Some may worry about their personal safety in another country. Be sure to take your children's worries seriously and offer positive suggestions, rather than dismissing their concerns.

Interesting and upbeat information about your new country can help calm children's fears and encourage them to look forward to the move. Concrete information about daily life and their new neighborhood and school is especially useful, if you can find it. Try to get in contact with families already living in your new country, through your employer, expatriate groups, or the local international school. Direct e-mail contact with families who have kids your age is best. Older kids may be able to find contacts themselves, perhaps through a school website or social networking site. In addition, research your new country on the Internet and at your local library. Look for children's stories, legends, recipes, photos and videos, and anything else that will help make the new place come to life in your children's imagination. For younger children, of course, you should focus on positive images and stories. However, be careful not to build their expectations too high. For example, if tourist brochures about the country show beautiful beaches but you won't be living near the beach, make that clear. Some experienced families make a scrapbook for each overseas move. The book may begin with photographs and drawings of your current home, school, neighborhood, and friends. Leave space for friends to add farewell messages. For younger children, add pictures of moving vans, airplanes, and so forth. The information and pictures about your new country that you find through research can also be included. A travel journal, written during your journey to your new home, can be an enjoyable family project and can be added to the scrapbook. Finally, after you arrive, the scrapbook can be completed with pictures of your new home, school, neighborhood, and friends.

The same principle can be used to create a family website to be shared with friends and extended family, perhaps password-protected for privacy. Update the site with your ongoing travels and adventures, as well as "local color" from your daily lives. Consider adding some ordinary and even ugly scenes, so viewers can gain a truer picture of your routine abroad, rather than envying what appears to be an extended exotic vacation. Teens may take on this project with enthusiasm as a way of keeping in touch with friends, perhaps even adding their own video clips. Although the decision to move overseas was probably made without the children's input, if children feel that they have some control over the process and believe that their opinions are respected, they are less likely to feel help-less, resentful, and angry about the move. Here are some ways that you might consider to involve your children.

- Hold periodic family meetings to review the progress of move preparations. Encourage children to ask questions, state their opin-ions and express their feelings.
- Involve your children in as many decisions as possible, taking their ages into account. For instance, they can help choose some of the things you are buying to take to the new home. If your itinerary includes a vacation or other stop on the way to the new country, let your children help decide how the family should spend that time.

- If you need to get rid of some household goods before the move, involve your children in the process. They can help with a yard sale or box up giveaways for charity. Recognize, however, that most children have a hard time letting go of their own possessions, especially when they are facing the upheaval of a move. Try to refrain from a major purge of their belongings around the time of a move.

Something to look forward to

No matter how excited you might be about the move, your children will probably view it as a misfortune, even a catastrophe. Try to make it a little easier by giving them something specific about the move to look forward to.

When Patricia and her husband were getting ready to move to Germany, for example, they promised their two boys bunk beds, which the boys had always wanted, along with new bicycles, since they hadn't done much biking in the tropical country they were leaving. Patricia knew that bunk beds and bicycles would be easy to find in Germany, and the prospect of these new things made the boys more eager to arrive there and made the first months of settling in a bit easier.

This "something to look forward to" is not a bribe for good behavior during the move. Instead, it should be something that fits in naturally with the advantages of the new place. It may be hockey skates in Canada, snorkeling equipment in Barbados, or horseback riding lessons in Argentina. It might be a new pet to help ease your children's loneliness for friends and extended family (perhaps acquired in the new country to avoid issues such as quarantine; see chapter 6), or perhaps a trip to a special place near your destination: the pyramids in Egypt or Disneyland in California. Get creative in thinking of ways to help your children view your overseas move as an opportunity and not just a loss.

Schooling options

If you have school-aged children, a very important variable is added to your overseas move. Is schooling in English available in your new location? Are local schools an option? Perhaps no adequate school is available; then what? Homeschooling and boarding schools are further options for internationally mobile families.

It is wise to gather information about potential schools from three sources: the school itself, reference materials such as guidebooks and websites, and families with students currently attending the school. The schools themselves will, of course, put you in touch with families who will express positive opinions. Network through expatriate groups and websites, and perhaps your colleagues, to find others. Be sure to talk to several families, because perspectives can vary greatly. Check out the websites of schools in your new location—but remember to take them with a grain of salt. Excellent schools can have rudimentary websites (or none at all), while some institutions cheerfully inflate their offerings. The photo of the smiling swim team may hide the fact that the school's pool was closed down five years ago.

If your children are in middle or high school, you will have to consider the academic offerings of overseas schools even more carefully. Although most expatriate students do very well abroad and after their return, we have known several cases where students had to repeat a year or more because of inadequate schooling abroad. Families facing this situation should be proactive. Research the requirements of your next school or university, and consider supplementing your student's schoolwork with tutoring, online or correspondence courses, or summer school. Boarding school may be the best option in some cases.

The social environment of overseas schools also becomes more important for older students. While most international schools are diverse and welcoming places, some expats have encountered tensions between national, ethnic, native-language, or religious groups. Be alert for these issues as you talk to families and tour potential schools. Keep in mind, however, that problems you hear about may be caused by a certain clique or a few individuals and not be widespread within the school.

The following sections describe potential schooling choices for internationally mobile families. Even if your organization tries to steer you toward a particular school and even pays the tuition, it is worthwhile to check out all of the available options. You may find one that suits your family better.

Children with special needs

If your child has a physical handicap, learning disability, or other challenge that requires accommodation during the school day, you will need to do even more research as you make your decisions about overseas education. Many international and foreign schools are simply not equipped to accommodate special needs, and there is no legal requirement for them to accept and assist your child.

Be honest and up-front about your child's situation when you talk to school administrators. Some expats have minimized or not mentioned a child's emotional or learning difficulties to school personnel, only to face a crisis several months later when teachers became aware of the problem and the child was expelled. Some families recommend bringing the child along on an exploratory trip, so that he or she can be evaluated by school counselors and you can assess the "fit" between child and school.

Some school administrators may be helpful and flexible in trying to provide an appropriate learning environment for your child. However, others may not have the resources—or the desire—to make special accommodations. Still others may seem to have little understanding of your child's needs. You may have to work out a creative solution, perhaps involving homeschooling, distance learning and/or supplementary tutors.

International or third-country schools

International, British, or American schools (as well as French, German, and Spanish schools and others) have been established in many foreign cities with significant expatriate populations. These schools are often an attractive option for mobile families. However, they can vary greatly in their academic quality, social atmosphere, and costs. An "American school" may have a large population of students from the United States and follow a U.S. curriculum—or it may simply have been founded by an American entrepreneur to provide local students with an opportunity to be educated in English. Thus, it is important for parents to carefully investigate a school before enrolling their children.

Instruction at international schools is generally in English or in a combination of English and the local language (sometimes with half a day in each). Secondary students may be able to choose from an American, British, or International Baccalaureate (IB) degree program. The IB program is a rigorous, internationally designed curriculum that prepares its graduates to attend university in a range of countries. It is highly respected, but we have heard that not every school implements it to the same extent, especially in the lower grades.

International school classes tend to be small, and the student body usually includes children from many different countries—25 nationalities is a typical number. These students' international experience gives them something in common with your children, and schooling becomes a true cross-cultural or multicultural exchange.

Many international, British, American, and local private schools are filled to capacity each year, so it is important to contact schools as early as you can to apply for admission. Some schools require an entrance examination as well.

One potential drawback of international or even "American" schools is that the classes may have a high proportion of nonnative speakers of English. If your children are native speakers, you may fear that they might be held back while other students struggle with the language. If this is a concern for you, ask how the school handles this issue. Some parents decide to send younger children to schools in the local language if they face a situation like this. Better, they think, to have their children be challenged by a foreign language than to be bored while classmates strain to catch up in English.

Local schools

In some places, local schools may be a viable educational option for your children. Public schools may be appreciably less expensive than an international school, and they provide an opportunity for your child to become immersed in the local language and culture.

At the preschool level, local schools may be your only option. Preschoolers have a special advantage in learning language through the immersion method because they are not expected to do academic work, and their peers won't be bothered if they are at a loss for words at the beginning.

Patricia reports:

One of my sons attended preschool in Spanish, the other in German. A few months after we arrived in Germany, a pair of psychology students sat in on my younger son's preschool class. After the session, the teacher pointed out the little American in her class; they answered that they hadn't noticed anything different about him at all!

At higher grade levels, adaptation to a foreign-language environment becomes a progressively more difficult challenge. A lonely and frustrating period must be expected at the beginning of the school year. Yet many (but not all) children younger than about 12 seem almost miraculous in their ability to pick up languages. After struggling for a few months, they are suddenly able to do the work and keep up with their class. We have known expat children who became the best students in the class because they were concentrating so hard on understanding the lessons.

Aside from language, culture must also be considered in a local school. Will your children be the only foreigners in their classes? Are there aspects of the local culture that make you uncomfortable? (You may find that your own country has no monopoly on social snobbery, sexism, or racism, for example. Both of us have encountered worse examples of all of these abroad than at home.)

In addition, will you have any further contact with that country or culture in the future? Or do you expect to move on to a completely different part of the world? We have known North American parents with Hispanic roots who were very happy for the opportunity to place their kids in Spanish-speaking schools overseas. On the other hand, if the family will be moving to a different country every few years, it may be a heavy burden on the children to immerse themselves in a new language and culture each time.

We share the opinion that if the children are young, if the family's overseas experience will be concentrated in a single cultural region, or if the family strongly wishes their kids to become fluent in the local language, local schools can offer a very valuable experience. However, if you plan to move frequently, if your children are already in the middle grades, and/or if the local language and culture will have little relevance to your children's future, an international school is likely a better choice.

Home study options

If no school meets your family's needs—or if you're interested in trying out the growing phenomenon of homeschooling—the best option may be to create your own school at home. Many overseas parents have become successful home teachers, working with regular school curricula from their home district or with textbooks, workbooks, and tests from correspondence schools or specialized publishers. If you feel the need for additional help in teaching, tutors can often be found locally (perhaps a university student from your home country).

Some correspondence schools provide comprehensive materials, even including videos or DVDs that do not require the parent to serve as a teacher (although parents always need to provide help and supervision). Assignments and tests are e-mailed or mailed to teachers in the home country, who provide correction and comments. Online schooling options are also quickly expanding. Students can participate in interactive courses via computer and even have virtual discussions with their fellow learners.

Check your host country's regulations before making plans for home-schooling. In some countries, all children must be enrolled in a school. If this is the case where you are, find out if you can satisfy the requirements by signing your child up for a recognized distance-learning program. The authorities may consider that an acceptable "private school." You may also face testing requirements in the host country.

For students and parents who are willing and able to put in the effort, homeschooling can offer numerous advantages. You can agree to an assignment on a tiny tropical island in the Pacific, as one diplomatic family did, without worrying about the availability of schools. Because you are not tied to a school schedule, you will have the freedom to travel when it's convenient for you and to visit museums and other sites of interest during the workday rather than on crowded weekends. Patricia home-schooled her sons for one year and took them on trips to Germany and Guatemala, teaching math on the plane and refreshing the German and Spanish they'd learned abroad. Homeschooling families often find themselves growing closer and feeling that their lives are less hectic. (Of course, as Patricia's sons will tell you, there are also times when they get on each other's nerves and wonder why they ever agreed to the arrangement!)

One common worry for new homeschooling families is the availability of social interaction for their children. This may indeed be a problem on tiny Pacific islands, but in most places, homeschooling children will be able to join sports teams, volunteer or Scout groups, religious youth groups, and other associations where they can make friends and learn social skills. It's also especially important for homeschooling parents abroad to make friends with other families with children of similar ages.

Homeschooling is not for everyone, but it is increasingly recognized as a viable option for overseas families. Many children schooled in this way have gone on to brilliant university and professional careers. If you are interested in this option, a quick Internet search will turn up numerous homeschooling organizations and websites that can provide guidance. Some have a religious orientation, others focus on rigorous classical learning, while yet others advocate "unschooling" or letting your child choose his or her own interests and activities. Choose those that most closely fit your family's educational philosophy.

Boarding schools

Many internationally mobile families send their children of high-school age, or even younger, to boarding schools. The school may be in the home country or closer to the parents' place of assignment. For example, one missionary family working in Nepal sent their teenaged daughter to boarding school in India.

Good boarding schools offer top-notch academics and a nurturing environment. If you consider this option, be sure to visit several schools to find the right one for your child. Numerous directories and guides to boarding schools are available in libraries and on the Internet. One warning passed along to us by experienced families is that it is easier to find a good boarding school environment for girls than it is for boys. Boys' schools sometimes develop an unhealthy atmosphere in which bullying and even abuse can occur. Try to talk to some of the school's current students and recent graduates to make sure it offers an appropriate social as well as academic environment.

If you have more than one child, keep in mind that different schooling options may best suit their individual needs and temperaments. For example, a family we know in a Middle Eastern country was not completely satisfied with the international school there. They chose to homeschool one of their teenagers, an introvert who enjoys independent study. However, their two other children, who are more outgoing and interested in school activities, decided to attend the school, supplemented by extra study at home.

Helping children learn the language

As with adults, your children may need to start learning the language in advance, depending on the environment in your new country and their school situation. Will your daily life involve interactions with local people from the very beginning, or will you be living in a compound for expatriates? Will your children attend an English-speaking school or go to a school where they are taught in the local language?

Language study is usually much easier for children after they actually arrive in the new country. Just being in the environment will help them learn. In addition, tutors and classes may be cheaper and easier to find, the school may offer a bilingual program, and your children may begin to make friends who speak the target language. In most cases, however, we think it is important for children to have at least some idea of the language before they arrive. At a minimum, you should make sure they learn some basic words, phrases, and greetings.

The importance of prior study also depends on your children's ages. At around 10 to 12 years of age, depending on the individual, a major shift occurs in a child's ability to learn languages. Before age 10, children can usually pick up languages "by ear" quite rapidly and without much effort when immersed in an environment where that language is spoken. These early language learners tend to speak the language with perfect pronunciation, although their speech may be peppered with grammatical mistakes.

After about age 12, however, a young person's brain becomes less receptive to picking up a language from the environment. Those who start learning a language at this time or later will probably always have a foreign accent. On the other hand, older children are better than their younger counterparts at studying languages in an academic setting, either with a teacher or with self-study materials.

If you have children younger than 10, you can expect them to pick up the language quickly after they arrive in the country. Introducing them to a bit of vocabulary in advance, in an enjoyable way, is probably enough. Depending on the language, you might find computer programs, books, songs, and stories designed to help children learn the language. If your children will be going to school in the target language, more effort is called for: perhaps a class is available in your area, or you might hire a native speaker of the language to spend time with your children—not tutoring them, but just doing something enjoyable together while speaking only the target language. (Don't let your children hear the person speaking English—children are very practical, and they will see no need to struggle with French if they know their companion understands English perfectly well!)

If your children are older than 10 or 11, learning the language will be more of an academic undertaking. Check online booksellers, distance learning programs, bookstores, and libraries together, and choose a few materials—computer or online courses, book and CD sets, DVDs, and/or self-study manuals. Also look for items from the country that will help motivate your young learner—perhaps pop songs, teen magazines or a school newsletter (ask colleagues or other expats in your new country for help). Set aside at least 3 hours a week for study; an hour a day is better. You may also consider enrolling your older children in a language class or hiring a trained tutor. Choose a teacher who can take an academic approach but who also has a sense of humor and can make the sessions fun.

You will face the greatest challenge of all if your children are older than 10 and will have to go to school full-time in a new language. Because both schoolwork and language learning become harder at this age, your children will need all the advantages you can give them. Work with a language school or tutor to design a learning program for them, including the study of specifically academic language, such as the vocabulary of science and math. (This can get expensive, but if a company or organization is sending you abroad, they may be persuaded to pay for it.) In this case, consider arriving in the new country at the beginning of the summer vacation to give your children extra time in the country to learn and practice the language before school starts.

Preparing for the move

The importance of a sponsor for your children

As we discussed in chapter 1, we feel strongly that every family moving overseas should have a sponsor in the new country. This is someone—ideally another family—who helps with the transition by providing advance information, getting things ready on the ground, greeting you when you arrive, and helping you get settled. The following are some factors for ideal sponsorship of a family with children.

- The sponsor should have spent at least six months in the country and feel relatively comfortable there.
- The sponsor should also have children, if possible.
- If the actual sponsor does not have children, another family with children should be asked to volunteer some support in child-related matters.
- The sponsoring family should be willing and able to devote some time to helping your family, especially right after arrival.
- The sponsor should live relatively near your new quarters.
- The sponsor should be assigned as early as possible before your arrival, so that you can communicate beforehand.

As you communicate with your sponsor or the other people assisting you before arrival, ask if he, she, or they would be willing to do the following:

- Meet with you during an exploratory trip
- Collect information for you about play groups for younger children and other families with kids in your new neighborhood
- Assist you with schooling decisions
- E-mail you photos of their own kids, local kid-friendly places, the school your children will attend, and even your new home (if you have chosen it in advance or have been assigned to organizational housing); this will give your kids a head start on gaining a sense of familiarity with the new country
- Encourage communication between their children and yours, such as exchanging e-mails, photos, and perhaps letters and small gifts

- Lend you some age-appropriate toys, games, and books until your shipments arrive

Don't feel guilty about "bothering" your sponsor—just make sure you provide as much help when the next family arrives.

Moving children's belongings

When a family moves within a single country, the parents can often pull off a "magical transformation." After a few days of uprootedness, children find that their furniture, belongings, and toys have all moved with them to the new house. All the familiar decorations and objects, set up pretty much as they were before, provide a sense that this is home now, and children quickly begin to adapt.

An overseas move is another story entirely. It can take months for all of those familiar things to reassemble themselves. Meanwhile, children, especially young ones, wonder where home is and if they are there or not.

It helps if the children are told from the beginning what to expect and are involved in the planning. If you will be separating your belongings into different shipments—such as a large sea crate and a faster air shipment—let them pick some important items to place in the air shipment. Slip some new surprises into the air shipment as well—especially things like books, games, art materials, craft supplies, CDs, and electronic games, which can help keep kids busy on arrival when they have few friends and activities.

Each child should set aside a few of his or her most important possessions to be carried in a backpack or suitcase with you throughout the trip. A child's room, even if it is shared with siblings, is a special haven. Let your kids participate in planning for their new space. A teen looking back on several international transfers recalls: "Every time we move, my parents let me get a new bedspread. My dad and I always paint my new room to match the bedspread and it helps make the space mine."

If you will be living in a rented apartment and can't paint the walls or build in shelves, the following are just a few of the many ways to quickly personalize their new space.

- Pictures and posters reflecting your child's interests
- Removable wallpaper borders

- Colorful sheets, bedspreads, pillows, and comforters
- Bulletin boards, chalkboards, etc.
- A throw rug to cover existing flooring or carpet (young children especially love the kind with a town depicted on them for floor play)
- Colorful boxes to help keep possessions organized (and in tropical countries, to protect them from mold and bugs)

Many of these items are not heavy and can be sent in airfreight to help your children feel at home as quickly as possible. Even if you must spend a long period in temporary housing, these items can easily be set up and later moved to your permanent quarters.

Besides the items just mentioned to help personalize your children's room(s), experienced families usually ship a large amount of children's supplies overseas. Before you pack, carefully investigate the availability—and prices—of children's clothes, toys, and other needs in the new country. In many cases it will make sense to bring along a supply of children's items to last through your entire stay. Things to consider taking with you, depending, of course, on the age(s) of your children, include the following:

- All of the endless range of baby needs, from disposable diapers to strollers
- Educational toys and games
- Children's books and workbooks
- A multisystem, multivoltage TV and "codeless" DVD player (if you are going to a country with a different system), so you can watch programming and movies from both countries
- Electronic game systems and video games—note that some systems have regional codes, so you may need to purchase a new console to play games purchased locally
- Clothes to grow into (consider seasons and sizes carefully)
- Birthday gifts for other kids (consider gifts that appeal to a wide range of interests)
- Gifts for your own child, for future holidays and birthdays
- Holiday decorations and supplies
- Sports equipment

- Beach and pool toys and equipment, if appropriate
- Child-sized furniture
- Kids' toiletries such as shampoo, toothpaste, and bath soap
- Children's vitamins and familiar over-the-counter medications (check expiration dates); check with your pediatrician about fluoride supplements and other special recommendations
- Guidebooks on children's health and development
- A supply of some of your kids' favorite nonperishable foods, if permitted—of course, they will eventually have to get used to the foods available in your new country; however, some familiar treats will help ease the transition
- Large play equipment, such as climber and swing sets, paddling pools, and covered sandboxes—however, tire swings and wooden playhouses built by a handy parent or a skilled local carpenter can often substitute for the toy-company versions

If you will be living in an apartment, or if the weather is too hot or cold in your new country to spend much time outdoors, consider setting up an indoor playroom for active young children. One British family with three young boys put down gymnastics-type mats in their playroom and set up a sturdy climbing apparatus. During tropical summers, when the heat outside was unbearable, the boys happily swung and hung upside down in their air-conditioned "playground."

Sea shipments to faraway countries can take months to arrive. Your crate may have to wait for a ship to fill up, or it may be mired in endless customs delays. Meanwhile, the period without familiar objects and toys can seem like forever for children, especially young ones.

Investigate possible options for sending your children's most important equipment and possessions by a faster method. Perhaps you can send part of your shipment by air (which, however, can also take a long-time if customs delays are part of the problem). Look into charges for excess baggage; they may be cheaper than international shipping. If you can receive packages at your new destination, consider packing up some boxes and mailing them to your sponsor or a helpful colleague in advance. Having familiar objects (and a few new surprises) waiting for your kids—and for you—can help turn even the dreariest, emptiest new quarters into home.

The family pet

It may be difficult or expensive to take a cat or dog with you as you move overseas. However, if your children are attached to your family pet, make every effort to take it along. A familiar, beloved pet can help provide children with security and reassurance as they move. A pet can be a faithful friend and good listener when a child feels scared and lonely in a new place. (See chapter 6 for details on taking animals overseas.)

If you feel you absolutely must find another home for a family pet before moving, try to do this as early as possible. Although it is tempting to postpone the tears and heartache, it is best to allow children a period of grief for the loss of the pet that does not overlap with the stresses of the move. In addition, you need not tell very young children that the loss of the pet is related to the move. Simply tell them that your family cannot keep the pet any longer.

If you have given away a beloved pet, consider acquiring some sort of animal after you arrive overseas. Of course, a new pet will not erase the memory of the one left behind, but it will help turn the child's mind in a positive direction.

Moving with children of various ages

Babies

During the first eight months of life, an infant will hardly notice a move at all. The burden will all fall on you, as you lug a mountain of baby supplies and equipment through airports and try to juggle interrupted naps and feeding times.

When Patricia moved abroad with a seven-week-old baby, she was lucky enough to be able to mail boxes of supplies to herself in advance, including disposable diapers, toys, medicines, and so forth. If mailing is not an option, consider airfreight or excess baggage. Even if similar items are available in your new country, having a supply of familiar brands will help ease the transition to new products. Perhaps they will be labeled in a language you don't know . . . and shopping is never an easy task with a baby along.

Patricia was also breast-feeding at the time, which she recommends highly to internationally mobile moms. Breast-feeding eliminates the need to ship large amounts of formula or switch to foreign brands (she sent a small supply anyway, just in case) as well as the need to constantly sterilize water, bottles, and rubber nipples. In some developing countries, tap water may require five-minute boiling plus filtering to remove contaminants such as heavy metals. Bottled water can be used to mix formula, but have it tested if you can, since the quality varies greatly. Or boil and filter it regardless.

Patricia also found breast-feeding to be highly convenient during the move itself, on airplanes, and in hotels. If you plan to leave the baby with a sitter for extended periods, find a breast pump that works for you and take it along. Many moms report that the handheld ones work just as well as electric models, once you get the hang of it.

If you are formula feeding, consider using disposable bottle liners or buying a countertop bottle sterilizer (with compatible voltage or a transformer). Investigate the kinds of formula available at your destination. In some countries, special kinds such as soy-based formulas for allergic children are not available, so you might have to ship a full supply. Even if you plan to use local formula, take along a good amount of the brand your baby is used to, so that you can make a gradual transition to the local version.

One of Patricia's favorite pieces of equipment during her move with a baby in tow was a small, inflatable bathtub. It took up practically no space in the suitcase and could be blown up in seconds. A combination car seat and carrier also plays many essential roles during the moving period. It serves well for napping on the move, for a comfortable seat, and even for feeding an older baby. A stroller attachment or comfortable handle will be especially important as you hurry through airports and find your way around an unfamiliar city.

Equipment Patricia shipped for the baby in her household effects included a baby swing, portable playpen, stroller, and screened shade tent (it was a tropical country). She also took along a baby backpack but never used it in the sun and heat; it would have been much more practical in a temperate country. The playpen also saw much use as a travel crib. Hotels may or may not offer cribs, or the ones they provide may not be up to the safety standards you expect. We've seen some that appeared about to collapse, while others had spaces between the bars wide enough for the baby's head to poke through!

Toddlers and preschoolers

Once a baby reaches the toddling stage, moving becomes more difficult. Keeping up with a mobile baby during a move—or anytime—is a challenge, and many more dangers await a baby on the move than at home. More important, new fears set in at this time: about strangers, about losing you, and about new things in general.

Home, at this age, is the primary focus of life; its people, routines, and objects are the foundation of the toddlers' world. They like to find the same objects in the same place and do the same activities in the same order. This is part of the way they achieve a feeling of confidence and mastery of their environment.

For toddlers who are not talking yet, a major disruption in the household must be a frightening mystery. They are old enough to realize that something big is happening, but not old enough to ask you what, exactly, is going on. Still, even one-year-olds can begin to understand the idea of boxing things up to send to a new place.

Make an effort to explain the process in simple terms. You can even make a game out of it. Help a doll or stuffed animal family move to a "new home" in another part of your house. Pack up some ordinary household items in a box and ship them on top of a toy truck. Be creative: if you will be staying in a hotel en route, have the stuffed animal family do the same. Show how they unpack and are glad to see their things again.

The young child's tendency to be embedded in the present moment can also be an advantage, however. One family with one- and two-year-old children was pleasantly surprised after packout to find the children playing happily in their empty home without showing signs of distress at the disappearance of so many familiar objects. At this age, children take the world at face value; a new "status quo" can be rapidly accepted.

Some young children, however, react fearfully to a move. In Patricia's new home in Chile, her 17-month-old son visibly panicked when the family's shipment arrived. He had associated moving trucks and big cardboard boxes with the mysterious disaster that had struck his orderly life several months before, and now it seemed to be happening all over again.

Continuity in four general areas can help young children feel secure: people, routines, objects, and concepts. Here's how to provide support in each area during a move.

People are the most important source of stability for young children. During a move, they "lose" everybody they know outside the nuclear family. This is bound to be stressful. To help compensate, spend extra time with them before, during, and right after the move. Try to avoid unusual separations, such as traveling without them or starting work if you have not worked before (wait until several months after the move, if possible). Finally, work on building relationships with new friends and neighbors as quickly as possible.

Start the search for caregivers—babysitters, day care, or preschool—as soon as possible. Even if you're not employed, you may need time to do a number of things (such as unpack!) without your children. Meanwhile, they may be clinging to you with extra force because of the disruptions in their lives. Identifying appropriate caregivers as soon as possible gives your children the maximum time to become accustomed to the situation. Both before and after you move, ask other expat parents for recommendations and advice.

Routines are disrupted most during the period of actual travel to your new home. Children function best if they can stay as close to their regular schedule as possible, even while traveling, and can reestablish their usual routines in the new home. Before you move, make a note of your children's normal routines and regular activities. As you travel, try to stick to these comforting, familiar activities as closely as possible. In fact, this is so helpful that you may even consider adding additional routines to existing ones before you move, if you have time. Choose things that can be done no matter where you are, such as a blessing to be said before meals, a special puppet who tucks the child in at night, or a song for bath time.

When you reach your new home, establish new routines and rituals quickly. For example, you might take a walk together every day after breakfast. Seeing the same things happening day after day in the new country will help your children feel that they "know what to expect" there—that it is a familiar and comfortable place rather than a strange and unpredictable one.

Objects necessarily get packed up and disappear. Choose a few strategic objects from your children's everyday life to carry with you or to send by a rapid method. Look for a high level of "comfort value" relative to weight. Besides the obvious stuffed animals and toys, consider the following:

- A special plate, cup, spoon, placemat, and so forth
- Familiar bath toys and supplies
- Photographs of special people
- A favorite decorated pillowcase
- DVDs and a portable player
- A portable music player and favorite songs and lullabies, as well as music they are used to hearing *you* play around the house

Concepts are often neglected because they seem obvious, but they can be a great ally in helping children feel comfortable in a new place. On the most basic level, red is still red and a triangle is still a triangle no matter where you go. With a little help, your children will enjoy recognizing things that are the same or similar in a new place. Ask them to identify objects and furniture and to tell you what they are for. Show them where things "go" in the new home. Very rapidly they will feel that they "know the place." The following are some examples to build on.

- What are the kitchen appliances like? The stove, refrigerator, and dishwasher (if there is one!) may look different, but they have the same functions.
- Where do different things belong in the house: toothbrushes, silverware, towels, cookies? Where does the trash go?
- Where do people sit, eat, sleep, play, bathe?
- Where are the windows and doors? How many are there?

If you play this game at home a few times *before* you move, your children will be even more likely to derive a sense of familiarity and mastery from it.

Grade-school children

School-aged children's horizons extend beyond the home, with friends and school taking on more significance. Activities such as sports and lessons also become more important. At this age, information about a new country begins to interest children. Together, you can research topics such as the foods, customs, history, and geography of your new country. Information about daily life—perhaps provided by your sponsor—is especially helpful. The Internet is an excellent source of information about other countries—surf with your child and learn together. The challenges of a move with grade-school children include

- helping them cope with the loss of friends and find new ones,
- getting them settled in school, and
- getting them involved in new activities.

The pain of leaving friends increases greatly at this age. While preschoolers forget the friends they leave behind rather quickly, school-aged children miss them intensely. The ritual of "saying good-bye," discussed later in this chapter, becomes especially important. Encourage your children to maintain contact with old friends—through e-mail, letters, or other means. Eventual visits, if possible, can be very helpful to show children that their friends are not lost forever.

At the same time, new friends can be the best remedy for children's blues. Be proactive in helping your children find new playmates. Encourage them to invite classmates home to play. If you move during the summer, take the initiative in seeking out other families, perhaps colleagues at work or members of expatriate groups, who have children of similar ages.

Choosing the right school for your children was discussed earlier in this chapter. Once you have made your decision, stay involved in the schooling process. The way things are done in an overseas school may surprise both you and your children. Try to equip them with the same kinds of supplies that the other kids use, even if you have home-country substitutes on hand. Keep lines of communication open with your children's teachers. If you don't speak the teacher's language, find a friend or colleague who is willing to help you communicate.

Enjoyable activities outside the home can help school-aged children adjust more quickly to a new place. If possible, offer your children the opportunity to do something they have been wanting to try. Activities to consider include music lessons, swimming lessons, sports lessons (such as tennis), horseback riding, team sports, scouting, drama clubs, art, crafts, and so on.

If these activities are offered exclusively in a language your children don't know, encourage them to give a favorite activity a try, but don't push too hard. If they refuse, offer again in six months. They may be more comfortable with the language by that time and willing to try. If there are no suitable group activities available, be creative about making your own fun. Go swimming, hiking, or biking together after school or on weekends. Visit museums. Find out what unique opportunities your host country offers and take advantage of them regularly. Look for interesting things that you couldn't do back home.

At the same time, try to avoid overscheduling your children. A move causes stress, no matter how well children seem to be handling it, and school-aged children need "downtime" during the week.

Teenagers

Some teenagers welcome a new adventure or the chance to escape a dull school routine, especially if your stay abroad will only be temporary. However, many may feel as if their lives are being ruined forever. If a girl-friend or boyfriend is in the picture, the prospect of separation will be painful. In addition, teens may have plans for the next few years (perhaps playing on a sports team, taking advanced courses in school, and learning to drive) that don't include moving to Ouagadougou.

Teens usually have a harder time moving abroad than younger children, for three main reasons:

- Their schooling decisions and performance become more important as they look ahead to university studies or a career
- Their relationships with friends and romantic attachments are deeper, and separation is more painful
- Their activities and interests, inside and outside of school, tend to be even more important to them and may be directed toward a future career

While the schooling issue is especially touchy for teens, students of this age also have a wider range of options. For instance, let's imagine an

English-speaking family with a teenager—call her Anna—moving from Canada to Dakar, Senegal. As of 2007, Anna would have two schools in the city to consider: the International School of Dakar and the religiously affiliated Dakar Academy. If resources permit (perhaps with the employer's help), the family might consider sending her to a quality boarding school back in Canada or in a closer location such as Great Britain or Switzerland. Another option would be to allow Anna to live with a host family or relative in Canada, attending her previous high school or a different one. If a parent will have time to provide support, Anna might also choose to homeschool abroad, perhaps using an online program, since high-speed Internet connections are available in Dakar. She might also learn fluent French in Senegal and get involved in volunteer work that helps boost her application to the university of her choice.

The final decision for Anna and her family will depend on her particular interests, needs, and plans for the future. If at all possible, visit potential high schools (including boarding schools) with your teen. Attend classes and talk to a range of students and parents. Investigate possible activities for your teen both inside and outside of school.

An older teen's first impulse might be to plead to stay behind. This may indeed be possible, as just discussed. This is a difficult decision, involving factors such as schooling, concerns about adequate supervision, and the desire to keep the family together. You might consider having your teen come along for a trial period. The high-school-aged son of a friend of ours moving from Rome to Brussels wanted to stay with his friends in Rome. His school offered a boarding option, so this would have been possible. However, his parents convinced him to give Brussels a try for a year, promising that he could return to Rome if he remained miserable. He adjusted well and graduated from high school in Brussels. The knowledge that he had another option may have been a positive factor in this teen's adjustment abroad.

Teens' friendships are strong and the pain of separation is intense, especially if they are involved in a romantic relationship. During and after the move, you may find them glued to a laptop or wanting to spend hours in an Internet café, instant-messaging and e-mailing their friends. The telephone is another lifeline for teenaged friends; one recalls: "My parents got an amazing phone plan in Germany, so calling the United States only costs about a dollar per hour. When I first moved here, they allowed me to call my best friends in the U.S. as much as I wanted."

This contact can be quite helpful in easing the pain of the transition, of course, but as we advise the adults in the family in chapter 7, relying completely on a long-distance social network is not conducive to good adjustment in the new environment. Explain this to your teens and encourage them to branch out. Allowing teens' best friends to plan a visit, if this is possible, can also be helpful. Supporting teens in their efforts to connect in a new place can be a bit tricky. You can't just make playdates for them as you could when they were younger; they need to build relationships on their own. One of the best ways to help is to do your own research into available activities (for example, local sports teams, lessons, volunteer opportunities, and youth groups) and offer them choices.

Two 14-year-old girls in Casablanca report:

> We wish our parents would tell us about all the opportunities and let us choose. Not just put us in the activity without asking. It makes us feel like we have no control over our lives and maybe we'd rather do a different activity in the new place, be different people or try something new.

Clubs, sports, and lessons can help your teen build self-esteem and self-confidence, avoid boredom, identify interests for the future, build a positive attachment to the new place, and meet others who share their interests. It's ideal when you can find interesting new activities (such as scuba diving, skiing, or wildlife photography) that they couldn't have pursued at home.

Some teens already have a particular activity or interest that they take very seriously and may even be planning to turn into a career or lifelong occupation. If this is true for your teen, do your best to make sure he or she can continue to pursue the activity abroad. This consideration may even affect your decisions about schooling or allowing your teen to stay behind in your home country. We do not think it is wise to force a teen who is truly serious about an activity to give it up. Your teen may have big dreams for the future—as a symphony violinist, famous ballet dancer, or professional athlete—and if these dreams don't materialize, you don't want your teen to blame you for the rest of his or her life. We know a man in his 40s who still believes that his prospects for a professional baseball career were ruined because his parents moved him to Cairo for high school.

Fortunately, you may be successful in finding ways for your teen to practice a special interest abroad—perhaps even more effectively than at home. If the activity is not offered at school, your teen may be able to pursue it among adults in the community. Another option is to start your own group. A teen skilled in debating might start her international school's first debate club—which may look just as good on her university application as winning a competition at home. A talented athlete may organize a sports team for underprivileged children in the host country, providing uniforms and equipment donated by people back home.

A mom in Croatia reports:

> *Our 17-year-old daughter, who has been horseback riding and competing since she was 5 years old, trained with an Olympic gold medalist on her spring break from school. I don't think we would ever have been able to arrange something like this if we were in the U.S. The sport is so expensive, and the top riders are practically celebrities.*

When you move with teens, involve them in the process as much as possible. Assign them topics for study and research. Give them the opportunity to learn the new language. Let them help choose new household supplies and equipment, especially for their own room(s). Give them responsibilities, such as organizing a moving sale—and perhaps keeping some of the profits.

Once you arrive, allow your teens to explore as much as possible (within safety limits) and help you find grocery stores, pharmacies, parks, and so forth. The more involved they feel, the more likely they are to feel positive about the move. Look for new privileges that can be granted to your teens in the new environment.

Although you may be distracted by your own adjustment process and the hundreds of tasks involved in moving, not to mention younger children, remember that teens are vulnerable after a move and need extra support and supervision. In their quest to find friends, they might experiment with risky behavior, hoping to gain attention and acceptance. Get to know your teens' new friends and invite them to your home, even if it is still full of boxes. Make time to talk, listen and sympathize with their concerns.

You may find the teen culture in your new country very different from what you are used to. In Argentina, for example, even preteens often get together for late-night parties that start at 11 P.M.! Local sexual mores may be either looser or stricter than those at home. Be sure to get advice from other parents of teens already in the country as you set rules for your family.

The good news for families with teens is that many young people draw closer to their parents and siblings during and after their overseas experience. In the early weeks overseas, the family unit is a kind of "lifeboat," isolated from others. Family members must rely on each other, perhaps more than ever before. The strong ties that develop in such a situation (similar to the feelings shared by members of a wilderness survival course) can be enduring, permanently strengthening the family.

Many teens with overseas experience also exhibit more mature judgment than their untraveled peers. Their horizons have been expanded through exposure to different cultures and ways of life as well as through the challenges of adjusting to a foreign place. They are more likely to be tolerant, understanding, diplomatic, and realistic about the world and their place in it.

Older teens often complain about the lack of work opportunities overseas. The kinds of part-time jobs available to teens at home may not exist where you are going—or perhaps your teen lacks a work permit, or the pay scales in your new country are ridiculously low. If your teen wants to work but cannot, here are some solutions to consider.

- Encourage your teen to offer services such as tutoring, babysitting, or computer assistance to the expatriate community.
- Help your teen think of creative projects such as videodisks about the host country, homemade greeting cards, baked goods, or artwork that can be sold to other expatriates or used to raise money for charitable projects.
- Encourage your teen to become involved in community service work, as appropriate in your host country: volunteering at a local

animal shelter, holding babies at an orphanage, visiting the elderly, or tutoring younger children in school. The International
Baccalaureate program actually requires a certain number of community service hours. Be sure to document your teens' volunteer
work for future résumés or university applications.

- Pay your teen for completing challenging projects around the
  house.
- Give your teen a generous allowance and encourage him or her to
  focus on schoolwork, hobbies, and outside activities.

Driving can be another problem area for older teens. The minimum
driving age in your host country may be higher than at home. Furthermore, driving may be impractical in a large foreign city. Encourage your
older teens to use other appropriate means of transportation—bicycle,
subway, bus, and so forth. Meanwhile, remember that when you return
home, teens of driving age will be expected to know how to drive. Try to
give your teen the opportunity to acquire his or her license—perhaps during a summer visit back home.

Last days, first days

Packing for the trip

Besides the obvious clothes and toiletries for your children, you may want
to consider carrying the following with you wherever you go:

- Books and activities for long airplane rides; a travel journal is a
  great project for older kids
- Portable game systems and DVD players or a laptop
- Prepackaged foods for times when traveling disrupts young children's regular mealtimes (unpackaged foods must usually be consumed or discarded before you go through customs)
- Your children's school transcripts, immunization records, and
  other medical and dental records
- A portable music player with headphones and music and/or audio-
  books (you won't have to worry about this for a teenager permanently glued to his or her iPod)

- Supplies for writing, drawing, and coloring
- Favorite stuffed animals and a few favorite toys
- Postcards and addresses of friends and family
- A small photo album with pictures of your children's favorite people
- First-aid kit and medical supplies, such as prescription medicines and anti-nausea medications
- Tape and magnets to quickly personalize your new quarters with your children's drawings after you arrive (Patricia reports that her children's artwork has sometimes been the only personal touch in their new home for several weeks!)

When traveling with younger children, especially toddlers, pack a change of clothes for *both the child and yourself* in your carry-on bag. Include plenty of cleanup cloths and plastic bags as well for the inevitable spills and messes. Bring a plastic cup with a lid and immediately transfer drinks offered on the plane into it. Those flimsy airline cups are an accident waiting to happen.

Prepare yourself mentally to give your full attention to younger children during the trip. Tell stories, play cards, play with puppets, color together, make some simple crafts (such as clay sculptures), and so forth. Think of it as particularly intense "quality time," not a missed opportunity to read the in-flight magazine!

Packout day

When packout time comes, it may be tempting to send the children off for the day and box up the household without their interference, questions, and protests. But children, especially young ones, need to see things concretely in order to understand them. Let them see at least part of the process firsthand so they can visualize what is happening. After packout, celebrate with a special family outing or a restaurant meal. Let the children share your excitement, relief, and the strange new sense of freedom that arises as your possessions are finally on their way.

Patricia reports:

When my children were young, I liked to have them around at the beginning, when things started to be wrapped up and put into boxes, and also at the end, when a huge wooden crate with our name on it was nailed shut and driven away on a flatbed truck. For the middle of the process—the endless sorting, boxing, taping, and labeling—we tried to find another family who would invite them over.

Saying good-bye

For some children, the move may be the first time that they are confronting a significant loss in their lives. *Grief* is not too strong a word for the feeling of losing friends and a familiar environment. The severity of the loss increases with age.

Experienced families agree that it is psychologically helpful for children (and adults too—see the section "Saying a Proper Good-Bye" in chapter 3) to say a proper good-bye when they leave people and places. Before your packout at home, take pictures of your house and the rooms inside. Walk through it to say good-bye one last time before the movers come and box everything up. Encourage your children to take photos and collect farewell messages from their friends. Make up cards or slips of paper with your new address and e-mail address for your children to hand out. Some families even prepare self-addressed envelopes with the proper postage to encourage friends to write soon. Invite your older kids' friends to visit you in the new country—and be prepared for them to do so! Say good-bye to familiar places as well: the local park, beach, or ice cream stand. Think together about some things you *won't* be sad to leave. Good-bye, stinging nettles. Good-bye, neighborhood bully. Good-bye, mosquitoes.

Safety and security issues

In spite of the high level of media attention paid to terrorist attacks and kidnappings, such events are extremely rare. In addition, many foreign cities may be safer than those you are accustomed to. However, there are sensible precautions to take while traveling and living abroad, wherever it may be.

Experts agree that it is unwise to label your children's backpacks, shirts, or caps with a visible name. Strangers can win a child's confidence too easily by using his or her name.

Before traveling through busy airports, have young children put on brightly colored, highly visible shirts. Write your family name and flight information on slips of paper, and tuck them in children's pockets.

Telling your children not to talk to strangers has little meaning. What are they to think when you encourage them to say hello to someone you have just met in an airport waiting area? Some young children also have the mistaken idea that the "strangers" they are supposed to watch out for always look sinister or even wear masks and scary costumes!

Instead, teach your children to be on the alert for dangerous *situations*, such as getting lost or being approached by someone they don't know. Explain that if you are separated in an airport, on a city street, or elsewhere, children should stay put and wait for you to find them. Emphasize that adults don't normally ask children they don't know for help, offer them treats, or ask them to come with them. These are dangerous situations, and your children should refuse, even if the adult is dressed in a uniform or says that he or she has instructions from you. Some families make up a code word that only someone sent by the parents would know. However, this can backfire with small children, who might blurt out, "But you're supposed to say 'Max the cat'!"

In your new country, safety and security issues may be different from those back home. Get advice from colleagues and other people living in your new country about what you and your children may safely do and what you should watch out for (see chapter 8 for further suggestions).

Helping the family get settled

The most important piece of advice for families with children arriving in a new place is the same as our advice to anyone else involved in an international move: be patient. Expect setbacks, difficulties, and frustrations. Try not to be hard on yourselves or on the kids. Adjusting to a new country is a long and difficult process. Ultimately, you will most likely look back on your time overseas as a highly rewarding experience for you and your children, but don't expect the rewards to be obvious at first.

Moving internationally is a bit like having a baby; the first six weeks can be the most difficult, a roller coaster of emotions as you adjust to the demands of a new situation. While you are exhausted from packing and traveling and unpacking again, and stressed-out because everything is new and unfamiliar, the kids are whining and acting up. They are just as stressed as you are, only they may show it more openly. Stress in children is often manifested through

- regression and immature behavior,
- increased fears, clinginess, and whining, and
- changes in activity level—they may become either withdrawn or hyperactive.

If you prepare yourself in advance by expecting these changes in your children's behavior, you are more likely to react with understanding than with anger or annoyance. Even though the last thing you probably need is clinging, whining children, don't give in to the temptation to push them away. Getting on your nerves is their way of telling you that they need more emotional support than usual. To provide it, try these suggestions.

- Offer extra physical closeness, such as hugging or reading books snuggled side by side. Even teens appreciate this more than they'll admit.
- Listen; let them talk about whatever they want to. Sometimes it's easier for children to open up when you're doing something together, like cooking or playing a card game.
- Be especially calm and understanding about "mistakes" such as bed-wetting; however, do not relax important family rules or standards of discipline.
- Invite them to do everyday things with you, such as shopping or taking a walk; even if they say no, you are showing them by asking that you value their company.

A 14-year-old French girl in Morocco advises parents: "Don't take your stress out on the kids! We know you have a lot to do but don't yell at us. When we arrive at the new house we feel overwhelmed, like babies, and we can't help or think. Try to be more understanding then."

When you have just arrived, *put your family first*, not the messy new house or the boxes crying out to be unpacked. Turn down adult-oriented invitations if your kids aren't yet ready to stay with a strange sitter, or alternate with your spouse when attending social events. Here are some tips for making the settling in easier on your family—and therefore for you.

- At home you may find yourself frustrated by children "in the way," preventing you from getting everything organized. When you feel this way, hug them and think how lonely you would be in a new country without them.
- Keep your children's room(s) free of boxes, so that they have a comfortable and settled place for playing, reading, doing homework, and sleeping. Join them there often for a game or story. Two teenage girls living abroad gave us this tip: "It's nice when you've been in your new room for a while, unpacking alone, when your mom comes in and tells you she loves you and makes a compliment about what you've done or how you've set up the room and tells you that it's all going to be OK and then gives you a big hug."
- Establish a routine as quickly as possible to make life in your new home predictable and secure for your children. And as soon as you can after you arrive, arrange a fun outing as a family. It will help turn everyone's mind away from what was left behind and toward the new adventures ahead. Relax and enjoy the good times!

Stuck with kids and no stuff?

If you are lucky, your shipments will arrive quickly, your sponsor will have provided or lent you many useful items, and you will perhaps have had the chance to mail ahead or carry a load of your children's special belongings. If you are less fortunate, you may be playing hide-and-seek among the drapes in a barren house for many weeks to come.

Being stuck with children in temporary housing or in your home without your belongings for a long period is undoubtedly one of the worst phases of an international move. Expect boredom, anger, and frustration—both from the children and from you! Still, there can be something special about this time. It is a bit like camping, like homesteading, like traveling across the Old West in a covered wagon. It is a time that can bring everyone in the family closer as you face difficult times and explore a new country together.

When Patricia arrived in Cuba with a newborn and a three-year-old, the family had to spend five months in temporary housing, an apartment that smelled strongly of mold. It was a frustrating time, and there were plenty of arguments and tears. However, her memories of that time are positive as well as negative.

Patricia notes:

> Since the apartment was so dismal, we traveled somewhere almost every weekend. Even a cheap hotel in a not-so-exciting town was better than staying home, and these trips really helped us to get to know the country. Back home, without many toys or other distractions, we sang songs, made up stories, and ate by candlelight. We were also gratified at how people pitched in to help us. People I hardly knew drove my son to preschool, brought me homemade food, and even went grocery shopping for me.

Making a success of it

Helping children find new friends

Making new friends can be a crucial factor in the speed of your adjustment. Families who become friends with other families not only offer the opportunity for good times together, but are also sources of much-needed help and advice. Fortunately, expatriate families tend to seek each other out and form friendships quickly. However, there are several steps you might take to speed up the process.

- Ask your sponsor or a colleague at work to give you the names of families who have children near the age of yours. E-mail them in advance or call them once you've arrived and introduce yourself.
- Try not to be shy! If you can't imagine inviting someone to your empty house, invite people to meet at a public place such as a local playground, shopping mall, swimming pool, and so on. Rent a car, or take a taxi if necessary. Don't let anything stand in the way of forming new friendships.

- If you are in a country where people speak a foreign language, listen for people speaking English to their children in public. (People usually speak their native language with their kids, even if they speak the local language with everyone else.) Strike up a conversation. They'll probably be delighted to meet you.
- If your children are small, ask around about expatriate or host-country play groups in your area.
- Join any and all organizations that interest you, whether they involve children or not. Look for expatriate clubs; church groups; sports, craft, and hobby clubs; and volunteer groups. American, Canadian, and British clubs sometimes welcome associate members from other English-speaking countries.

As you seek out friends in the new country, don't be surprised if you find it much easier to meet other expatriate families than local ones. While in some cultures local families are very open to friendship with foreigners, in others they are not. This is generally not a question of prejudice or xenophobia but of different habits and expectations.

Take Santiago, Chile, for example. Since Chilean families are large, people have a multitude of brothers, sisters, aunts, uncles, and cousins. Furthermore, they tend to live close to each other. With so many relatives and long-time friends about, Chileans simply don't need to meet anyone new. Furthermore, mother-child activities are uncommon, since nannies watch the children in middle- and upper-class households. Finally, the Chilean culture seems more European than South American in many ways: people are reserved with strangers and slow to make friends. It's no wonder, then (although she was disappointed at the time), that most of the friends Patricia made during her two years there were other expatriates. Because they were foreigners too, they needed friends, just as Patricia did.

Still, it is worth the effort to help your children make local friends. They offer a genuine window into the culture of your host country. And unlike expatriates, they probably won't move away in a year or two. Keeping in touch with them after you leave will help your children maintain their connection with the country, which will surely come to mean a lot to them (perhaps more than it does to you, since they will have spent a greater proportion of their lives there than you have).

As you widen your circle of friends among expatriates, don't neglect people whose children are different ages from yours, or those who don't have children at all. Often, a kind of "extended family" takes shape among friends overseas. A childless couple may miss their nieces and nephews and be happy to spend time with your children. Children of different ages may start to feel like cousins as they travel together and celebrate holidays as a group. Especially in a small expatriate community, these ties can become deep and long-lasting.

A mom in Mexico reports:

> *One of the true joys of being around expat kids is how well they all play together—from age 2 to age 16! I have watched groups of incredibly varied ages all have fun at the pool, on a playground, or even while the moms were having a Bible study.*

Caregivers overseas

In countries where wage scales are low, household help may be quite affordable, and you may hire someone to help with the children as well as with the household. This can be a great advantage, especially if you have children below school age. Parents who work full-time will be under more time pressure as they deal with all of the issues discussed in this chapter. Since many developing countries lack adequate day-care centers, overseas parents often rely on household help to care for young children and watch older kids after school. Choosing the right caregiver is especially important in this situation.

If both parents are employed, we advise that one parent take time off from work—perhaps a month or more—upon arrival in the new country. This will allow you to provide extra emotional support to the children and to take your time in choosing child care, if necessary.

A South African expatriate and mother reports:

> *To help the kids cope, I promised them that I would not look for work for six months after we arrived. That way, I was around for them to talk to*

about all the traumas of new schools, new social rules, misunderstandings, and so on. It meant that I was quite lonely, but it paid off in terms of how well they settled in.

If you are a single parent or if both parents must work full-time soon after arrival, consider asking a close relative to accompany you to the new country for the first month or two. Another option is to hire a well-recommended caregiver on a temporary basis when you arrive, but to continue to interview other candidates. Some families who make frequent international moves hire a live-in nanny who is willing to accompany them from country to country (although visas can be tricky in this situation). This can be an excellent solution, since the child does not have to say good-bye to a beloved caregiver in the course of each move.

Even if hiring a caregiver is not new to you, there are a few issues to consider overseas that you might not have considered at home (see chapter 4 for more suggestions regarding domestic help overseas).

Health and safety. Don't assume your new caregiver is familiar with first-aid techniques, child safety guidelines, and hygienic practices. If your caregiver has never had any training in these areas, make whatever provisions you can to provide at least rudimentary training, even if you have to do it yourself. Courses may be available locally, or you may be able to arrange a seminar for caregivers from several families. Also, we suggest that you require prospective or newly hired household help who will be working with your children to have a physical examination and provide you with the results. Offering to pay for the exam makes it a benefit for your employee rather than a burden.

The relationship between child and caregiver. In a developing country, domestic workers may have very low social status. You, as a seemingly "rich" foreigner, may be considered near the top of the hierarchy, socially speaking. Your caregiver may see your children as "masters," treating them with exaggerated respect, giving them anything they want, and cleaning up after them. The children won't complain, of course, but this is probably not the kind of cultural experience you want them to have abroad. Some families are able to convince such a caregiver to demand respect from the children; however, ingrained cultural patterns are hard to change. You may simply have to supervise the relationship and intervene when the balance shifts too far in favor of the children. At least when you are with your kids, you can treat them as you always have, including requiring them to do chores appropriate for their ages. Otherwise, they will be in for a rude shock when they return home.

Cultural clashes. A strong relationship with a local caregiver can expose a child to a new culture, with its nursery songs and games, traditional foods, and daily customs. This is a wonderful opportunity. However, there may be some elements of the foreign culture that you would rather not have passed on to your children. Attitudes toward women, superstitions, and methods of discipline are common problem areas. Be alert to influences or practices you consider harmful. In some cultures, people tell children that a monster such as a huge spider will come and eat them if they are naughty. One housekeeper Patricia knew in Chile would pull the children in her charge by the ear and lock them in their rooms when they misbehaved. Another would give the kids alcohol to calm them down.

For all of these reasons, hiring a caregiver overseas is a delicate and difficult task. Take the time to interview a number of candidates, and get detailed recommendations from previous employers.

Problems with prejudice

Back home, your family may have been perfectly ordinary; abroad, your children may find themselves suddenly conspicuous and "different." You may be considered very wealthy compared with the average citizen of your host country. Your lifestyle, language, and perhaps your hair and skin color may brand you as an outsider. This can be a difficult adjustment, especially for older children and teens.

Children are easily influenced and confused by ethnic, class, and national prejudices. Sometimes they even come up with their own misguided stereotypes. "Spanish people like dirty houses," announced a four-year-old daughter of a friend one day in Cuba, after a visit to her nanny's home. Not understanding that the Spanish-speaking people she knew were too poor to paint and repair their homes, she concluded that they must prefer things that way.

Counteracting prejudices that your children may pick up overseas requires alertness and creativity on your part. Be careful about criticizing your host country and its people in front of your kids (even if you are exasperated with local drivers or have just been cheated at the vegetable market!). Expose your child to a wide range of people from all social classes and ethnic groups in your host country. If your child encounters prejudiced attitudes, explain your own beliefs firmly and clearly. When buying or ordering children's books, look for ones that reinforce tolerance and respect for others. Make sure that the school environment supports these values as well. Local children may also have misguided ideas about your home country. Equip your kids with positive, correct information. If the teacher agrees, it can also be helpful for younger school-aged children to present a report on their home country in school, complete with some typical foods to share.

Keeping your kids in touch

As children become settled in a new country, with new activities and new friends, the place they left behind can seem very far away. However, regular contact with the people and the culture "back home" remains important, for three reasons:

1. To maintain close ties with extended family and with friends in the home country
2. To make the eventual return move, or reentry, easier
3. To maintain a strong "home base" for the inevitable times when your child will wonder, "Who am I? Where do I belong?"

For children, an overseas assignment lasting two or three years can seem eternally long. If they have no contact with family members back home during this time, they may view them as strangers when they return. The family back home will hardly recognize your five-year-old if they last saw her at age two. Long periods of total separation can affect the way family members feel about each other for years to come.

Parents may be eager to give children an "authentic" cultural experience overseas, without fast food, advertisements, or TV programs from home. However, if children (especially older ones) are isolated from friends back home and their home culture for a long period, they may end up feeling like foreigners when they return. Fortunately, however, there are numerous measures you can take to avoid these problems by keeping in close contact with friends, relatives, and your home culture.

Encourage visits. Invite relatives and friends to visit you; although being a host takes effort, it is almost always worth the trouble. Visits from friends help show your children that the people they left behind have not disappeared permanently from their lives. Relatives who visit are suddenly included in your overseas adventure. In the future, when your children mention things that happened abroad, those family members who visited will have a clear picture of what your kids are talking about.

Take home leave once a year. Although you might prefer to spend your money and vacation time exploring new places, children need to touch base regularly with the extended family and with their home culture. Remember that a year seems much longer to them than it does to you. Try to make these visits long enough so that you don't just spend them rushing from relative to relative and shopping for things to take back with you. Take time to relax in one location for a while—at a relative's home or in a rented place. Ask relatives and friends to come visit you so your children are not always on the move.

One cautionary note about home leave: it is easy to fall into the trap of making these trips a nonstop carnival of fun, with excursions to amusement parks and other attractions, visits to relatives who spoil the kids with food and gifts, and lots of new toys to take back overseas. This leaves the unfortunate impression that your home country is one big amusement park. The overseas environment can't help but appear dull in comparison. Furthermore, the children are bound to be disappointed when they move back eventually and find that everything isn't quite as wonderful as they had remembered. Consider the following:

- Emphasize practical and cultural activities on your trip rather than pure "fun." Have your kids help on a relative's farm, visit museums or historical sites, pick apples or berries, go camping at a national park, or record an elderly relative's stories.
- Pack up gifts and new purchases immediately, to be saved until you get back overseas. This also serves as a pleasant "reward" for returning abroad.

- During your trip, talk about a few things you enjoy overseas that you can't do at home.
- Send postcards from your home country to friends at your overseas location and elsewhere in the world.
- Let your children spend unstructured time with cousins and friends, just hanging out and even being bored.

Use technology to keep in touch. Today's overseas families can keep in contact with people back home much more easily and cheaply than in the past (see chapter 10). When asked what his parents can do to make an international move easier, a 10-year-old boy answered: "It helps me when you tell me when we leave one place that those friends don't disappear; we can still e-mail them and keep in touch." Kids old enough to write should be encouraged to send weekly or monthly e-mail updates to close family members and friends (the same message can be sent to everyone, or parts of it can be modified for each recipient). If your kids are younger, write regularly to grandparents and others on their behalf. Include not just their latest accomplishments but also what they have been saying and feeling. Encourage relatives and friends to reply with e-mails that can be read out loud to the child.

When Patricia's kids were small, she loved to take dictation from them for a note to the grandparents. What came out was always unique and definitely in their own voice. Here is an e-mail from her younger son, Zachary, at age four to his grandparents:

> *I love you Grandma and I miss you, then when I'm four and a half, I'll miss you even at Christmas. And Grandpa, I love you even when I'm not there, and I love you even when you're in your house, and when I'm in my house, and Grandma, you too.*

This message was especially precious because Zack hated to talk on the phone at that age; he would generally squeak a quick "Hi" and hand the receiver back.

Many families create their own websites and post news, photos, travel reports, kids' artwork, and other items of interest to relatives and friends. Others publish and send out regular family newsletters. Patricia had her kids record cassette tapes with family news, jokes, pieces played on the piano, and so forth to send to their great-grandmother whose eyesight was too poor to read letters.

A video clip or cassette recorded by the children makes a special holiday gift for relatives. They might sing holiday songs, talk about what they have done over the past year, and include their wishes for the year to come. Movies can be sent via e-mail or on DVDs, or posted to your family website.

Keep reminders of relatives close at hand. Decorate your home with photos of family and friends. Change them around often; slip new photos into frames or rearrange them on the shelf. The new arrangement will attract children's attention. Keep photo albums on accessible shelves, where even small children can flip through them. Get them out often yourself and talk about them together. Watch family home movies frequently. When you receive an e-mail or letter from someone, get out his or her picture and have the kids look at it as you read.

When one of your children plays with or uses something that was a gift, ask if he or she remembers who sent it. Get out a picture of the person. Consider writing a card or e-mail together to tell the person you are still enjoying the gift.

Ask relatives and friends to record their voices on tape. Many grandparents video or tape themselves reading a bedtime story.

Choose symbolic items or foods that remind you of close relatives. For example, a children's book might be a certain aunt's favorite. Talk about her when you read the story. If Grandpa loves raspberry jam, mention him when you eat some. Teach the kids a game a relative taught you to play, and name the game after him or her.

Before a visit home, take the children shopping to pick out small souvenirs to take to close relatives. Don't just buy ten identical key chains; really think about each individual and what he or she likes.

Keep current with your home culture. As well adapted as your children might become overseas, the time will eventually come for them to return home. Will they feel like foreigners? Will they be put back a grade because they don't know your country's history? Will they be considered hopelessly "uncool" and out of date? You can help them avoid these reentry difficulties by taking a few simple measures overseas.

- If you know when and where you will be returning home, ask the local school administration to give you information on your child's expected curriculum. See if you can purchase new or used textbooks (check online booksellers) in areas that might not be covered overseas, such as national or regional history and government. If this is not possible, look for catalogues or supply stores serving homeschooling parents and purchase relevant materials.

- Look for children's books, workbooks, historical novels, websites, and computer games that teach your country's history and government in an enjoyable way. Hang a map of your home country on the wall, with pins in places you have visited and where friends and relatives live. Play games together such as memorizing the names of cities, states, or provinces; teach your kids folk songs with historical content; quiz them about your country's history and challenge them to find the answers. If you feel that you are not keeping up with your children's needs in this area, hire a tutor to fill in the gaps.

- Help your kids' independent studies "come alive" on home-leave trips by visiting historical sites and attending cultural events. Go to a cricket match or baseball game; eat some traditional foods; attend a classical, folk, or traditional concert.

- Let your children surf the Internet (with proper precautions such as supervision and protective software). Help them to keep current on subjects of interest to their age groups such as music, television, sports, fashion, environmental issues, and so on. Encourage them to communicate with kids back home via e-mail, instant messaging, and appropriate chat groups.

- Allow your children to subscribe to a couple of age-appropriate magazines from your home country, if possible.

- If you don't have satellite or cable TV offering familiar programs, see if you can get them over the Internet. Or ask a generous friend or family member to record your kids' favorite shows from time to time. Purchase or rent DVDs of the most significant new movies appealing to your children's age groups.

- Celebrate traditional holidays from home while overseas. Be creative in adapting home-country traditions to local conditions.

Coming home

Reentry, the move back home, has been called the hardest move of all by many international travelers, both for adults and for children. First, people expect the move back home to be easy, whereas it is just as hard as—or even harder than—moving out of the country. Second, little or no support is offered to families moving back home (unwisely, we think), while those moving overseas can usually rely on support from their organization and from other expatriates.

Families with children can prepare for reentry by expecting all the stresses that accompanied their outward move and by taking proactive steps to seek support before they arrive. (Most of the advice given in this chapter for the outward move also applies to a reentry move.)

As with an outward move, the best time to arrive back home is probably in late summer, allowing a short adjustment period before school starts. If your children have kept in touch with your home culture through regular visits, correspondence with friends, magazines, TV shows, the Internet, and so forth, their sense of strangeness will be lessened, but some feeling of being "foreign" is inevitable. Reassure them that these feelings will decline over time, and help them make new friends and get settled as quickly as possible.

Older children, especially those who have spent several years abroad, may find that they never completely "fit in" again at home; they have become third-culture kids, as we discussed at the beginning of this chapter. They may feel most comfortable in schools with diverse student populations, including families from other countries, regions, and ethnic groups.

Your children may have looked forward very much to coming home, and they may at the same time feel disappointed and even homesick for the country they have left behind. Assure them that these feelings are normal. Encourage them to keep in touch with their overseas friends and to remember their good experiences abroad.

At the same time, your children may be surprised and disappointed that their peers are not very interested in hearing their stories about overseas life. Many people who have never lived abroad simply can't relate to tales of scorpions in the bathroom, school classes with kids from ten different nationalities, and twenty-hour airplane rides. Or they may simply think your kids are bragging about their great adventures. Visiting a home-country zoo with friends, one mom had to gently pull her 8-year-old son aside and ask him to stop saying "This is nothing. I've seen these animals in the wild lots of times." Encourage your children to talk with friends about subjects of common interest, such as hobbies, sports, and schoolwork.

Also, find people they *can* share their stories with. Look for families with international experience or people from the country you just left. With them, you and your children can talk about the things you miss, practice the language you expended so much effort to learn, share foods you came to love abroad, keep current with the news from your "adopted" country—and feel that somebody else understands how strange it is to come home.

Eventually, of course, your children will become adapted again to their home country (or wherever you settle), but their broadened horizons will stay with them. The mother of an American teen who has lived in Africa was pleased to hear her daughter say that she appreciated knowing more about the world than most of her peers:

> *This made me feel a bit vindicated because she rarely was happy when I dragged her off to various volunteer projects in Niger and Uganda. We started talking and she remembered things we'd done in Uganda, a Christmas party for kids at the rehabilitation hospital, and a party for kids in the Banda slum, and she was much more positive about these things in hindsight than she was at the time.*

Living in a foreign culture will change your children's lives; they will meet new people, try new foods, see new sights and gain new language and cultural skills. Consistent understanding and support from you before, during, and after the move will help provide a stable and nurturing foundation from which they can venture out, learn, and grow from experiences in their new country. So what are you doing to your children by taking them abroad? You're helping to make them third-culture kids, global citizens, cross-cultural ambassadors; in short, exactly the kind of people our troubled world needs. They will never be the same again . . . nor would you want them to be.

CHAPTER 6

Moving Pets Overseas

No, you don't need to feel frantic when flying with a furry friend to a foreign country, at least not if you plan carefully. Proper preplanning prevents pet problems. Preplanning is the single most important step pet owners can take to ensure that Max or Mittens will have a successful move overseas.

First, though, comes the decision as to whether it is wise to take your companion animals abroad. Start by examining whether taking a pet overseas is in the animal's best interest. You will want to consider any cultural issues or health concerns that might make your pet's life abroad unpleasant or difficult.

Much will depend on where you will be living. In Western Europe, dogs are often a regular part of the daily routine. For example, in France many dog owners bring their pets with them to cafés or fine restaurants. In Germany, dogs often accompany their owners inside stores while the owners shop. However, other parts of the world may have an entirely different view of animals; the notion of a dog or cat as a pet and a companion is not a universal one. In some countries, dogs and cats are eaten as food and are even raised for that purpose. You may be moving to a country where the concept of a dog as "man's best friend" is not an accepted cultural belief. In the Middle East, for example, dogs are considered dirty animals. Don't assume that all cultures will share your affection and concern for pets.

Veterinary care abroad may also be an issue, as it can put pets at risk. We know of a couple who took their cat to Peru with them to a small village in the Andes. Although the cat was initially healthy, it later developed a urinary tract infection and a blocked bladder. Unfortunately, the only veterinary care available was in Lima, a considerable distance away. Without treatment, the cat died.

In fairness to your pet, learn as much as you can about your future living conditions; they may greatly influence the quality of the animal's life. If there are cultural or health concerns, having this information will enable you to make a more informed decision that could ultimately affect the happiness and health of your pet.

If your pet is healthy and you are moving to a country with a pet-friendly culture, then making your decision will be easier. The companionship pets provide is especially meaningful when you are living in a foreign environment. They make you smile with their antics and their personality quirks, lower your level of stress, and make a house really feel like a home. Pets are always glad to see you. You can't help but feel happy when a furry little face greets you at the door or a tail starts to wag simply at the sight of you! Having a beloved pet as part of your overseas experience can be worthwhile for everyone in your family and can sometimes help with making new friends.

So, what does this preplanning entail? The next section will get you started with essentials you need to know as well as important travel considerations that can affect your pet's welfare overseas.

Pet entry requirements and quarantine restrictions

Pet entry requirements vary by country and may be subject to change at any time. To obtain the most current and relevant information, check with the embassy of the country where you will be working. You can easily find embassy contact information on the Internet or at your local library. To obtain information on importing animals, contact your host country's embassy in the country you are departing from. Your organization may provide information as well, but it is always a good idea to double-check with host-country authorities; regulations can change. The same holds true for taking pets back home with you when your overseas assignment ends. Do the research to see if there are any rules or regulations you need to be aware of when exporting a pet back to your home country.

Be sure to ask what kinds of vaccinations or health certificates are required to import an animal. Sometimes entry requirements can be as simple as obtaining a vaccination record from your local vet. In other cases, requirements may be more complicated and require an accredited vet to examine an animal and then issue an official health certificate from a state veterinary institute in the country you are departing from.

If your pet is a dog, mention the animal's breed and size and ask if there are any restrictions on bringing that particular breed into the country. In some countries, certain breeds of dogs are not allowed. For example, France generally allows the importation of dogs; however, the country strictly forbids the importation of pit bulls, mastiffs, and some other large breeds. Requirements in China are even more complicated. Each city has its own regulations regarding the importation of animals! Beijing, for example, has specific size restrictions on large dogs. Any dog over the limit cannot live in the city. Be sure to clarify if any restrictions will apply in your pet's case.

Quarantine restrictions vary widely as well. Some countries do not allow the importation of animals at all—quarantine or no quarantine! Other countries have no restrictions. In still others, such as island countries, imported animals may face a six-month quarantine. If your new country has such restrictions, you may have to quarantine your pet for the required amount of time and to pay for your animal's stay in an approved kennel. Plan to reserve kennel space far in advance of arrival. Quarantine restrictions will not be waived, even for those traveling with diplomatic passports.

Most important, start as early as possible to obtain information about requirements and possible quarantine so that you have sufficient time to schedule an appointment with your vet, get paperwork in order, and complete any other arrangements.

The Pet Travel Scheme

If you will be moving to the UK, you should be aware of the Pet Travel Scheme (PETS). PETS permits some dogs, cats, and ferrets to enter the United Kingdom without having to spend six months in quarantine, provided the animal meets the rules and requirements of the Scheme. The rules require a pet to have a microchip, blood test, specific vaccinations, documentation, and treatment for ticks and tapeworm. These animals must come from other EU countries. Pets coming from third (non-EU) countries must be quarantined for six months. For more specifics, log on to *www.defra.gov.uk*.

When en route to your new country, if you have a connecting flight through an EU country, you may avoid the EU requirements if you make the transfer without taking possession of your pet. Check directly with your airline for more information.

Microchips

EU countries (and some others) now require pets to have ISO microchips implanted. It is important to know that EU transponders will read only ISO microchips. If you do not live in the EU and plan to have your pet microchipped before you leave, be sure that your veterinarian uses ISO-compliant microchips.

A pre-travel checkup with a veterinarian

Regardless of what requirements and restrictions apply to taking your pet abroad, a checkup with your veterinarian is always a good idea. Before you arrive at the vet's office, your research on pet entry requirements should be complete. Tell the vet exactly what is required, and he or she can examine your pet accordingly, vaccinate if necessary, and prepare the papers you need.

In addition to getting papers in order, a pretravel checkup with a vet is a good idea to determine if there are any hidden problems that can jeopardize your pet's health after you leave. This is particularly important if you are going to a country where veterinary care for pets is marginal or nonexistent. Use this time to ask your vet any questions you have regarding your pet's travel. Tranquilizing, withholding food prior to travel, and obtaining medicines to take with you are a few of the topics you may want to discuss. Although we have included basic information on these issues in the discussion that follows, you will want to ask your vet what is best for your individual pet.

Airline requirements for transportation of animals

After September 11, 2001, airlines around the world revised their security policies or implemented new ones. How these changes affect the transportation of animals depends on each airline. Since new regulations may be implemented at any time, we suggest contacting your airline directly for the most up-to-date information on any security issues that relate to traveling with pets. The policies and procedures for transporting animals vary widely worldwide. Talk to airline representatives not only at the time you make your reservation, but check with them again closer to your departure date to see if any policies have changed. Always reserve space for your pet as early as possible. What do you need to ask? Here are some guidelines to help you.

Pets in the cabin. Not all airlines allow pets in the cabin. Some will allow one or two in-cabin pets per aircraft; once a passenger has a confirmed reservation for an animal in-cabin, other pets on that flight must be shipped as excess baggage in the cargo hold. If you plan to travel with your pet in the passenger cabin, reserve as early as possible and be ready to pay an additional charge. Remember, also, if your overseas flight requires you to change planes to complete your journey on another airline, you will need to check the policy of each airline. For example, it is possible that a passenger could take a pet in-cabin on a domestic airline, change planes, then be required to ship the pet in the cargo hold for the international portion of the flight. This could be an unpleasant surprise, so be sure to check the policy of each airline ahead of time and get a confirmed in-cabin pet reservation for each segment of your flight.

The airline is likely to ask you for the dimensions (length, width, and height) of the carrier you plan to use as well as the combined weight of your pet and the carrier. The limits are quite restricted, because the carrier must fit under the airline seat. Have this information ready when you make your reservation and keep it with you when you check in at the airport.

Pets as excess baggage. The airlines will ask the dimensions of your carrier and the weight of your pet traveling in the cargo hold, just as they do for in-cabin pets. Make sure the carrier is sturdy, airline-approved, and large enough for your pet to stand up, lie down, and turn around. You should also be sure that the animal is wearing a collar with a tag that has the pet's name and phone numbers where you can be reached. In addition, have your pet's name, as well as your name and address, on the carrier. (We suggest writing it on the carrier itself.) Be sure to ask if the airline has any special food or watering requirements for the animal prior to departure. Usually, only one animal will be allowed per kennel. There will be an additional charge for each pet shipped this way.

Pets as cargo. Shipping a pet, unaccompanied, as airfreight is the most expensive way to transport an animal. Though some airlines will offer passengers the option of making arrangements themselves, many accept cargo shipments of pets only through a licensed shipper. This increases costs even more. If you must ship your animal at a time other than when you are traveling, ask your airline for details. You will also want to find out how animals are handled and transported as cargo. In some cases cargo is handled in an entirely different manner from passenger baggage and in a separate area of the airport. For your pet's comfort and for your own peace of mind, be sure to get all the specifics.

Temperature extremes. A pet may be denied travel as excess baggage in periods of extreme temperatures, particularly in months when heat poses health risks. Some airlines impose a summer embargo between May and September and will not accept pets at all during that time. Also, keep in mind that summer months in the southern hemisphere will be different than in the northern hemisphere. Unfortunately, there is no easy answer to the problem of heat-related restrictions. The best you can do is talk to the airline as early as possible, get the specifics on their summer pet travel policy, and find out what options are available to you if your pet is denied travel permission. You won't want to be faced with a dilemma at the airport, so formulate a plan of action ahead of time in the event pets are not accepted on your travel date.

Health requirements. Ask if the airline requires any special health certificate, veterinary papers, or other documentation. Some airlines want a veterinary certificate bearing the seal of a state veterinary institution from the country you are departing from. If documentation is necessary, ask if there is a time restriction on when this needs to be done. For example, if you wait until the last minute and then find out that the certificate must be issued over 10 days prior to departure, you may have to delay your travel.

Carrying on versus checking

Traveling with a pet in-cabin has several advantages. Should delays occur, the animal will not be left sitting in its carrier somewhere in the airport or on the tarmac. In-cabin pets will not be subjected to extremes in temperature, if you happen to be flying on a very cold or hot day. In addition, if there is little time to make a connecting flight, you and your pet will be together whether you successfully make the transfer or not.

Disadvantages exist as well. In any travel situation, animals normally experience some degree of fear, which could potentially present problems in the passenger cabin. An unhappy pet may bark or meow more than usual, which could disturb passengers around you. Before you decide to take your pet onboard with you, consider the pet's temperament. If your dog has a tendency to bark incessantly when nervous or your cat "yowls" when fearful, you may want to consider checking the animal as excess baggage. In addition, some animals experience motion sickness and may vomit when traveling in a car or plane. This would be a problem for you and all those seated near you in the cabin!

If you decide to take your pet on board, we recommend that you put a harness on your pet and take a leash that you can snap onto the harness in case you have to take the animal out of the carrier to pass through security. Having your pet in a harness gives you greater control if the animal is frightened and tries to run away. If a pet is so scared that it tries to bolt, a collar might possibly slip off the animal. It is more difficult for an animal to slip out of a harness.

Checking your pet as excess baggage has advantages also. You will be freer to stretch your legs, eat, or get up and walk around the cabin if your pet is not with you. Some airlines may even allow you to do a "gate check-in," where the animal (in its carrier) stays with you until boarding time, then is checked in at the boarding gate as you get on the plane. When you reach your final destination, you simply claim your pet at the arrival gate.

On the downside, a pet checked as excess baggage is out of sight but not out of mind. You hope that airport personnel are properly caring for the animal, but your pet is not with you, so there is no way to know for sure what is happening at any given moment. This may create anxiety for some pet owners. Also, if you have a connection to make, you will have to check with airport personnel to find out if your pet also made the transfer. If the connection is tight, there is always the possibility that airline personnel cannot transfer the pet in time.

What does the pet experience when traveling in the cargo hold? Some vets suggest that once the plane has taken off, the unfamiliar things that frighten pets are over. Except for a few bumps and loud noises, air travel is rather monotonous. Most pets likely sleep in their carriers.

All things considered, having your pet in-cabin, if this is possible, will probably give you the greatest peace of mind. It will be up to you to weigh the pros and cons, though, and then decide what works best for your pet and for your travel situation.

Equipment and supplies for pet air travel

Whether you decide to take your pet in the passenger cabin or check the animal as excess baggage in the cargo hold, you will want to have certain items on hand:

- A sturdy, airline-approved carrier (with your name, telephone number, and destination written on the carrier)
- Some type of soft bedding for the animal to lie on, such as old towels
- Newspaper to line the bottom of the carrier
- Collar and/or harness for your pet
- Pet tag (with your name and an emergency phone number)
- Leash
- Small water dish and bottle (to be refilled within the airport if liquids cannot be taken through security)
- Current photo of your pet (optional, but a good idea)

If you are taking your pet in the passenger cabin, you will need to purchase a carrier large enough to accommodate your pet but small enough to fit under the seat in front of you. Many styles are available at pet stores, from catalogues, or over the Internet, including leather "suitcase" types with handles. If a pet is traveling as excess baggage, attach a plastic water dish to the carrier and fill the dish with some water or ice cubes. As an extra precaution, mention to a flight attendant that you have a pet in the cargo hold. If the plane is delayed and has to sit on the tarmac, it is important the crew knows there is an animal onboard.

Prior to air travel

Feeding pets

Many veterinarians suggest providing water but withholding food from pets prior to air travel. Withholding food before travel and then feeding at the final destination reduces the chances of an animal having to travel in a messy cage. To determine the best timing to withhold food, check with your vet. The answer will vary depending on the age and health of the animal and the season of the year when you are traveling.

You will also want to check with the airline. Some, as part of their pet policy, require that food or water be given to an animal during the last four hours before departure. We were surprised to learn that airlines have instituted such specific requirements. However, Melissa learned from an airline agent with an international carrier about a case where a dog was not given water prior to a long international flight and became so dehydrated that he died during the trip. This sad incident prompted litigation, and as a result, some airlines have established new policies.

Pet owners should use common sense. If you are traveling on a hot day and know that your flight will be a long one, make sure your pet has water in the dish of the carrier, airline permitting. As for food, dogs and cats are by nature carnivores and scavengers and have adapted to going without food for periods of time. In the wild, they sometimes eat only one out of three or four days. We are not suggesting that you should withhold food that long from a domestic pet; just remember that cats and dogs are able to tolerate intervals when they cannot be fed. Traveling for a *reasonable* period of time without food should not pose undue health risks—unless your pet is very young, diabetic, or has some other medical problem.

To tranquilize or not to tranquilize?

The decision to tranquilize your pet prior to air travel should always be made in consultation with a vet. The vet will want to examine the animal, determine its current state of health, and find out if there are any previously unknown medical problems. For example, if you discover that your pet has a heart condition, then sedation is not an option. Even if your pet is healthy, you will still want to consider additional factors.

Pets generally cope better with traveling when they have their wits about them. Being awake and alert is one of their best defense mechanisms. Therefore, many vets do not recommend tranquilizing pets during travel unless there is some compelling reason.

In making your decision, consider your pet's temperament and personality. If the animal is calm and easygoing by nature, a tranquilizer is probably unnecessary. Likewise, if your pet travels well in a car, then it will likely travel well by air. Animals that tend to be excitable, fearful, or overly vocal or those that constantly try to get out of the carrier may be good candidates for sedation. Melissa's cat, found as a feral kitten in the Egyptian desert, falls into this category. The animal fights against being placed in a carrier and will bolt at any available opportunity. With a tranquilizer, however, she calms down, goes to sleep, and can be placed in a carrier and transported without difficulty.

Every animal is different. You and your vet can best determine if tranquilizing is right for your pet.

Concerns about older pets

Older pets, in particular, should be examined by a veterinarian for health conditions that could affect travel and their stay abroad. If your vet identifies a serious problem, then traveling is probably not in the animal's best interest. However, if older pets are healthy, they will likely do well.

Consider an example that occurred while Melissa was living in Leningrad. She had agreed to "cat-sit" for a new family that would be arriving soon. The family, who had a twenty-year-old Siamese, sent the cat two weeks ahead of their arrival. Melissa had no idea what to expect when she went to the airport with her husband. The flight arrived and there was the old Siamese, looking a bit bewildered but stable. Although the cat was old, he had successfully made the trip with only one minor mishap: He had meowed himself hoarse! Fortunately, within a day or so, his voice returned to normal and he no longer sounded like a bullfrog croaking "meow."

Another example of an old animal successfully traveling overseas occurred when Melissa's eighteen-year-old cat traveled from Washington, D.C., to Kiev, Ukraine. The cat had traveled in the cargo hold as excess baggage. Since there were no direct flights to Kiev, the plane had to make a stopover in Frankfurt. Unfortunately, delays caused the plane to land in Frankfurt with only ten minutes left to make the connection to Kiev. Melissa and her husband made the transfer, but the cat didn't. He spent the night, alone, in his cat carrier in the Frankfurt airport. When he arrived in Kiev the next day, Melissa was worried about his condition. She was relieved to find him resting quietly in his cat carrier. When she took him home, he acted as if nothing had happened. He walked out of his carrier, ate some food, then took a nap. Apparently, his unexpected overnight in Frankfurt had not caused him any undue harm, even at his advanced age.

These examples are not meant to show that older pets always travel well. They do indicate, however, that there are cases where the age of the animal does not interfere with successful overseas travel. If you check with a vet and then decide to take an older—and still healthy—pet overseas, chances are the pet will be able to tolerate the trip.

Surprisingly, the flight itself may be less stressful to an older animal than having to adapt to a new place. Like older people, older pets are comfortable with their daily routines. When taken from the home they have known and placed in a new environment in a new country, some of them may be disoriented at first. Most adapt, however (with their owner's help), and eventually establish a new routine.

Pets in hotels

For most animal lovers, staying in a hotel with their pets is not a major inconvenience. Your stay with a pet will go more smoothly, however, if you do a little homework and preparation ahead of time.

Check before you check in. Before you make your reservation, ask about the hotel's pet policy. Some hotels accept pets; others do not. Some will require a deposit for possible damage. Sometimes the deposit will be refunded, sometimes not. Hotels may also limit the number of pets to a room. If you have two dogs and a cat, finding accommodations for all of you might be a problem. Do your homework so there are no surprises.

Bring pet food and supplies with you. To save time, money, and unnecessary hassles, we recommend that you take pet food and other necessary pet supplies with you. Consider your pet's individual needs and the length of time you will be in a hotel. Your suitcases are likely to already be full, so bring only what your pet will need. Don't forget to pack a leash, a familiar toy or bone, and a trash bag big enough to hold what you will discard. Empty pet food cans, used cat litter, or discarded litter boxes crammed into tiny hotel wastebaskets or—worse—left where they stand leave the room looking unsightly. You are less likely to pay a fine for pet damage or lose a pet deposit if your pet trash is bagged neatly and you leave the room looking orderly.

"Animal-proof" the hotel room. Cats, and sometimes dogs, can become frightened in an unfamiliar environment. On one trip, Melissa's cat became so spooked in a hotel room that he hid for an hour, unseen, under the metal cover of a radiator. Melissa thought she had lost him, but he finally calmed down and ventured out from his hiding place. Luckily, there were no holes in the wall where he could have been trapped.

For a pet's protection, always do a safety check of the room before letting the animal out of its carrier. Check the bathroom floor and wall for holes in the tiles or areas where there may be exposed pipes. Cats feel safer in smaller, confined spaces, and they may be attracted to such areas. Do the same for the main room.

If you have a puppy or small dog who likes to chew objects, unplug electrical cords that could attract the dog's attention. Taking a few minutes to do a safety check will protect your pet and lessen the chance of an accident that could harm your pet and ruin your stay.

Melissa reports:

While living in the Sinai, I adopted a beautiful Egyptian cat. When my husband's assignment ended and the time came to take her home to the States with us, our travel itinerary required one overnight in a Tel Aviv hotel. Although I knew I could purchase pet food and supplies in Israel, I didn't want to waste time walking around looking for places to buy what I needed. To make things easier for all of us, I packed my cat's favorite food and toy, a paper plate and plastic spoon, a small amount of cat litter, a litter box (made from the lid of a cardboard box), and a trash bag. Having these things with me saved time and made taking care of the cat easy. When it came time to check out of the hotel, I simply sealed the trash neatly in the bag.

If you go out, leave your pet in its carrier. If you are not in the room, your pet will be safer left in its carrier. Maids or other hotel personnel who need to enter your room may frighten pets and trigger the instinct to flee. If a maid starts cleaning your room, the door may be left open, inadvertently creating an escape route for your pet. The sound of a vacuum cleaner can be particularly disturbing to cats, causing them to run for cover. Since you have no control over what might happen to your pet during your absence, play it safe. A pet left in its carrier cannot escape or become lost.

If you have a cat, put him or her in the carrier in the bathroom when you are ready to leave. Then turn out the light and close the bathroom door. In a familiar carrier—your pet's safe haven—the cat will feel more secure and will likely go to sleep while you are away.

When you need to leave your hotel room, try not to be gone any longer than necessary. A dog left unattended in a carrier for hours may start to howl or bark and disturb other guests. Use your own best judgment. Do what you need to do, but keep the time away from your pet to a minimum. In an unfamiliar environment, your pet will feel happiest and most secure when you are there.

Living in the Third World with pets

For animal lovers, the benefits of having their pets accompany them far outweigh the inconveniences encountered when traveling or living in less-developed countries. If you decide to take your pet with you, be aware that pet products and supplies commonly found in Western countries are often scarce or unavailable in developing countries.

If you want to maintain a high standard of care, plan to purchase all your pet's necessities ahead of time. To help you get started, in this section we present information regarding what you and your pet may encounter in the Third World, along with pet supplies and medicines you may want to bring with you.

Because each country is different, we can't give you definitive information that applies 100 percent of the time. Your best resources are colleagues or other expatriates already living in your target country. If you have the opportunity to contact them and ask about the situation for pets well before you depart, you will have a more realistic picture of what you need to do ahead of time. The more information you have specific to your situation, the better you will be able to plan. Both you and your pet will have an easier trip and transition if you are well-informed and prepared.

Your pet's arrival. Unfortunately, customs officials in some developing countries may see the arrival of an expatriate's pet as an opportunity to supplement their personal income and may require an "unofficial fee" before passing a pet through customs. If you are traveling on a diplomatic passport, this will not likely happen to you; otherwise, you may find yourself a target. Your best solution to such a potential problem is to find out ahead of time if others in your organization have experienced problems clearing their pets through customs. Please note that such corruption does not occur in all Third-World countries, and hopefully this type of incident will never happen to you. However, being forewarned and forearmed will increase your chances of a smoother and less stressful arrival for both you and your pet.

Pet food. Commercial pet food is not always available in the Third World, and if you can find it, the cost will be far higher than what you pay at home. If you are able to ship consumables with your household effects, then feeding your pet will not be a problem. For many, however, shipping food is not an option.

If pet food is not available locally, you may be able to travel intermittently to purchase what you need or ask other expatriates to bring back a supply when they travel. However, this can be expensive as well as a hassle and may not be feasible. Another option is to make your own pet food. Every dog or cat will have individual food preferences, so you may have to experiment to find what works best for your pet. For example, when Melissa first moved to Nigeria, she purchased canned sardines locally and tried mixing various combinations of the sardines, cooked meats, and rice to feed her two cats. It didn't take long to find a recipe the cats liked. If you know ahead of time that you will be in a country where pet food is unavailable, you may want to ask your vet for suggestions. You know your pet better than anyone else. See what ingredients are available locally and go from there. You can also do an Internet search to find recipes for home-made pet food. In addition to food, water is worth mentioning because it plays a major role in keeping your animal healthy. In many developing countries, tap water is unsafe to drink. If you can't drink it, don't give it to your pet. Safeguard your pet's health by providing clean, safe drinking water—either from bottles, a filter, or a distiller.

A word about medicines. Don't assume that you will be able to pur-chase veterinary medications. As with pet food, veterinary medicines for small animals are not available in many Third-World countries. To main-tain your pet's health, bring medications with you. Having medications on hand and ready when needed will greatly increase your pet's comfort and well-being, and in extreme cases this may even save your pet's life.

Melissa reports:

> *When I lived in Russia, I found a tiny, six-week-old kitten on the street. The animal was covered with fleas and had a nasty eye infection, with one eye completely swollen shut and the other so crusted over that only a tiny slit remained open. I didn't have cats at the time, so I hadn't brought any vet supplies with me. Unfortunately, there were no veterinary medicines available in Russia. Thanks to other expatriate pet owners, I was able to borrow some antibiotic eye salve and flea spray. Both of these products were highly effective. Within a very short time, the kitten's eyes were cleared of the infection and he was rid of fleas.*

A pet first-aid kit. When putting together a first-aid kit for your pet, begin by considering your pet's overall state of health. If the animal has specific medical problems that you need to treat on a regular basis, plan to take an ample supply of medicine(s) for that condition. The following is a list of basic supplies and medications for a first-aid kit. Use it as a start-ing point, and add or subtract items according to the needs of your indi-vidual pet and advice from your vet.

- Gauze pads and rolls
- Cotton pads

- Scissors
- Tweezers
- Alcohol prep pads
- Triple antibiotic ointment for wounds
- Antibiotic ophthalmic ointment
- Anti-itch cream
- Eyewash
- Ear miticide (for cats)
- Ear wash or ear-cleaning pads
- Topical flea treatment (the type applied between shoulder blades of pets)
- Flea/tick spray
- Flea shampoo
- Broad-spectrum antibiotics (either tablets or injectable form)
- Antihistamines
- Worm tablets or paste
- Hairball treatment for cats (comes as paste in a tube)
- Cold pack
- Elizabethan collar
- Eyedropper
- Pill cutter
- Syringes (may not be necessary, depending on country)
- Latex gloves (or nonlatex, if you prefer)
- Cotton swabs
- Blanket
- A pet first-aid book (check your local bookstore or the Internet, or ask your vet)
- Antibacterial soap or wipes to disinfect your hands

What happens if your pet develops a medical problem abroad, one that you don't know how to treat? Resources are available to help you get the answers you need.

Establish a rapport with your vet in your home country before you move, and ask if he or she would be willing to answer e-mail questions regarding pet medical problems. Melissa did this while living in Kiev, and her vet provided invaluable information needed to treat her pets. The

Internet is also an excellent resource for veterinary information—numerous sites address animal welfare and health. Use keywords such as "dog health" or "cat care" to start your search. If you are in a place where small-animal vet care is nonexistent, you may be able to ask your family physician in the country to answer medical questions or acquire medications needed for your pet. In most cases, if the physician is used to working with expatriates, he or she will likely be willing to help.

Melissa reports:

> *When I lived in Nigeria, most expatriates lived in homes with big backyards. Sadly, several of my friends experienced the loss of their pets, simply by letting the animals run loose in their yards. One family I knew had a beautiful Irish setter who was found dead after being bitten by a poisonous snake. Another family, with a black retriever, also found their dog dead in the yard, and attributed his death to a snakebite. In another case, a friend let her small kitten roam freely, wherever the kitten wanted. Unfortunately, within a few weeks, the kitten was found dead after being struck by a car.*

Your pet's safety. Wherever they live, pets lead longer lives when kept inside rather than outside. If you have cats or small dogs, life indoors is usually not a problem. For larger dogs that need space to run or cats that are left to roam around on their own, be aware that there can be hidden dangers outdoors. Cars are always a problem no matter where in the world you live, and in some countries, predators can be especially hazardous to your pet's health.

Before you take a pet to *any* country, consider what your housing situation will be and how it will affect the life of your pet. If you know you will be living in a small apartment in a busy, crowded city with few parks and lots of heavy traffic, do you really want to bring a big dog with you? Even if you will live in a large house with a backyard, will it be a safe environment for your pet? If you are going to live in a guarded, walled compound, maybe the answer is yes. If not, you may want to carefully consider what is best for your pet and, ultimately, for you. The loss of a family pet is always difficult, but it can be especially devastating when you are living in a foreign culture.

So, is all the trouble and expense it takes to move overseas with a pet worth it? Expats who love their "expets" think so!

Melissa reports:

Little did I know that day when I was walking down the street in Russia that I would find the cat of a lifetime. That tiny, dirty kitten, eyes crusted over with an infection and body covered with fleas, grew into a beautiful Maine coon cat with a mane and tail that made him look like a little lion. One of the Russian employees at the American consulate where my husband worked named him "Smokey," and another, seeing how plump and healthy he had become, remarked, "He looks like a rich person's cat!" "He's an American fat cat," I used to say. I think he must have been grateful. Whenever I was home, he had to be in the same room with me. He would follow me around if I got up to go to another part of the house. He loved being close, and I enjoyed his companionship. Smokey traveled the world with us, living in Russia, Washington, D.C., Algeria, and Arizona. We had 16 years together, filled with international adventures and unforgettable memories. He was a special member of our family. The small amount of additional work and expense to have him travel with us was insignificant compared with the happiness he brought into our lives.

CHAPTER 7

Adapting to Your New Environment

Patricia reports:

Our first five months in Cuba, with a new baby and a three-year-old, were spent in a temporary apartment. The place had mildew on the walls and frequent water and power outages. People were constantly ringing the doorbell to sell us something or ask for money. As a U.S. diplomatic family in Cuba (yes, there is such a thing), we were told that we had microphones in the walls, and local people were either forbidden to associate with us or required to spy on us. One night I was so filled with frustration that I smashed several plates in the kitchen.

But I also remember those months as a time of family closeness, adventure, and discovery. Stranded without TV or other distractions, my husband and I found ourselves focusing more on each other and the kids. A single colleague, Steve, who lived upstairs, practically became part of the family too; he would hold the baby while I made dinner, and then he would eat with us. We escaped from our unpleasant housing by traveling nearly every weekend, exploring beaches and old colonial towns. One night we were swimming in the pool at a simple concrete-block hotel, and the power went off in the whole complex. Floating in the warm water under a breathtaking star-filled sky, I felt myself recharging, gathering the strength to face the challenges of our new assignment.

By the way, years later we all still think of Steve as part of the family—we communicate and visit regularly, even though we live in

different countries. The bonds we formed in that moldy building in
Havana were strong and enduring.

Settling in is a time when moments are lived intensely and new impressions burn themselves into your memory. It is also a stressful, bewildering time of great change when you may find yourself tested to your limits. As cross-cultural expert Janet Bennett has noted,* *culture shock*—the anxiety that occurs when people are plunged into a new and unfamiliar cultural environment—is only part of the challenge of moving overseas.

Major life changes—even positive ones—always involve stress. Think of some of the stressful times in an average person's life: moving to a new community, changing jobs, separating from loved ones. Moving overseas is the equivalent of facing several of these changes at once—while surrounded by an unfamiliar language and culture, and lacking the support systems you relied on at home. It is only natural for expatriates—and not only those going abroad for the first time!—to react to this kind of upheaval with a temporary case of what Bennett calls *transition shock*.

Moving to a new country is a bit like moving a multi-part computer system to a new location. Moving a computer may involve disengaging the cables and connections for the display, modem, printer, electrical input, and so forth, and then properly reconnecting and configuring each of them again. If you neglect even one, the system won't work. For human beings, much of the difficulty of adjusting to a new country arises from being "disengaged" from one environment but not yet fully "reconnected" in a new one. We have found that five basic elements are necessary for true adjustment in a new place:

- Language and cross-cultural skills
- A comfortable home base
- A support network and new friends
- The ability to navigate your new environment with confidence
- Meaningful and enjoyable activities

*See "Transition Shock: Putting Culture Shock in Perspective," in *Basic Concepts of Intercultural Communication: Selected Readings* edited by Milton J. Bennett (Intercultural Press, 1998).

Some people will be able to "reconfigure these connections" more quickly than others. An employee with a satisfying job, supportive colleagues, language and cultural training, and a family to greet at the end of the day may wonder what the fuss is all about. But most expatriates— including, most likely, the spouse of that very same employee—will be missing several, if not all, of these essential elements when they first arrive.

As you make progress in each of these areas—which we call the "five components of adjustment"—you will find stress and homesickness decreasing and your confidence increasing. Many of the preparatory measures we have recommended in this book so far should give you a head start on this process by equipping you with language skills, cultural knowledge, links to supportive people, and so forth. Yet no amount of preparation is enough to shield you completely from transition shock. In this chapter, we present detailed suggestions from our own experiences and that of other expatriates to help you through the adjustment process as quickly as possible once you have arrived.

At the end of the chapter, we provide a checklist of questions to help you assess your adjustment as well as advice for those of you who find that you are not making progress. We do not mean to scare you with the descriptions of stress and negative emotions in this chapter, but it would be misleading to suggest that adapting to a new country is easy. No new and difficult endeavor is—whether it's taking on a challenging new work assignment, getting married, earning an advanced degree, or becoming a parent. And as with those undertakings, the rewards of adapting to a new country are great. If you can weather a temporary phase of transition shock and achieve the five key elements of adjustment mentioned here, new experiences, friendships, and adventures await you that will make all of your hardships seem worthwhile.

The ups and downs of adjustment

Cross-cultural experts have identified three typical phases of adjustment to a new country:

- an early period of optimism known as the "vacation" or "honeymoon" phase,

- a "slump" as the stresses of the transition become overwhelming, and
- the gradual progression to reconnection (your internal "system" is now running smoothly) as you adjust to the new environment.

We have followed this general pattern in the organization of this chapter.

One note of caution, though: individual experiences vary greatly. A few experience an initial "crash landing" and go directly into the slump without even a hint of a honeymoon. Many report ups and downs, such as two slumps separated by more positive times. Some lucky people don't notice a drop in morale at all and simply ride the gradual upward curve of adjustment. And some unfortunate souls get stuck in the slump phase for the remainder of their stay overseas, counting the days until they can go home or even opting for early termination.

For those of you with family members, keep in mind that each member of the family may react differently to the move, confront varying issues during the adjustment period, and experience the phases of adjustment on a different schedule. Encourage all family members to acknowledge their feelings and problems and to support each other. The trust and closeness you build together during this challenging time can strengthen your family bonds. The opposite may occur, however, if family members feel that their concerns are ignored or their feelings dismissed.

The first few days: rest and recuperate

Even if you haven't stayed up late night after night to pack, clean, finish up work projects, and attend farewell parties, you may be exhausted from the trip itself and suffering from jet lag. Your first priority upon arrival should be to rest, recuperate, and stay healthy. A continued state of exhaustion will make you more prone to illness, less effective at work, and more irritable about having to face the constant new challenges of daily life. Worst of all, illness and exhaustion can sap your morale, souring your attitude toward this adventure you have embarked upon.

Politely postpone invitations from well-meaning colleagues to late dinners and evening parties, if possible, until you have rested for a few nights.

People who are eager to meet you can come by during the day, take you for a walk around the neighborhood or on a short tour of the shopping district, or invite you (and your family) for a casual afternoon get-together. If you are the employee, try to avoid separations from family members during the first few days after arrival, as this will increase everyone's stress. Arriving just before a weekend or taking off the first few days from work is a good idea. Teamwork and togetherness will help promote the family's adjustment; feelings of abandonment and resentment will hinder it.

If your move takes you across several time zones, work on adjusting to the new schedule as quickly as possible. We have found the "forced wake-up" method to be helpful in overcoming jet lag: for your second morning after arrival, set an alarm for your new target wake-up time, and force yourself to get up then. Stay active during the day and expose yourself to a lot of sunlight; this helps reset your internal clock. Keep yourself awake until an early but reasonable bedtime (say, 8:00 P.M. local time). If you are able to sleep through the night, you're home free. If not, try the same schedule again the next day.

In addition to being deprived of rest, your body may be exposed to new environmental conditions (such as temperature, humidity, increased pollution, and/or altitude) as well as unfamiliar germs in your new country. Intestinal upsets, colds, and flu are extremely common after arrival in a new country. To avoid or minimize illnesses, adjust gradually to the local food and water. Even if tap water is considered safe to drink, use filtered or quality bottled water at first and avoid ice cubes. If tap water is unsafe in your new country, take extra care; you should even brush your teeth with bottled water. Avoid salads. Fruits and raw vegetables that can be peeled (preferably by you) are fine, or wash raw produce in an antibacterial solution. Although it may seem like a chore, it is imperative that you find out right away how to avoid contaminated food and water, how to keep safe on the streets, and what to do in an emergency (see the discussions of health, safety, and security in chapter 8).

The "vacation" period

After catching up on your rest during the first few days, you may experience a few weeks of excitement and energy. Like a tourist taking an adventure vacation abroad, you may focus on the positive things in your new environment and think, "This isn't so bad; I can handle this."

Now is a great time to get moving, explore your new environment, build up your competence in the new country, and make new friends. The more "plugged in" you can get during this period, the better you will manage the slump that probably lies ahead.

Of course, this "vacation" can also feel a lot like a camping trip. You may be living out of a suitcase, not sure how to cook, or even what to eat. The physical hardships can be considerable—tropical heat, high altitude, noisy streets, or just small annoyances like lumpy beds, unfamiliar foods, and wheezing air conditioners. Yet as long as your basic needs are met, these early weeks will certainly be memorable, perhaps even fun if you begin to explore your new surroundings and don't take problems too seriously. As Patricia discovered in Havana, family members or friends who have experienced this time together share a permanent bond, like fellow graduates of a wilderness survival course.

Vacations are enjoyable, but by the time they end, the weary adventurers are usually relieved to sleep in their own beds again and get back to their old routines. Around the time that a normal vacation would certainly be over—perhaps four to six weeks—you may start to wish you could do the same. But this *is* your bed now, and the new routines are here to stay.

Transition shock: the "slump"

Up to this point, you may have been drawing on a kind of psychological "reserve tank" stocked with security, self-confidence, and energy from your previous life. But eventually you will exhaust these reserves, and you may find yourself sinking into the "slump" of transition shock.

Typical symptoms of transition shock include feelings of being overwhelmed by change, homesickness, a drop in self-confidence, mild depression, irritation, and hostility. We will discuss each of these in turn.

Change overload. Human beings make sense of the world and their lives by following routines and taking familiar things for granted. However, during an international move, there are no comforting routines or familiar things. Everything changes at once. The physical environment assaults you with new sights, sounds, and smells. The time zone and climate may be different. The rhythms of daily life are unfamiliar. You may face a new job—or no job. You may have moved from a suburban house to a big-city apartment or vice versa. Even the habits and expectations of the people around you are confusing. Nothing is obvious anymore; everything takes work to figure out, and much more work to actually accomplish.

When babies are overstimulated, they cry or turn away. Adults are not so different: we may become irritable or seek to withdraw from this unrelenting assault on our senses. Some expatriates fall into a pattern of working late, staying at home reading or watching satellite TV, and generally avoiding confrontation with the host-country environment. The trouble with avoidance, however, is that it rarely produces a satisfying lifestyle—in fact, it offers all the disadvantages and none of the advantages of being abroad. In a worst-case scenario, it can lead to the ultimate withdrawal: failure of the assignment and an early return to the home country.

We offer a few practical suggestions to minimize sensory overload and ease yourself into the new environment, ideas we often learned the hard way ourselves.

- As you prepare for your new country, seek out sensory impressions along with information: practice the language, sample the food, rent movies, and read novels about the country. This will lessen your sense of alienation in the new place.
- When you arrive, consciously put structure and predictability into your uprooted life by establishing new daily routines for meals, exercise, and free time.
- Try to strike a balance between withdrawal and exploration. Learning about your new environment will help you feel more comfortable and confident there; however, don't overwhelm yourself by trying to learn and experience everything at once; explore and try new things steadily but gradually.

A friend and long-time expat, currently in Cyprus, reports:

I've been surprised at how intense those first six to eight weeks are compared to the rest of an overseas tour. How, for me, in my highly stressed state, every confusing or difficult thing is magnified. Trying to figure out how the hot water works and how to regulate the temperature in the house, not knowing which keys work for what doors, driving on the "wrong" side of the road, needing to ask where the restroom is but not knowing the Greek word for toilet . . . and I remember thinking how I just couldn't tolerate how noisy the refrigerator was. At those times, I wonder if I'm really cut out for this life and I wonder if I'm the only one thrown so very off-balance by the unfamiliar day-to-day moving parts of my new life . . . I lie on my bed and try to relax but feel as if a bag of concrete mix is lying on my chest.

Then, two months later, when all the familiar sounds and tasks and conditions are digested and catalogued and I can dial my family's phone numbers without thinking, I start to be okay again. Then I can enjoy the bright, bold lines of a Mediterranean cityscape, the sounds of new birds in the trees, kids outside playing basketball in the weedy lot across the street, and the wonderful new cheeses and wines and shorelines and weather. The reward, I guess, for my time of trial.

Homesickness for the place left behind. As the strangeness of the new environment sinks in, you may find yourself missing family, friends, neighbors, familiar places and activities, your former work environment, and even some of the quite ordinary aspects of your previous life more strongly. At least you knew what to do with the garbage back home! Grief for these losses is natural and real, and as you would manage other kinds of grief, you must face and work through the loss of a former home and lifestyle gradually. The following measures may help:

- Communicate regularly with people back home, by phone, voice-over-Internet, e-mail, instant messaging, and so forth. This will help you think of the world as an interconnected whole, in which you have not disappeared but are simply out of town. (See chapter 10 for further discussion of the importance of maintaining ties to your home base.) However, beware of focusing all of your attention on faraway social networks. You will also need to get out and face the challenge of building friendships in your new environment.

- Look forward to home leave, even if it's a year in the future, and invite loved ones to visit you.
- Think of ways to satisfy your cravings for something familiar. A South African in the United States notes, "Even though I am not and never have been much of a sports fan, I missed the sports of home. I longed to see cricket, soccer, and rugby, not just baseball, basketball, football, and golf on the TV." If you have a high-speed Internet connection, you may be able to access sports or other home-country programming. Fellow expats may know of a specialty market where you can find a food from home that you crave. If all else fails, make plans to enjoy the things you miss on your next home leave or vacation trip. Simply knowing you will have access to them again someday can help.
- Try not to romanticize your previous lifestyle. Regularly remind yourself of the aspects of your home, neighborhood, or workplace that you were quite happy to leave behind.

What happened to your self-confidence? A cross-cultural move can be a heavy blow to the ego. When you arrive, you may not even know how to get around, buy bathroom tissue, or ask directions. You may find yourself stumbling over cultural blunders and language errors that a six-year-old local child wouldn't make in the host culture.

Patricia reports:

Back in Washington, I had been a normal, middle-class person, but in Trinidad, everyone on the street stared at me, and not necessarily in a friendly way: my pale skin, my accent, and my clothes were like a sign around my neck saying, "I don't belong in this country." I even collided regularly with people on the sidewalk, because they walked, as they drove, on the left.

The first few months on the job can be a shock for someone accustomed to success and quick results—which is precisely the kind of person usually sent abroad in the first place. Working late hours, struggling with language and cultural barriers, and dealing with the stress of a new job may cause you to wonder whether you will ever be able to accomplish what you set out to do.

At the same time, the easy sense of belonging that you may have taken for granted at home is nowhere to be found. Your sense of being in control of your own life can also suffer greatly during this period. You may find yourself dependent upon other people to help you call a taxi or locate a pharmacy. Your housing and furniture may be provided by your employer; incomprehensible local rules and laws may limit your activities.

Accompanying spouses, especially if not employed, face particular challenges to self-confidence and identity. You may suddenly find yourself considered what some still call a "dependent" or "trailing spouse"— defined in terms of your husband's or wife's job (see chapter 9 for an in-depth discussion of issues affecting accompanying spouses).

To help build self-confidence and regain your sense of identity, try these techniques.

- Prepare yourself in advance with cross-cultural and language training. This spares you the "stupid and helpless" feeling that expatriates arriving without these skills regularly report.
- As soon as you arrive, work on becoming an "expert" on aspects of the host country that interest you. Learn to cook local foods, identify the wild birds in your neighborhood, study the history of nearby ruins, take up lessons on a popular local instrument, or take an architectural tour.
- Find ways to remain "true to yourself." If you love the outdoors but find yourself stuck in a polluted city or enjoy interior design but have to live in drab furnished quarters, get creative about following the inclinations that help define your sense of self. Join a weekend hiking club, become an expert on local textiles, or at least link up with like-minded people over the Internet.

Temporary depression. Homesickness and the insecurity of the first months are obvious triggers for feelings of sadness and self-doubt. Many expatriates exhibit signs of depression during this time, such as insomnia or excessive sleeping, not eating or overindulging, bouts of crying, and excessive self-criticism. Progress in the five components of adjustment (see pages 180–196) will help ease these symptoms. Other measures may also help.

- Keep busy and involved with other people. On the night before a free day, make sure you have arranged a reason to get up the next morning: schedule a language class or plan to meet a friend.
- Try not to bottle up your negative feelings. Express them in conversations, letters, e-mails, or a diary. Most of all, admit them to yourself and acknowledge them as normal.
- Eat right, spend time outdoors, and get enough exercise. These physical factors definitely have an effect on mood. If unsafe streets or pollution prevent walking and jogging, join a health club or use a hotel pool.

An Austrian-American in Taiwan recalls:

An experienced expat told me upon my arrival that I should go out and do something every day. Staying in the security of your home for a longer time makes it more and more frightening to go out into an alien environment. Go out, even if you only go to the grocery store or the dry cleaner. I believe that forcing myself to interact with people even on my "low" or homesick days kept me from getting depressed.

Most likely, your depression will be mild and will lift as you make progress toward adjustment. If you begin to feel seriously depressed, however, with the inability to perform everyday tasks or with thoughts of suicide, you should seek medical help (see "If You're Still Not Adjusting," page 196).

Irritation and hostility. If you find yourself snapping at your spouse or sobbing over the nonsensical arrangement of electrical outlets in your apartment (as one woman was startled to catch herself doing), remember that it is a normal part of the adjustment process. And when you are feeling this way, it is natural to experience negative thoughts about the people who put you in this situation: your organization, your spouse, the moving company, or the local people with their confusing and frustrating ways. When you start to feel like pounding something out of sheer frustration (or to prevent yourself from reaching that point), try these ideas for reducing your stress.

- Cultivate your sense of humor. Laughter reduces stress and helps you keep a broader perspective when every little thing seems to go wrong.
- Take regular breaks from work or family chores to do things you enjoy. Especially if you find yourself in a high-pressure environment, travel regularly to give yourself a break. Even a weekend away can make a big difference.
- Practice stress-reducing techniques that work for you: perhaps meditation, deep breathing, yoga, massage, friendly sports competition, dance, aerobics, running or walking, visiting parks or nature sanctuaries, listening to music, or prayer. (Smashing plates is not recommended, but it worked for Patricia in Havana—her adjustment gradually improved after that low point!)

Stress, unfortunately, doesn't magically disappear after your initial adjustment is behind you. It may continue throughout your overseas assignment, especially if the host-country environment is difficult for you, if your work is frustrating, or if you have trouble advancing in one or more of the components of adjustment (see pages 180–196). Be sure to make stress-relieving activities like the ones just suggested part of your regular routine overseas. If you find yourself feeling angry and hostile, take stock of your situation. What is bothering you most? Asking your colleagues or spouse for help, rather than blaming them, may be the most effective route to a solution.

Coping with a "crash landing"

A few expatriates are so shocked on arrival in their new country that there is no question of a "honeymoon" period—all they want to do is jump on the next plane and go home. Depressing poverty, in-your-face beggars, traffic, pollution, a high crime rate, seemingly hostile stares from the local people, or a rat dropping out of a coconut palm right onto your head—as happened to a woman we know—may provoke an intense emotional reaction. The natural instinct to protect yourself and your family can go into high gear, overriding any concerns about career advancement and inconvenience to your organization. One family selected for a university exchange program in Trinidad took one look at their new home, with its barred windows and surrounding fence topped with barbed wire and embedded bits of broken glass—and promptly booked their return ticket. Risk factors for a "crash landing" include the following:

- Never having moved before, even within your own country
- Moving from a very safe, familiar environment to a dangerous, stressful one
- Moving to a culture that is radically different from your own
- Not knowing the local language
- Having little or no support from an organization
- Going through a major life change at the same time as the move (such as having your first baby, or being without a job for the first time)

Even if one or more of these categories describe your situation, adequate preparation, a preliminary visit, and strong support in the host country (from fellow expatriates, if it is not provided by an organization) can greatly lower the risk that you will "crash and burn." If you do find yourself in this situation, though, try some of these measures.

- If you are being sent abroad by an organization, ask for additional support. The people who sent you (or your partner) abroad have a vested interest in the success of your assignment.
- Take steps to increase your comfort and security. If you feel unsafe in an isolated house, move into a hotel or apartment. If driving scares you, take a taxi for a while.
- Spend as much time as you can with other people. An invitation to the home of experienced expatriates who have successfully adjusted to your host country can help lessen your fears. So can a new local friend who can show you around, translate for you, and explain "strange" customs (see "Building a support network and making friends" on page 185).

- Ask a relative or good friend to come stay with you for a while, if this is feasible.
- If you are not yet comfortable in your home, find a "safe haven" where you can feel insulated from the stresses of your new environment. This may be a hotel swimming pool, a health club, an expatriate club, or even a friend's home. Arrange to spend at least a little time there each day or several times a week.
- Discover the enjoyable things your country has to offer. Spend the weekend at a beach resort, on a photo safari, or at a regional or national park. Take a tour of the cultural highlights. Expatriate groups may also offer outings and tours.
- Give yourself a fixed period—perhaps a month—to decide whether or not to stay. Simply realizing that you have control over whether or not you stay can help. Also, you may find you feel much better by then. Even if you eventually decide to give up on your overseas employment or assignment, you'll know you gave it a fair trial.

One more thought: in asking for help from your organization (or your spouse!), specific requests are always more effective than vague complaints and expressions of resentment. Although your emotions may understandably be raw, alienating people at the office or fighting with your spouse will only make things worse. Concrete, positive suggestions (such as "I'd like to hire a driver, because I'm not yet confident with driving but I need to get around") are more likely to get the results you want.

Confronting poverty and suffering

If you are moving from a wealthy country to an impoverished one, the human and animal suffering you will confront may be the most profoundly disturbing change in your environment. In Kaduna, Nigeria, for example, Melissa shopped in markets where disfigured lepers begged for money and polio victims crawled along the dusty ground on wooden supports strapped to their bent knees.

In addition, in a poor country, where human lives are fragile and easily lost, concern for animals and the environment may be considered an unaffordable luxury. Expatriates who have grown up with a sensitivity to environmental issues and animal welfare may be shocked to see litter and trash everywhere, vehicles billowing out black smoke, and mangy, homeless animals slinking through the streets, while local residents consider these conditions a normal part of daily life.

If you have never encountered these conditions before, you may find such sights extremely disturbing and even guilt-provoking. Quite naturally, you may wish to shield yourself from these unpleasant realities as much as possible, but it is neither possible nor desirable to cut yourself off from ordinary life in your host country. Part of the transition-shock process in this case will involve learning to understand and face, if not accept, these conditions.

In some countries, aggressive beggars and vendors offering trinkets for sale make walking in public areas difficult and uncomfortable. Ask experienced people about the best ways to fend off unwanted attention. Beggars in obvious need also pose an ethical dilemma. It is clearly undesirable to encourage begging, and children asking for money may have been sent out by unscrupulous "handlers." However, impoverished people may have no other choice but to beg. Learning about local conditions before you arrive can help you decide whether giving to beggars is appropriate, or if you can help more effectively in other ways.

Many expatriates have found that the best way to cope with their shock at the suffering in a poor country is to contribute, even in a small way, to relieving it. Local expatriates' groups may already be involved in charitable work and will welcome your assistance. Or find your own way to help. Melissa and a friend founded a charity group to support Ukrainians in need. In Algeria, Melissa took in cats from the streets, nursed them back to health, paid for their sterilization, and found homes for them. A British woman started the Society for the Protection of Animals in North Africa to promote better treatment and care of donkeys, horses, and mules, the beasts of burden in the region.

An expatriate in a less-developed country reports:

> *One of the expats here just could not get over the trash everywhere.*
> *Her comments have toned down a bit since she located a charity which*

collects recyclable materials and uses them to fund a community initiative that works with sight-impaired children. Now she uses her energy to encourage both expats and nationals to bring their recyclables to her home, where they are picked up twice a month by this charity.

Efforts like these will help you feel like an active participant in your host culture, not just a helpless bystander. In addition, many expatriates find their encounters with poverty and suffering to be an opportunity for personal growth, as they gain a sobering view of global problems and humankind's capacity to face them. One surprising discovery noted by many expatriates from wealthy countries is the resilience of human dignity and joy, even under squalid conditions. Encounters with the truly needy can also be effective antidotes against the small complaints of expatriate life. For example, after Patricia helped scrub down orphans infected with scabies at an orphanage in Trinidad and experienced their smiles and songs of gratitude, little annoyances like malfunctioning air conditioners and the absence of beef in the local grocery stores didn't seem to matter anymore.

Strategies for singles

Going abroad on your own offers many advantages and lots of freedom. However, the arrival period may feel like an especially lonely ordeal. You may have to figure everything out by yourself—from opening a bank account to getting an Internet connection installed—while working full-time or longer hours. And at the end of the day, you'll come home to an empty house or apartment, perhaps depressingly filled with boxes or only a couple of messy suitcases. Here are a few strategies that may help.

Prioritize logistics during the first month. As Margaret Malewski points out in the book *GenXpat: The Young Professional's Guide to Making a Successful Life Abroad* (Intercultural Press, 2005), employers generally understand that you will need to take some time for house hunting and similar tasks when you first arrive. If you postpone these chores, you may still be distracted by them months later, when you're expected to be fully productive at work.

Network like you've never networked before. Spread your net far and wide, before and after you arrive, for fellow expatriates (from your country or a third country) and local people. Maybe the first people you meet won't become your good friends, help you with practical tasks, or prove useful for your professional network, but they may introduce you to people who will. Start with the suggestions in chapter 1 and those later in this chapter in the section "Building a support network and making friends." For an in-depth look at the issue of dating across cultures, see chapter 8 of *GenXpat*.

Ignore demographics. At home, you probably look for other singles, people close to your own age, and colleagues in your profession to spend time with. In an expatriate community, you might find yourself attending a lecture in English with university students, retirees, international school teachers, young parents, diplomats, and missionaries—who are all learning from each other and enjoying each other's company.

Like Patricia's friend Steve from the anecdote that began this chapter—and many others we have known—you may find yourself making friends with families (whether foreign or local) who will invite you for meals, holiday celebrations, and even weekend trips. Retired expats can be rich sources of knowledge and fascinating companions. And students can show you the local dance clubs and other places to meet fellow singles.

Set up a welcoming home. As we noted in chapter 3, research has shown that expats—singles as well as couples—feel more settled and have a more positive view of their time overseas if they do things like hang pictures, set up furniture, and invite guests to their home sooner rather than later. Consider the suggestions in chapter 3 and those later in this chapter in the section "Creating a comfortable home base."

Take along a partner. Is there someone close to you who would be willing to accompany you abroad for the first month? Perhaps a good friend, a sibling, your university roommate, or even your mother? As this chapter describes, the settling-in period is no vacation—but it *is* an adventure. The right partner—someone flexible, supportive, and reliable who knows you well—can be a big practical help as well as a welcome companion. A beloved cat or dog can also be a good "transition partner" if it is feasible to take a pet with you and if you will have enough time to provide proper care.

On the other hand, there is a lot to be said for independence without a demanding roommate or stressed-out spouse. This time on your own to explore a new country can provide a new sense of freedom, a positive test of your inner resources, and ongoing opportunities for self-discovery. Go out and conquer the world!

The five components of adjustment

As we have witnessed in the impoverished countries where we have lived, human happiness does not derive mainly from material luxury—at least once the basic needs of survival have been fulfilled. Instead, it seems to arise from more intangible factors, making up what author Gail Sheehy has called the "well-being scale." These include an overall feeling of self-confidence, the comfort of a familiar environment, good relationships with family and friends, a sense of accomplishment in productive activity, and the excitement of adventure.

Unfortunately, except for the last item (where we expatriates do have the advantage!), these are precisely the elements that tend to be disrupted in an overseas move. As mentioned in the introduction to this chapter, we have identified five basic areas on which most expatriates will need to work in order to adjust successfully:

- Developing your language and cross-cultural skills
- Creating a comfortable home base
- Building a support network and making friends
- Learning to function in your new environment
- Finding meaningful and enjoyable activities

These are not steps to be followed in order; they are complementary tasks that all point in the same direction: feeling at home in the new environment and regaining a comfortable position on the "well-being scale."

A British spouse, looking back on her time in Moscow, recalls:

I found it helpful, arriving in what looked to be a bleak and horrible place with a new baby and two small children, to make a list of things that I thought would make my life bearable. For instance, taking music lessons, taking language lessons, finding somewhere I could regularly get fresh flowers to brighten up the gloom, getting my confidence up about exploring the city alone, seeing specific things, learning specific things about Moscow. I did in fact accomplish all the things on the list that I set out to do, and they did make my life there happy and productive.

As you work toward these general goals, consider making a list, as our British friend did in Moscow, of what will make your life at least bearable and, hopefully, happy. Give yourself credit for your accomplishments, no matter how small. Reflect on your progress often and see how far you have come.

Developing your language and cross-cultural skills

After arrival, as you continue the language learning process described in chapter 2, you will likely make more rapid progress than before because the host-country environment around you will provide both motivation and reinforcement for your studies. If you are able to take formal training, both individual and group classes have advantages.

- A host-country tutor or "mentor," aside from teaching you the language, can become a very valuable resource, answering your questions about practical and cultural matters that arise from everyday life in the country (see our discussion on choosing a teacher in chapter 2).
- Attending a language class with other foreigners can offer a pool of potential friends as well as progress in the language.

An expatriate from Mexico living in Germany reports:

My German-language class included students from Japan, Taiwan, Switzerland, and Australia. We'd go out for coffee after class and have parties where we cooked our national dishes. We spoke German together because it was the only language we had in common. Ten years later, I still keep in touch with some of those people.

You will also make more rapid progress with the culture once you arrive—but you may also be dismayed by the realization of how much there is to learn. It is one thing to learn about foreign ways in a cultural seminar, but quite another to become a foreigner yourself, surrounded by people who take invisible rules of behavior for granted and wonder why *you* don't fit in.

An accompanying male spouse in India says:

> *The first morning we moved into our apartment, a man rang our doorbell around 9:00. He said "Cataclak," or something like it, and waited for me to do something. I stared at him. He repeated himself. I asked, "Garbage?" He repeated himself. "One second," I said, and I retrieved the trash from our kitchen. He took the bag and left. For all I knew he was the laundry man.*

It may be a shock—but ultimately a horizon-expanding experience—to realize that the local version of "common sense" leads people in your host country to conclusions that are quite different from yours (see chapter 4). It may be especially hard to get your bearings if social signals and feedback mechanisms have different meanings than they did in your home culture. For example, a laugh may signify amusement, disdain, or embarrassment.

It is important to find people who can act as mentors and cultural interpreters as you seek to understand the behavior and customs around you. Local colleagues, new friends, and fellow expatriates who have successfully adjusted will probably be happy to explain host-country customs to you. Be sure to phrase your requests as positive questions, such as "How can I make a good impression when I first meet someone?" rather than complaints about local ways.

Inevitably, as you gain knowledge of the local culture, some behaviors and rules may appear nonsensical or misguided to you. Local people may also regularly act in ways that would be considered offensive or insulting in your home country, such as spitting on the street or asking why you don't have children. (It is no consolation to realize that some of the things you do may be just as offensive to the people of your host country!)

Patricia reports:

> *In Cuba, an acquaintance who hadn't seen me for a while observed that*
> *I was looking "muy gorda" (very fat). I felt hurt and insulted. Then it*
> *happened a few more times, and I realized from the speakers' smiling*
> *faces that they meant no offense. I then assumed they were making gentle*
> *fun of me and responded with self-deprecating comments about how*
> *I needed to get more exercise. They only looked confused. It took me*
> *months to realize that the comment was a compliment: I was looking*
> *strong and healthy in their eyes, something very desirable in a country*
> *of scarcity and rationed food.*

Encounters with new ways of doing things are not always negative, however. Although we human beings tend to feel most comfortable with people like ourselves, we are also intrigued by new ideas and "exotic" ways. Some customs in your host country may seem pleasant and refreshing. For example, a Swiss couple in Latin America was delighted by the easy physical affection among friends they encountered in that region.

Your own personality will play a role here. Cultures are not rigid molds that produce stereotyped Brazilians, Russians, Americans, or Australians. You may well find that some of your own personality traits and preferences make you feel a closer affinity to your host culture than your native one. Some expatriates even say they feel like they were "born in the wrong country." Make the most of these delightful surprises as you get to know local people.

As you acquire a deeper understanding of the host culture, you will begin to adjust your actions—and your reactions—to the cultural context as you deal with local people. You will be on your way to becoming bicultural—a significant achievement and one that can enrich your life, your career, and ultimately even our globalizing but still-divided world.

Creating a comfortable home base

Your home—whether it is a hotel room, a temporary apartment, or your permanent quarters—plays an essential role during the transition period. Let it become a haven where you can retreat from the demands of the foreign world outside.

Set it up as soon as you can with decorations and other favorite items that will soothe your jangled senses and create a cheerful sense of home (see chapter 3 for suggestions). Add some pleasant touches from your host country, such as flowers, houseplants, a local painting or sculpture, or a bowl of local fruit. Even if you have very little control over the way your home is furnished and decorated, personalizing it in small ways can make it feel like home.

Consider inviting colleagues or new friends to your home as soon as possible, even if it is just a bare temporary apartment. Having guests over will give you a reason to brighten up the place and will help create a sense of home.

When your shipments arrive, manage the unpacking process with care. This may seem like a trivial issue, but we have noticed with ourselves and others that household effects tend to arrive in the middle of the slump period, when the stresses of adjustment are piling up and seem as if they will never end. Living amid endless piles of messy, half-emptied boxes can undermine your hard-won sense of adjustment during this vulnerable period and hold you back from what you need to be doing: exploring, making friends, and looking for enjoyable activities. We suggest two alternative unpacking strategies that have worked for us.

The "put it away" method. If your shipment is relatively small and the service of unpacking is in your mover's contract (ask; it often is), consider having the movers get rid of the boxes for you. Before your shipment arrives, plan where the larger pieces of furniture will go. Have the movers place your furniture and boxes in the proper rooms. Then ask them to unpack your belongings and put them away somewhere in the room. Pots and pans can be placed in any kitchen cabinet, books on the nearest shelf. Later, you can gradually organize your shelves, drawers, and cabinets.

Don't let the movers just pile things up on the floor! A newcomer in Chile made this mistake and found herself despondently wading through a sea of mixed-up stuff for weeks, while her small children gleefully spread it around further.

The "warehouse" method. Before the movers arrive, identify a room or area in your home that is accessible but not necessary for daily life (such as a guest room). This will serve as your "warehouse." Have the movers place pieces of furniture and particularly large and heavy things (such as wardrobe boxes of clothes) directly in the rooms where they belong. However, ask them to place all the rest of your boxes in your warehouse room. If there is enough space, have them make separate piles for each category, such as kitchen items, personal care items, and so on.

After the movers leave, you can then take out and unpack the boxes at your own pace. Set yourself a reasonable goal—perhaps five or ten boxes a day. When you're not unpacking, you can close the door to your warehouse room and enjoy your uncluttered, box-free home!

By the time your shipments have arrived and your belongings have been put away, you will probably be feeling more comfortable in your new quarters. One test of this is your reaction when you return from a trip away: the feeling of familiarity and relief at being home may take you by surprise.

Building a support network and making friends

Back at home, you probably had many people to turn to for advice, support, or help in an emergency: friends, colleagues, neighbors, extended family, a religious community, a family doctor, and so forth. If you wanted to go out for lunch or coffee, play tennis, or discuss a personal issue, you probably had numerous people to turn to. As you adjust to a new place, this support network must somehow be reconstructed—and quickly.

An important early step is to locate medical professionals and emergency facilities. Your colleagues, a local expatriates' group, or your embassy will probably be able to provide names of doctors and dentists who speak English. Identify and start building a relationship with these professional people as soon as you can, before an emergency occurs.

If you live among locals, you may find that they introduce themselves and welcome you as soon as you arrive. In many countries, however, newcomers are expected to take the initiative. Ask a knowledgeable source about the best ways to "break the ice" in your host country.

Your workplace is an obvious element in your support network. There may be a staff member or consultant specifically assigned to help newcomers settle in. Don't be shy about taking advantage of these services. If you have colleagues who are also expatriates, you may find that you have more contact with them outside of work than you normally would at home. Like you, they are lacking their usual sources of support, and forming a community outside of the office can be mutually advantageous.

If you are among the rising number of expatriates who plan to telecommute or work independently via Internet, you may need to put extra effort into building a support network. Be sure not to neglect this task. Besides helping you with everyday tasks, your network in the host country will provide you with opportunities for social interaction, which has been shown to be vital for psychological and even physical health. If you are working full-time on your computer, we recommend getting out and interacting with people each day in some form or another—perhaps breakfast or lunch with a local friend, exercising with a runners' group, or volunteering at an international school. Perhaps you can find professional contacts to meet regularly in the host country, even if you are not paid to do so. Don't think of the time spent away from your computer as "lost billing hours," but as a necessary component of your adjustment and well-being abroad.

Other expatriates in your host city—from your home country and from third countries—will likely be key components of your support network abroad. In fact, the willingness of expatriates to pitch in and help each other, especially in countries with difficult living conditions or those that aren't particularly welcoming to foreigners, can be one of the most agreeable aspects of living abroad.

To find fellow expatriates, look for groups catering to foreigners in your host city, including international clubs, service clubs, women's clubs, online communities, language classes, playgroups for parents with young children, special-interest clubs (sports, crafts, theater, etc.), volunteer or charitable associations, religious communities, international friendship groups, and so forth. Your colleagues may have information on these groups, or check a local English-language newspaper or the Internet.

A Swiss expatriate in Brazil states:

> *When we arrived in Salvador da Bahia, I felt so alone and depressed.*
> *I spoke English and German but not much Portuguese. My husband knew*
> *people, but they were his friends, his contacts, not mine. Finally I found*
> *out about a group of German-speaking people: a Lutheran church group.*

I wasn't even a Lutheran, but I started going to their meetings. And it worked: I found some friends, and things went much better after that.

Even if you do not consider yourself a "joiner" or a typical group member, attend at least a few sessions of the groups that most closely correspond to your interests. Even if the group itself seems dull or not your type, you may meet potential friends or gain important information.

Beware, however, of expatriates who have developed a negative attitude toward the host country. Some even seem eager to spread their gloom to newcomers, as if to justify their own experience. Avoid these people or groups, especially during the adjustment period. Attitudes, both positive and negative, are contagious. Throughout your time overseas, try to surround yourself with local people and expatriates who have adjusted well to your host country and are enthusiastic about living there.

If you find yourself isolated, with no interesting expatriate groups (or no groups at all) available, you may have to be more creative about developing a support network. Focus on the connections that are most important to you—perhaps a religious community or people with whom you can practice your favorite sport. We all gravitate toward those with whom we have something in common—and culture is certainly not the only thing people can have in common. Look for local people with interests similar to yours, perhaps at a community center or adult education classes.

A woman recently returned from two years in Caracas recalls:

I had many interests in Venezuela—swimming, lunch with my Venezuelan friends, theater, concerts, ballet, flamenco dance lessons, and women's clubs—so connections with people were occurring. Speaking the language was a big plus!

Using the Internet to connect with international expatriate networks and keep in touch with friends and family back home can also help ease a sense of isolation. However, your morale can suffer if most of your human contacts are electronic ones. Make an effort to develop flesh-and-blood contacts as well, even if the people you meet aren't precisely the ones you would have chosen as friends at home. In a recent study by the Interchange Institute, expatriate women who relied most on long-distance contacts such as e-mail for their social support had significantly lower levels of adjustment.*

A British woman in the United States notes:

> *I do feel that in one way recent advances in technology have made the transition to an expat lifestyle more difficult—it's very easy to fall into the trap of spending your social time keeping up with everyone "at home" by e-mail or instant messaging instead of getting out there and making new friends. I did fall into this habit in the beginning and had to make a conscious effort to stop doing it once I realized that it wasn't doing me any good!*
>
> *I still chat to people back in the U.K. online, but I don't miss out on other opportunities just to make sure I'm there on the end of the computer.*

Networking skills are important for making friends quickly in a new place. Try not to be shy about introducing yourself and asking questions. Many friendships have developed out of a newcomer's request for help and advice. When you meet someone you think you might like, don't leave your next meeting to chance. Exchange phone numbers and/or e-mail addresses and follow up with an offer to get together.

Don't feel that you have to wait until your home is in perfect order to invite people in. Two months after arriving in Trinidad, Patricia invited practically everyone she had met so far for chili and beer. Her company didn't mind the plastic tableware and sparsely furnished house, and the party helped her cement several new friendships.

An ideal goal is to make friends with a range of people in your new country, including citizens of your home country, expatriates from other countries, and local people. It is often easier to make friends with

---

*"Many Women Many Voices" Study of Accompanying Spouses Around the World, conducted by Dr. Anne P. Copeland at The Interchange Institute, www.interchangeinstitute.org, and commissioned by Prudential Financial, 2004.

third-country expatriates abroad than at home, since you share the experience of being foreigners in your host country. Of course, each new friendship is unique and valuable in its own right. But your home-country, local, and third-country friends can all help enrich your overseas experience in different ways.

Friends from your home country may celebrate holidays with you and help keep other home-country traditions alive. They will eagerly share their discoveries of foods and recipes that remind you of home. The laughs you share in private over strange local customs and cultural misunderstandings can help reduce stress and reassure you that others face similar difficulties.

Third-country friends put your overseas experience in a fascinating perspective, helping you see both your own ways and the host country's practices through someone else's eyes. These friends also broaden your cultural experience by exposing you to their own customs. And finally, you may have the opportunity to visit them someday in their home country, or have them visit you in yours.

Local friends can initiate you into the cultural mysteries of their country, along with its cuisine and other highlights. Since they are proud of their country, they help you feel good about living there, too. Getting to know them can help you understand and appreciate your host country in a deeper, more authentic way. And after you've left, ongoing contact with your local friends will help nourish that small piece of your heart you have left in their country.

In some countries the local people might be eager to meet you. In many others, however, it may seem difficult or impossible at first to make local friends. Besides the language barrier, local people may be busy and caught up in their own activities. After all, they are surrounded by their friends and families and might not feel they have time for new friends. Try these tips for making local friends.

- Get advice, perhaps from a local colleague, about how local people typically make friends. Where do they meet? What do they do during the early stages of a friendship?
- Look for local people with previous international experience or a special interest in your country.

- Join local clubs or go to events that focus on a hobby, sport, or interest you enjoy. Consider art exhibits, adult education classes, dance lessons or clubs, poetry readings, and travel groups, among others.
- Find out what activities are particularly popular in the local culture and give them a try. You may discover something new, as well as increasing your chances of making local friends.

A long-time expat now living in Thailand reports:

I instantly have a lot of friends because of martial arts. They are locals, real locals, and often they are from different strata of the population than the people you work with, so you get a better cross-section of society. Aerobics, music, and chess are activities people like to do, but if you do those with locals, you won't be talking very much. So you need to find activities that produce real conversation and friendships.

A word should be said about local people who seem a bit *too* eager to meet you. Especially in an impoverished country or one where networks of contacts are culturally important, they may be angling for financial assistance or perhaps your help in getting a visa to your country. If a relationship makes you uncomfortable or seems excessively one-sided, don't maintain it just out of politeness. Get advice from more experienced expatriates about your admirer's possible motives as well as ways to break off the relationship as painlessly as possible.

Learning to function in your new environment

A newcomer in Rome notes:

When you're in a new country, it takes all your energy and time to do just one thing. A seemingly simple job, such as finding a broom or getting a document, can turn into a half-day procedure when you don't know the ropes and barely know the language. Depending on my mood (and my moods are quite changeable these days), it's either a terrific new adventure or a giant hassle.

Mailing a postcard, buying a bus ticket, shopping for household necessities, and cooking everyday meals are skills we often take for granted. In a new country, however, the level of knowledge required for these tasks soon becomes apparent. When shopping, you may find that not only are the stores, products, and labels different, but the whole system can be organized in a way that seems baffling: In some places, bargaining is expected even for the most basic items; in others, you must pay first and present the receipt to pick up your purchases.

A Scottish expatriate in the United States admits:

> *I needed to be very careful to find out the difference between a postbox and a trash bin! Postboxes looked very different in the U.S. and were difficult to spot at first.*

An American in Prague describes her first encounters with a Czech supermarket:

> *Shopping has been pretty amusing. There is all this weird shrink-wrapped seafood—including a whole octopus!—but I can't find plain old canned tuna. There is an entire aisle of chocolate (it appears to be a major food group) but no baking supplies like flour. I thought I bought dishwasher detergent the other day, but I wasn't really sure until I ran it through the dishwasher and everything came out clean. It could have been bubble bath for all I knew. All my kitchen appliances are labeled in German, and I don't speak a word of German, so I just have to push buttons and hope for the best.*

Many of your recipes from home may turn out to be useless because key ingredients are not available or are so different that they cannot be substituted. Different units of measurement, utensils, and appliances may add to the confusion. Don't put yourself through the torture of figuring all these things out by yourself; ask your colleagues and contacts for advice. A few excursions with an experienced expatriate or local person soon after you arrive can reveal things that would take you months to discover on your own. Expatriates' groups often publish extremely helpful shopping guides and cookbooks featuring international recipes made with local ingredients.

A Canadian expatriate in Japan notes:

> *There are no ovens here, and most conventional cookbooks from home are oriented toward ovens. Recipes from Asia, Africa, and South America have been much more useful. A cookbook published by a missionary organization has also helped.*

At the same time, try not to depend too much on a driver, household employee, or your spouse to manage everyday tasks. Although you will likely feel foolish and incompetent at first, forcing yourself to do errands on your own will help build your self-confidence in the new environment, allow you to practice your language skills, and—if approached with a sense of humor—add to the adventure of living overseas.

To explore your new city, invest in the best local maps you can find. Tourist guidebooks, however, are usually best purchased in your home country before arrival, since they will be tailored to your own cultural expectations. Don't be shy about accepting offers from new friends and colleagues who are willing to show you around. Or hire a driver, walk, or take public transportation. Riding a bus or streetcar all the way to the end of the line and back (if this is safe) provides an authentic tour of your new city at little cost.

Finding meaningful and enjoyable activities

A sense of purpose and enjoyment is essential to a satisfying life, no matter where you are. This includes both your work (paid or unpaid) and your leisure-time pursuits. Meaningful and enjoyable activities give you a reason to get up in the morning as well as an answer to the question that nearly all expatriates pose to themselves at one time or another: "What am I doing here?" Accompanying spouses who arrive without a job often face particular challenges in finding meaningful activities abroad (this issue is discussed in depth in chapter 9).

Helping others, whether needy local people or fellow expatriates, is an excellent way to add depth and meaning to your overseas experience.

Many expatriates, both employees and accompanying family members, make volunteer work a core element of their lives abroad. In addition, during the adjustment period, nothing will boost your self-confidence faster than helping expatriates who are even newer than you are.

One spouse already living overseas and facing an upcoming transfer to Australia took this impulse even farther by creating a website (*www.yellabrickroad.com*) to help others who might be moving to Australia. She gathered and published the helpful information she had found and set up an online support community, which received 40,000 visitors within a year. Although she was not paid to create the website, she happily reports, "I've got some fantastic new skills to fill what would otherwise have been a big blank space on my résumé, and I've made a whole host of new friends around the world."

As we pointed out earlier, one important element on the "well-being scale" for all people—not just expatriates—is the excitement of adventure. Living abroad, here is where our real advantages lie. This is what our friends and relatives back home are thinking about when they express their envy about our travels.

According to cross-cultural expert L. Robert Kohls, "There is a high correlation between those foreigners who function at their best overseas and those with the keenest interest in exploring the country to which they are assigned" (*Survival Kit for Overseas Living*, Intercultural Press, 2001, p. 67). Tourists may pay thousands of dollars just to get where you are now. What do they do there? Find out what your new country has to offer—historical sites, cultural events, architecture, craft markets, natural beauty, outdoor sports, the beach. Especially when you are feeling overwhelmed by piles of boxes, bureaucratic hassles, or cultural misunderstandings, get out and be a tourist for a while.

An American in Nagoya, Japan notes:

> *In Japan, my favorite memories have been things like watching sword making, learning how to make paper from mulberry pulp, and helping our daughters learn how to tie-dye in a village where they've been tie-dyeing for centuries. I come back from special excursions "jazzed" about living overseas again.*

As we have seen, moving abroad can be a traumatic process, and living and working in a foreign society poses unavoidable challenges. Your time overseas can be viewed either as an unpleasant duty or as an opportunity for personal growth and adventure. Throughout your adjustment, try to emphasize the positive: focus on what *is* available rather than what is not. Although you may miss family and friends and some of the material comforts of home, your time overseas offers unique opportunities. If you spend your time wishing you were somewhere else, these months or years of your life may seem pointless and empty. But if you take advantage of these opportunities, your life will be enriched by your time abroad. Try to cultivate the skill that many people in the fast-paced modern world seem to have forgotten: enjoying the moment, the here and now. As a wise saying attributed to Mark Twain reminds us:

> *Twenty years from now, you will be more disappointed by the things you didn't do than by the ones you did. So throw off the bowlines. Sail away from the safe harbor. Catch the trade winds in your sails. Explore. Dream. Discover.*

A quick checkup: have you adjusted?

Of course, the time it takes to "reconfigure" the five components we have discussed in this chapter varies. However, most expatriates seem to adjust (for the most part) within about six months or so. Patricia's family has established a tradition of celebrating the six-month anniversary of their arrival in a new country with a special dinner and cake. They talk about their achievements, their new friends, and the positive aspects of their new home—and they take time to discuss any remaining concerns.

After you have been in your new environment for several months, ask yourself the questions that follow. Any negative answers indicate areas that may still need work. If the advice in this chapter is not sufficient to guide you toward progress in all these areas, consider asking a counselor or an experienced expatriate for help. Difficulties in just one of these areas can undermine the adjustment process and prevent you from getting the most out of your time overseas.

- Are you continuing to make progress in the local language (if applicable)? Can you communicate with local people in everyday situations?
- Are you starting to be able to read the cultural signals of the local people that differ from yours and to understand what they mean in context?
- When you are with local people, are you learning to adapt your behavior to their cultural expectations?
- Do you have more positive than negative feelings about the local people and culture?
- Do you get regular exercise, and have you found other ways to reduce the stress of living overseas?
- Does your home feel like a comfortable oasis amidst the foreign environment?
- Do you maintain regular contact with people back home—but maintain local social contacts as well?
- Do you have a network of people you can turn to in an emergency or if you need support in other ways?
- Have you made friends outside the narrow circle of colleagues from your home country?
- Do you regularly get out and do things in your free time rather than isolating yourself at home?
- Do you feel that you know your way around and can find what you need?
- Do you feel as if you have a reason to get up in the morning? Is your work (whether paid or unpaid) meaningful and satisfying?
- Have you found enjoyable things to do in your free time, especially activities that were not possible back home?
- Do you view your overseas assignment as an opportunity for personal growth rather than an unpleasant duty?

Don't be surprised or dismayed if some time after the original adjustment period you find yourself losing ground in some of these areas again. It doesn't mean you've failed! Researchers have found a pattern of two "down" periods (or slumps) among many expatriates, with the second one falling somewhere near the middle of the overseas experience. It may be that the achievements of the original adjustment period were enough to reach a plateau of satisfaction for a year or so, but as the reality of a longer stay abroad sinks in, you may begin to expect more from yourself and your surroundings. The good news is that once people make it through the second slump, they tend to become more comfortable than ever before.

A British spouse notes:

> *If I'd been offered a chance to go home after two months, I would have taken it in an instant. One year on, a chance came up to go back to the U.K., and for a few minutes it sounded great, but when I thought for a few moments, I felt like the adventure was just beginning and I wasn't ready to give it up yet!*

Consider testing yourself periodically with these questions. The answers do change. Perhaps friends will have left the country; a work project may have become frustrating; you will have ceased to make progress with the language or culture; or maybe you will have just fallen into a routine and stopped looking for opportunities for adventure and personal growth. Periodic checkups can help you identify areas that need work in order to minimize the disruption of the second slump.

If you're still not adjusting

The shock of transition and adjustment to a new country can be dangerous in some cases. Its insidious combination of stress, sadness, and self-doubt may trigger a serious depression, substance abuse, or other problems. If measures such as the ones suggested in this chapter don't seem to be working for you, for a member of your family, or for someone you know, *get help*. Overseas assignments, marriages, careers, and even lives have been cut short by the effects of transition shock.

If you do not have access to professional, confidential counseling through your employer, consider seeking help from a local psychologist, religious organization, or other expatriates. Online support groups for expatriates can help point you in the right direction. Or consider talking to a trusted professional in your home country (even by e-mail or phone if necessary).

If your symptoms are not serious but you remain uncomfortable in your new environment, try the following.

- Be creative about ways to achieve the five components of adjustment. Identify expatriates who have reached the goals you hope to attain and ask for their advice. They might suggest options that had not occurred to you.
- Consider taking a trip away for a while, if possible. Stepping back from a difficult situation by taking a vacation to an enjoyable place or returning home for a short time and being surrounded by caring family members and/or friends can help give you the strength to return and face the challenges overseas.
- Try something new. Take on a volunteer job, join a new group, try a new sport, or learn a new skill. Forcing yourself out of a routine that has become frustrating or confining can be helpful.

One last but very important caveat: expatriate life is not for everyone. If you have given yourself a fair trial (perhaps 6 months) and you have used the support measures recommended in this book, but still find yourself miserable and ineffective at work or at home, it is no disgrace to give up and go home. You will not be alone—it has been estimated that about 20 percent of foreign assignments are ended early. There is no sense in continuing if your job performance is seriously suffering or if your family is strained beyond the limit.

"Home" at last

The adjustment process is never perfect or complete. Being well-adjusted may not mean that you feel you truly belong in your host country. You may still experience what one expatriate calls "those foreigner moments"—embarrassing cultural misunderstandings and head-on collisions with local ways.

The adjustment period can feel like wasted time because you have expended so much energy just to settle in. When you feel this way, keep in mind that you *have* accomplished some very significant goals. You've gained in-depth knowledge of a new country (which some have compared to earning a master's degree). You may have learned to speak a new language, which is a difficult and valuable achievement. Most important, perhaps, is that you have pushed yourself beyond your previous boundaries, learning to cope in a strange environment and opening yourself to new ways of thinking and living.

As you begin to understand the local language and culture, feel comfortable in your new home, build a support network, make friends, learn to function in your new environment, and find meaningful and enjoyable activities, the fragmented parts of your life will begin to come back together. And perhaps when you take your first trip away and return, or show visiting relatives around, or introduce local friends to something in their own country they have never discovered, you will realize that your new environment is becoming comfortable and familiar. As surprising as it seems, you'll be home.

CHAPTER 8

Staying Safe, Secure, and Healthy

Though most expats have a safe and healthy experience living abroad, crises can happen anywhere and at any time, and handling an emergency overseas will likely be more challenging than dealing with one at home. While it is impossible to plan for all crises that might occur while living in a foreign country, you can heighten your readiness level by educating yourself about the possible risks in your host country and by taking proactive steps to plan ahead. Whether you work for an organization or are on your own, you are the one who is ultimately responsible for your own safety, security, and well-being and that of your family members. The following sections outline steps you can take to make sure you are adequately prepared.

Safety and security

Research the security situation in your new country

A source of information widely used by expatriates and international travelers is the U.S. Department of State's website, *www.travel.state.gov.* The site contains a comprehensive list of travel warnings, public announcements, and specific information for each country in the world. To obtain the latest threat information for the country where you will be living, consult the list of Travel Warnings. Look on the home page in the Travel Information by Country section and you will find Consular Information Sheets containing information on the safety and security situation in your new country, as well as information on crime, traffic safety, road conditions, and more. You can check the Public Announcements section to read the latest alerts or advisories regarding ongoing security concerns in specific countries. Logging on to the website regularly will keep you up-to-date on the current security situation in your country, as well as others that you may visit.

Register with your embassy

Registering with your embassy enables officials from your country to contact you if there is an emergency. Should an in-country emergency occur, such as a natural disaster or political unrest, the embassy will be able to provide you with important information and instructions. Likewise, if there is a family emergency at home and one of your relatives has not been able to reach you, the embassy can assist. Embassies and consulates are resources that can provide information or assistance in a crisis; however, they cannot help if you have not registered and they are not aware that you are in the country.

You can register as soon as you arrive in your new country; in some cases, there are opportunities to register online. An Internet search can determine if such a service is available to you. If you are a U.S. citizen, you can register by logging on to the U.S. Department of State's website, www.travel.state.gov.

Be mindful of potential terrorist activity

Terrorist attacks are random, often occur without warning, and can happen anywhere in the world. Although one should not live in fear, expats should stay alert and be aware of what is going on around them. Keep up to date on current events, be aware of what is happening in your surroundings, and report any suspicious activity. If you are overseas and have concerns, contact your embassy. At times embassies may hold community meetings that can provide more information on the threat of terrorism in your area.

Inform yourself about local crime

Crime patterns in your new location may be different from those in your home country. Find out what kinds of crime are common in your new city and how to avoid them. Embassies sometimes give briefings for their citizens, or ask a relocation consultant or local expatriate for advice. Local law enforcement authorities may be willing to provide a briefing to your company or expat group.

Anywhere in the world, looking like a wealthy tourist can mark you as a target. Blending into the local scene as much as you can—dressing in the local style, trying out your language skills, and looking like you know where you are going when you walk the streets—will decrease your chances of becoming a target for pickpockets and other street criminals. Be wary of requests for help from strangers on the street. They may just want money, or they may be trying to distract you while their accomplice lifts your wallet. In addition, depending on where you live, be mindful of carrying laptops or PDAs (or even using your cell phone) on the street. In some countries, carrying or using these items in the open may make you a target for street thieves.

Copy important documents

Petty theft and pickpocketing can happen anywhere. Wherever you live, it is important to store a photocopy of your passport (the data page that includes the passport number, date of issue, etc.) and other important documents that you carry with you. If you have a visa, make a copy of that page as well. Should you ever become a victim, having this information in a safe place will save you time, help reconstruct what has been lost, and expedite getting replacements. Don't forget to copy both sides of your driver's license and credit cards. Also, whenever you travel, keep a photocopy of your passport in a separate place, such as in your suitcase.

While you are making copies of your documents, check the expiration date of your passport. In the flurry of activity in an international move, the expiration date is sometimes easy to overlook. Make sure that your passport is valid for a reasonable length of time. If a visa is required, this becomes even more important. Don't complicate your move by inadvertently letting your passport expire soon after you arrive abroad.

Safeguard your identity

Identity theft has become a global problem, and the victims of this type of crime may spend months or even years trying to get their accounts and credit ratings back in order. Reduce your chances of becoming a victim by staying informed about current scams. An Internet search can provide you with current information and steps you can take to protect yourself. In addition, talk to colleagues, experienced expats, or law enforcement authorities about crime and scams in your new location.

We know of a scam in one country where credit cards were stolen from Western tourists in a restaurant when they paid for their meals. After paying by credit card, tourists would sign their bill, but instead of having their own credit card returned, a stolen or expired card belonging to someone else would be given back to them. In the dim, candle-lit restaurant, guests did not think to look carefully at the card returned to them. By the time the error was discovered, unauthorized charges were already on the account.

Always keep a close watch on your credit cards and bank accounts—especially when using the Internet. Phishing (sending fraudulent e-mail or text messages to obtain personal information) has become a common practice, and if you are duped into giving your user ID, password, or other account information, your accounts and credit will be compromised. Checking your accounts regularly will enable you to see right away if any unauthorized activity has taken place.

Shred trash that contains account numbers or personal information. Even overseas, mail can be a source of information to an identity thief, so be mindful of what you are throwing out. Buy a document shredder if you don't have access to one at the office.

Create your own emergency action plan

An emergency action plan outlines actions to take if an unexpected crisis occurs. This is not only necessary in politically unstable countries or known "hot spots"; a crisis such as a natural disaster or terrorist activity can happen anywhere (even in your home country, so be sure to maintain your good security habits after reentry!).

Creating an emergency action plan reminds you to gather important information, keep it in one place, and have it when you need it most. The plan should contain a master contact list of people, local organizations, and resources that can be of assistance in the event of an emergency.

When creating an emergency action plan, you may also want to consider the following.

- In an emergency evacuation, to whom could you turn? Who are the people who would help you?
- What would you do if you had to get out of the country quickly for personal reasons?
- What documents would you take with you?
- What would happen to your household if you had to evacuate and leave the country? What kind of arrangements would you need to make?
- Would your employer or organization be able to help you? Does your organization have access to emergency evacuation services (other than medical evacuation)?
- If you have pets and cannot take them with you, what arrangements would you make? Identify local friends, colleagues, or a veterinary clinic with whom you could board your animals on a temporary basis.

In the event of a large-scale crisis in your country, it is likely that your embassy or consulate would provide some assistance. Hopefully, you have previously taken the step of registering. However, never assume that when an emergency occurs, the responsibility for managing the crisis lies solely with your embassy. Work with the embassy when assistance is available, but take ultimate responsibility for your own personal affairs. Some expats live in areas that are not near their embassy or consulate. It is especially important for them to have a plan. Even if you live in a capital city where your embassy is located, it is always prudent to think ahead and know what emergency resources are available locally.

As part of your emergency action plan, have a "grab-and-go bag" ready to take with you in case conditions in the host country or a personal crisis require you to leave the country quickly. Keep copies of your most important papers and documents in the bag so you can leave promptly. Besides our suggestions in chapter 3, the U.S. Department of State's website has useful information on contingency planning and evacuation resources, including a list of papers and documents to hand carry. For more information, log on to *www.state.gov/m/dghr/flo*, click the *FLO—A to Z Site Map* link, and look under the heading *Evacuations.*

Once your plan is complete, take the time to program important phone numbers into your cell phone (and keep your cell phone charged and accessible). In a crisis, there is no time to open an emergency action plan and start reading it. The real value of having a plan lies in the effort taken to create it. The process of formulating a plan (and keeping it updated) allows you to gather information and become familiar with local resources you can turn to when you need them most.

Take steps to heighten your security awareness

Developing security awareness means thinking ahead about potential emergency situations before they occur. Mentally anticipating what can happen by going over the types of actions to take in an emergency can help one react more quickly and take more decisive action when an actual crisis occurs. Studies have shown that the stress of an emergency situation can make it harder to think clearly and make good decisions. People who have practiced—even mentally—what to do in an emergency situation will respond more effectively than those who have not.

As an expat, one does not have to look far for opportunities to practice security awareness. For example, when traveling on a plane, look for the location of the nearest *two* exits, in the event there is an emergency and the exit closest to you is blocked. When you check into a hotel room, make it a habit to locate the nearest stairwell in case of a fire. Also, look to find an alternate escape route, should one be needed. In some countries, fire equipment may not reach the top floors, so if your hotel is in a tall building, you may want to request a room on a lower level.

These may sound like common sense suggestions; however, the more you travel, the easier it is to become desensitized to routine safety instructions or complacent when checking into a hotel. Taking steps to actively gather information and think about what to do in an emergency helps to develop crisis preparedness—a valuable asset that can make a difference in how effectively you deal with an actual emergency and may even save your life.

Be safety-minded in your home and community

Crisis preparedness also includes learning about day-to-day safety issues where you live. Safety standards in your host country may or may not be enforced the way you are used to at home. Even ordinary, everyday activities may pose safety concerns when you live overseas. For instance, there may be unmarked deep, open holes in streets and sidewalks, and playground equipment may be damaged and unsafe.

Expats who are accustomed to high levels of safety precautions, such as seat belt laws, lifeguards, and protective fences, may feel a sense of liberation in a less-restrictive country. You may be able to walk along the steep edge of a cliff or castle wall, snowboard without a helmet, or rent a motorbike for your 10-year-old. At home, you may have thought, "If it's allowed, it must be safe." In many places abroad, this is not the case. Enjoy the adventure, but never forget that the responsibility for your safety (and that of your children) lies with you and you alone.

Precautions you might expect to be taken against fire, such as sprinkler systems and fireproof construction, may not be present. Your ability to escape from your residence in case of fire may be blocked by burglar bars. Think ahead and purchase or request fire extinguishers, emergency escape gates, rope ladders, and other potentially life-saving equipment for your home.

Prepare to shelter in place

In the event of a political crisis, natural disaster, or pandemic (see the later section "The threat of a pandemic"), do not take it for granted that the local government in your country or your embassy or consulate will be able to help you. The ability to get help from anyone may be severely limited, depending on the actual situation. In a national emergency, air travel might be suspended and airports closed, so getting out of the country quickly might not be possible. Depending on the circumstances, the safest place to stay may be in your own home.

Take charge before a crisis occurs and make your own contingency plans. Do your own research to get suggestions and recommendations for sheltering in place. Simply put, to shelter in place means to remain in your home and take refuge in a room in the interior of your house as a means of protecting yourself from what is happening outside. Put together a disaster supply kit that contains nonperishable food, potable water, medications, flashlights, batteries, a radio, and other items you would need if you had to shelter in place.

Drive defensively

Fatal car accidents are much more common in some countries than in others. Seat belts (or their use) may be rare, and drivers may pass or change lanes recklessly or drive at night with no lights. Pedestrians and animals may cross the road, especially at night, with no warning. Drive defensively, and take extra precautions. In many countries it is wise to avoid driving at night.

Limit your speed in unfamiliar situations for your own, as well as everybody else's, safety. We know of a case in Egypt where an expatriate driver rounded a corner on the highway and there was a small baby sitting and crying in the road! Fortunately, the driver was traveling at a reasonable speed and was able to stop the car in time. A young girl who appeared to be the baby's caretaker was crying at the roadside. Finally, adults from the village came to the rescue and got the baby out of the road. Had the driver been speeding, there would have been no way to stop in time, and this could have been a tragedy for all concerned.

Learn the rules of the road. If you are not required to take a test to get a local driver's license, be sure to learn the local traffic rules and customs anyway. Also, observe other drivers' behavior— many "rules" are not written anywhere but are followed by custom. Every country has its own peculiarities in driving. An experienced expatriate or a colleague from work will probably be able to acquaint you with these.

Take care around water

Drowning is one of the leading causes of death for expatriate children, partly because they are more likely to have access to swimming pools in tropical countries. If you have children and a pool, fence it in and keep the fence locked unless you are there and paying full attention. Drowning can happen in seconds. Also, check the depth of the water before you dive into a swimming pool. We know of a case in Nigeria where an expatriate dived into a pool at a party, broke his neck, and was not able to get immediate emergency medical treatment. Unfortunately, he died a short time later. In addition, a beautiful, calm-looking sea can hide dangerous undertows or other hazards which may not be posted. Ask the local people or someone who knows the area before swimming anywhere.

Use caution with chemicals

Local pest control companies may use chemicals that are banned in your home country. If you feel you must use them in your home or yard, try to find out what the available chemicals are and what precautions you should take. Also, try to minimize your exposure to harmful chemicals by controlling pests in other ways—with traps and bait, by sealing cracks, and by eliminating food and water sources.

A word about photography

Taking pictures is usually not a problem in Western countries, but this may not be the case elsewhere. Some countries have strict regulations that forbid photographing certain restricted places, such as airports, bridges, or military installations. In some cases, an official permit is required before photographs of any kind can be taken. If you inadvertently snap a photo of one of these places, you may have your camera confiscated or even end up in jail. Unofficially, you may encounter situations where local people feel very uncomfortable about having their picture taken and will tell you not to do so. For your own safety, before you snap a picture, find out if any cultural biases or regulations against photography exist in your area.

Melissa reports:

> My husband and I were traveling in southern Algeria, in an area filled with old, abandoned French Foreign Legion posts. When we spotted a particularly interesting looking old fort, my husband stopped our car and took a picture of it from the window. The car behind us suddenly sped

around us, and then stopped a short distance ahead, where the driver said something to a soldier. As we pulled up, we were shocked to discover what looked like a charming piece of history was actually an Algerian military installation! To make a long story short, we were stopped, told to get out of the car, taken to an office where we were questioned separately, detained for hours, and ultimately had our film confiscated. We were lucky. The outcome could have been much worse.

The lesson learned is this: think before you take a picture. Even if you make an honest mistake as Melissa did, there may be unpleasant consequences. If you are living in a country with photography restrictions and have any doubts, don't take the picture!

Melissa recalls another unusual situation when taking photographs, this time in Nigeria:

As an expatriate in Nigeria, I found that taking photographs was always a challenge. Frequently, local people verbally objected to the sight of an expatriate with a camera—even before any pictures were taken. Some were fearful of having their picture taken. There is a belief in some areas that a camera can "steal the soul" of the person photographed. Others thought expatriates might be spies. It was my first time living in Africa, however, and I really wanted pictures to send to relatives back home. I mentioned my problem to a friend, a prominent Nigerian doctor, who agreed to make all the necessary arrangements and accompany me to the local open-air market, where we could both take photographs. When we arrived, I was surprised to see that a police escort had been provided. The policeman stood by, with a small whip in hand, as we snapped pictures of yams, wooden yam pounders, African baskets, and other ordinary, everyday items and market scenes. Occasionally, local people objected, and when they did, I was shocked to see the officer waving his whip to silence their protests. When necessary, he even swung his whip in the direction of old women, small children, or anyone else who voiced an objection. Fortunately, he never actually struck or injured anyone.

This may seem like an extreme example, but it clearly illustrates how the Western view of photography is not shared by all cultures. Expats living in developing countries should understand local regulations as well as how people in the culture feel about having their pictures taken. In Melissa's example, she did the right thing by enlisting the help of a prominent local person and obtaining permission from the police. Had she not done so and decided to walk around the market and take pictures on her own, she might have aroused suspicion, incited a crowd, risked her physical safety, or even been arrested by the police.

Staying on the right side of the law

Remember, when you live abroad you are a foreigner in someone else's country, and you are subject to local laws. Unless you have a diplomatic passport, you have no immunity. Traffic laws, drug laws, and other regulations apply to you—whether or not you are aware of them. Educate yourself with the help of your employer or colleagues, experienced expats, or local authorities.

If a problem occurs where you must deal with local officials, show them respect. In many cases, police and military officials in developing countries are not highly educated or well paid, and they have little tolerance for people they believe are acting condescendingly or treating them disrespectfully in any way. Showing respect means staying calm and courteous. Complaining, shouting, or getting angry and losing your temper will only make a bad situation worse. You won't necessarily be able to resolve a problem the way you would in your own country. Keep a clear head, assess the situation and the options available to resolve the issue, and then go from there. As a foreigner, you have the right to contact a consular officer from your country. As a precaution, always keep the phone number and address of your embassy with you.

Safeguarding your health

An ounce of prevention really is worth a pound of cure—especially when living in a foreign environment. Taking the time to educate yourself about the health conditions in your new country provides information that can help you make choices that maintain your health and lessen the chance of developing medical problems. This section will provide information on basic health issues encountered around the world and suggest ways to prepare yourself ahead of time. Use it as a starting point for your research as you learn more about your new country.

Checkups and vaccinations

Start with the basics. Schedule a predeparture physical exam and dental checkup to make sure you are healthy and fit to travel; then take care of any existing problems. Health risks may be different in your new country (malaria, tropical diseases, respiratory illnesses due to pollution, etc.), so you will want to let your physician know where you will be living and ask advice about vaccinations, preventive measures, and medications to take with you. Your doctor may be able to provide the necessary vaccinations. You can also check websites such as that for the international Centers for Disease Control (*www.cdc.gov*) for additional information.

Some countries, especially in Africa, require travelers to carry an international vaccination card or booklet. This is sometimes called a WHO (World Health Organization) card, yellow vaccination card, or shot record. Ask your doctor for one at the time of your vaccinations. When you arrive in-country, you may be asked to show your vaccination card when you present your passport to immigration officials. If you will be moving to a country where vaccinations are required for entry, be sure to keep your vaccination record with your passport when you travel, and have it easily accessible in case authorities ask to see it.

Prescription medicines and corrective lenses

If you take any prescription medications regularly, you will need to plan ahead with your doctor to take an adequate supply with you—don't assume that you will be able to purchase your medications in your new country. Find out if an identical or similar medication is available in your host country, perhaps under a different name. You may also be able to order medications online or through your home pharmacy. See if your doctor will be willing to continue writing prescriptions for you abroad. In any case, having at least a six-month supply of prescription medications and other preparations you are likely to use will save time and unnecessary stress when you or a member of your family is not feeling well.

If you wear glasses or contact lenses, don't forget to schedule an appointment with your eye doctor before you leave. You will probably want to take an extra pair of glasses or a box of contact lenses with you. Ask your doctor for a copy of your lens prescription to take with you as well.

First-aid kits

To be prepared in the event of a medical problem or emergency, have a well-equipped first-aid kit at home and one in your car. Being prepared is especially important if you are living in a developing country where the availability of medical supplies and emergency care may be limited. The following is a list of basic supplies to get you started. Check with your doctor or pharmacist—and your pediatrician, if you have children—for additional suggestions.

- Sterile gauze compresses and pads
- Gauze bandages in rolls or elastic crepe bandages
- Adhesive tape
- Sterile cotton and cotton-tipped applicators
- Antibacterial hand wipes and/or liquid
- Sterile gloves
- Adhesive bandages
- Scissors
- Tweezers
- Safety pins
- Thermometer
- Ice bag and hot water bottle
- First-aid cream or spray and antibiotic ointment
- Rubbing alcohol
- Laxative of your choice
- Calamine or some other anti-itch cream or lotion
- Syrup of ipecac
- Aspirin and other medicines for pain
- Antihistamine tablets

If you will be driving in a less-developed country, especially in rural areas, consider the possibility that you may be involved in—or witness—a car accident far from sources of help. Although this is an unpleasant sub-ject to consider, it is a situation that has been faced by many expatriates abroad. With this in mind, consider adding items to your kit such as a heat-reflecting blanket, reflector triangles, flares, emergency escape tools, and special trauma bandages that stop bleeding. A charged cell phone, satellite phone, or radio is also essential.

In addition to the first-aid items just listed, take a good supply of your favorite toothpaste, vitamins, deodorant, shaving cream, feminine hygiene products, and other items not likely to be available—at least in your favorite brand.

Preparing for self-care

Because you might face a language barrier, different standards of care, or different approaches to health care overseas, prepare yourself to identify your own and your family's health problems and treat minor ones your-self. Invest in a comprehensive medical reference manual that includes first-aid instructions to have as a reference as needed. The Internet is also an excellent resource to answer medical questions, but keep in mind that connections in developing countries may be slow or easily lost. In such cases, you do not want to rely solely on the Internet as your primary source of information.

If possible, enroll in a basic emergency medical training class before you go. Every family member over 12 should also have completed a basic first-aid and CPR course. Check with local community groups and emer-gency services to find courses. In addition, ask your doctor, dentist, and any specialists who provide your family with care if they are willing to be contacted by e-mail while you are overseas. If something serious develops, you may want his or her advice, or even to fly home for treatment.

If you have dietary restrictions or food allergies

Dietary restrictions or food allergies require extra vigilance when living in a foreign culture. Should you or a member of your family have to avoid certain foods, the prudent choice is often to prepare the food yourself at home. Knowing what ingredients are going into your food is the surest way to eat safely, although this is not always practical or feasible. When you are invited to someone's home or want to eat out in a foreign culture, think ahead. There are steps you can take to help stay healthy.

Always mention to your host or to your waiter that you have (or your family member has) a food allergy. Carry a card with a description of your allergic condition, the food(s) that trigger your allergy, and a list of ingredients that you cannot eat. Be sure the description is written in the local language as well as in English. Learn the local names for the ingredients you need to avoid so you can look for them on package labels. Most importantly, always have a supply of your medication with you. You never know when you may need it quickly.

Once, when Melissa was on a Nile cruise with a friend, a fellow passenger who was allergic to peanuts suddenly gasped and went into a panic when he discovered the creamy "nougat" dessert he had just eaten had ground nuts in it. Dinner was over, and everyone was about to board a bus to go to a sound and light show. The passenger knew he would have a problem if he did not go immediately to his cabin and get the medicine he needed. Melissa helped by explaining the situation to the tour leader and, though this delayed the group, the passenger took his medicine in time and was able to enjoy the evening without having an allergic reaction.

There are two important lessons to note:

- If you have a food allergy, never assume that a food is allergen free; always ask before you eat.
- When you are eating out, always carry a supply of your medication in your purse or pocket.

The threat of a pandemic

The possibility of a widespread outbreak, or pandemic, of a disease such as avian influenza (bird flu) is a global concern. Though the actual level of threat varies from country to country, it is prudent to keep up to date on the latest developments, no matter where you live. It is also wise to think about your own contingency plans should a pandemic become a reality. Here are some useful websites to get you started.

- The World Health Organization: *www.who.int*
- The Centers for Disease Control and Prevention: *www.cdc.gov*
- The Overseas Security Advisory Council: *www.osac.gov*
- The United States Department of Health and Human Services: *www.pandemicflu.gov*

Health insurance and local medical facilities

Make sure your health insurance plan covers adequate care in your new country. If you face an emergency far from a hospital or a condition that cannot be adequately treated locally, does your health insurance plan include medical evacuation coverage? If not, you may want to look into insurance plans that include helicopter or other type of emergency evacuation. If relatives come to visit you, make sure their policies cover health care abroad, or suggest that they purchase a supplemental traveler's policy for the time they spend with you.

As soon as you can after arrival, make contact with a local doctor and dentist. Visiting local clinics and hospitals is also an excellent idea. Find out if your insurance card will be accepted there, or if you will have to pay for services in advance. Also find out about the availability of ambulance services. Don't wait for an emergency to strike.

In some countries, antibiotics, antidepressants, sleeping pills, pain killers, and other drugs that may be prescription-restricted in your home country are available over the counter. Don't risk your health by taking medications that might hurt you or that you may not need. If you are ill and think that you need a specific medication, check with a doctor or other knowledgeable health professional in your area before you reach for a pill.

Food safety and clean drinking water

In many countries, due to the threat of hepatitis and other illnesses, vegetables and some raw fruits need to be disinfected before they can safely be consumed. For those fruits that can be peeled, disinfecting is not necessary. To disinfect fresh fruits and vegetables, rinse thoroughly in clean water (you can wash them with soap if it seems necessary), then place them in a solution of two drops bleach (sodium hypochlorite) per one quart or liter of water. Soak for 20 minutes, and then rinse with clean drinking water. There may also be local products on the market especially for disinfecting produce (such as Milton in African countries and Zonalin in South America).

To make water potable, bring it to a rolling boil for at least 10 minutes. If you will live in a country where tap water is unsafe to drink, consider investing in a water distiller. A water filter is another, less-expensive option you can use to treat previously boiled water.

There are many additional ways to practice safe food handling in your home. Clean and disinfect fresh produce and refrigerate fresh foods promptly. Keep raw meat separate from other fresh foods and wash your hands thoroughly after touching it. Use hot, soapy water and paper towels to clean your kitchen utensils, counter tops, and sink. You can further disinfect your kitchen by cleaning with a solution of chlorine bleach and water (one teaspoon of bleach mixed in a gallon or four liters of water). If you aren't sure if food is fresh or suspect that it may be spoiled, don't take a chance—throw it out. A wealth of information on safe food handling and preventing food-borne illness is available on the Internet.

An expatriate in Mexico recalls:

> An expat family who had lived in Spain moved to Torreon for a one-year assignment. No one in their company told them about issues with the purity of the water or properly cleansing fruits and vegetables!
>
> In our case, one of the best things our company did was to send us all to an international health clinic run by University Hospitals in Cleveland, Ohio. Not only did they give us the appropriate shots and check our medical records, they also did specific health counseling with my children and even gave us medications so that if we became ill in the first few weeks before we had really oriented ourselves, we could treat the basic illnesses (diarrhea, etc.) that we might encounter. It is well worth it for companies to provide this to employees. If they don't, the family should head to the Internet themselves and see if there is a university-related or corporate health center that does this type of counseling.

Be selective about where you eat. If you are living in a country where safe food handling is questionable, ask locals or other expats for their restaurant recommendations—before you go out to eat. You are not likely to see how food is prepared, so play it safe by only going only to places that are known to have adequate standards of cleanliness.

Hand washing

As mundane as it may sound, hand washing is a major deterrent to the spread of disease. If you live in a developing country, make frequent hand washing a habit. Before you eat at a restaurant or after coming home from a market or other public places, wash your hands. If you are traveling and do not have easy access to water, take along antibacterial hand wipes or gels that allow you to disinfect your hands without water. Melissa learned this lesson the hard way. After walking around an open-air market in Nigeria, she ate a bag lunch in her car without washing her hands. The next day she came down with a virulent stomach bug that kept her in bed for a week!

Educating yourself about safety, security, and health conditions in your new country is a proactive step to safeguard your health and well-being throughout your time abroad. The more you know and the more steps you take to prepare, the better off you will be in the event an unexpected health, safety, or security issue comes up while you are overseas.

CHAPTER 9

Special Issues for Spouses Abroad

Spouses accompanying their partners overseas can have the best of both worlds—the opportunity to live abroad and the freedom to enjoy it. Yet their stay abroad can also be the worst of times if they face a crisis over the loss of their independent lives and careers, or if their marriage weakens and they find themselves stuck in a strange country without a support system.

The stresses of the transition to a new country tend to be greater for accompanying spouses than for their employed partners. Spouses need to pay particular attention to the general adjustment issues discussed in chapter 7 of this book. In this chapter we address additional issues that can make an important difference in the well-being of accompanying spouses abroad: making their own decision to go (or not), finding employment or other meaningful activities, and keeping the marriage relationship strong. We also present a brief discussion of the challenges faced by "trailing males," who represent a small but growing category of accompanying partners.

Unmarried partners

Throughout this book, for simplicity we have usually referred to accompanying partners as spouses. Committed but unmarried partners overseas will face the same kinds of issues we cover here. In addition, they may encounter barriers that wouldn't have existed at home, such as difficulties obtaining a visa or work permit, the denial of organizational benefits, or the lack of diplomatic status for unmarried diplomats' partners.

However, many unmarried partners we know have managed to work out these problems—for example, leaving the host country every six months to reenter with a fresh tourist visa. A few have even found their status advantageous; in places where accompanying spouses are not permitted to work, they were able to enter the country independently on a professional contract or as self-employed businesspeople.

Same-sex partners may also face cultural barriers, depending on the country. The website Tales from a Small Planet (*www.talesmag.com*) includes notes from expats all over the world on conditions for gay and lesbian expatriates in their host countries.

If you are not married and are accompanying your partner overseas, be sure to investigate potential problems in advance, so you can make appropriate plans and arrangements. For further discussion of the challenges faced by unmarried partners, see the book *GenXpat: The Young Professional's Guide to Making a Successful Life Abroad* by Margaret Malewski (Intercultural Press, 2005).

The paradox of the "trailing" spouse

While some couples manage to go abroad on equal terms (for example, as "tandem couples" in the diplomatic service or missionaries working together), in most cases, a job opportunity overseas is presented to one partner and the other agrees to "trail" along.

If you are an accompanying spouse abroad, your situation is somewhat paradoxical. In some ways, you may find your life severely restricted. The host-country government may not permit you to get a local job. Your spouse's organization may control your housing and other aspects of your life, as Patricia experienced. The local culture and conditions may place additional restrictions on your lifestyle.

In other ways, however, you may find you have more freedom than you did at home. Higher salaries and allowances abroad may let one spouse remain at home without financial hardship. The inexpensive household help in many countries may give you more free time than ever before. Unlike your employed partner, you may find yourself free to travel, pursue your own interests, continue your education, take up a new career, stay home with your children, help others through volunteer work, or simply make friends and enjoy your host country.

Patricia reports:

> *Back in Washington, my husband and I were equal partners. We earned about the same amount of money and lived in a house we had chosen together. When we arrived in Trinidad, however, the balance changed completely. I had no job at first. My husband's employer provided our house and even (like it or not) our furniture. The visa allowing me to remain in the country depended on his job. Even my diplomatic passport was stamped: "The bearer is a dependent of . . ."*

The good news is that, especially since the advent of high-speed Internet connections, there are more opportunities for an accompanying spouse to find self-fulfillment overseas than ever before. The not-so-good news regards the difficulty of weathering the transition and finding a niche for yourself. The following sections address these issues.

An expatriate wife moving from Turkey to Italy explains:

> *Lower your expectations. No, I take that back. Have absolutely no expectations. I can't emphasize enough how important that is.*

Facing the transition

Transition shock is usually even more challenging for accompanying spouses than it is for employees. There are a number of reasons for this.

- A feeling of control over your own life is important for psychological well-being. If going abroad wasn't your choice, or if you have little control over your everyday life, this can add to your stress.
- You may suffer an identity crisis if you go abroad for your partner's job, not your own. In many industrialized societies, identity is linked strongly to work: we ask children what they want to "be" when they grow up. As a trailing spouse, you arrive overseas with no immediate function and no reputation.
- As an accompanying spouse, you may receive less language and cultural training than your employed partner. At the same time, while employees may interact with helpful, English-speaking colleagues at

the office, you are left to your own devices, to confront local sales-people, workers, and household staff with little patience for "stupid" foreigners making language and cultural mistakes.

- While employees (usually) gain self-confidence from doing a familiar job well, you may feel like a failure as you struggle to accomplish even a simple, everyday task in a new country.
- If you are an at-home spouse, especially with children, you may find yourself thrown into the role of the "family shock absorber," making sure that everyone else's needs are met but neglecting your own.

It is important to recognize what a demanding task it is to accompany your partner abroad. Think of the challenges faced by immigrants coming from another country, or by people who have been laid off from their jobs or who are retiring from work. In a sense, you are facing both kinds of challenges at the same time. The rewards do come. But recognizing the magnitude of what you are doing will help you go easy on yourself at the beginning, refrain from blaming yourself when things go wrong, and recognize the need to prepare adequately.

A Peruvian/Colombian graduate student accompanying her husband in the United States notes:

> In my case, what has made a difference in the way I manage this lifestyle is closely related to issues of control—or lack of it in this case—so what works for me is having information, to find out as much as I can about the situation I am in and where I am going to be sent to.

Making your own decision to go

If the overseas assignment was your partner's idea—or the idea of your partner's employer—you may naturally feel as if you are being "dragged along." This is a recipe for resentment and for feeling that you are not in control of your own life.

It is much better for both of you if the decision to go overseas—with all its advantages and disadvantages—is a joint one, made by equal partners and based on your best interests as a couple or as a family.

A British spouse, now in Brussels, says:

> *For family reasons, I stayed back for six months while my husband went ahead to Moscow. This turned out to be one of the best things that happened to us, because it made me realize that I didn't "have" to move. And if I could decide not to do it, then relocating to another country was a decision too. It became a decision not made by my husband's employer but by me. When I finally did move to Moscow with my new baby and two other children, I had a new feeling of commitment to my husband and overseas life.*

As soon as the opportunity to move overseas is presented to you, go over the realistic options with your spouse. Look at the advantages and disadvantages, not only for your employed partner, but also for you and your children. If your spouse is still negotiating with an employer about the overseas assignment, make sure your interests are represented as well.

Another helpful exercise is to negotiate with your spouse and take control in areas where possible. For example, you may agree to accompany your partner overseas for three years, but the following three will be focused on *your* career. Or agree on some benefits for you during the assignment abroad: perhaps you won't have to work (without complaints from your spouse about lost income!), or maybe you'll be able to travel to places you've always wanted to go. You might be able to continue your education or build a "portable career" with your spouse's support.

If you truly do not want to go, there *are* other options. You can stay in your home country while your spouse works abroad. Your spouse can quit and find another line of work. Even divorce may be on the negotiating table. These may not be pleasant alternatives, of course, but it may help to consider them, to realize that you are not being forced to move overseas.

Identity

The issue of identity is one that must be faced by all expatriates. More than we typically realize, our identities are shaped by the environment we live in.

Of course, you become a foreigner when you move abroad. Your relative wealth and social status may change. You may be considered part of a minority group in the host country (as Patricia was in Trinidad). You may lose professional and group affiliations that help define who you are (regional manager, swimming coach, or Scout leader). You may not find a way to practice free-time activities that form part of your sense of self (e.g., organic gardening, fixing up your house, or reading at the public library).

All of the information in this chapter will help you rebuild your sense of identity in your new environment. However, we recommend taking some time to focus on the issue of identity itself, especially if you are an accompanying partner.

In a recent study of female accompanying spouses abroad conducted by The Interchange Institute, the stress factor most closely related to the participants' level of adjustment abroad was "being able to be the kind of person I want to be." According to the study findings:

> . . . women who felt they were "not being able to be the kind of person [they wanted] to be" were most likely to have very poor adjustment, while women who did feel they could be the kind of person they wanted to be were likely to have very good adjustment.*

To examine your own identity challenges, first make a list or diagram of any elements you can think of that defined who you are or were in your "old" environment (for instance, your typical activities, groups you belong to, and the way you are seen by others). Think about how these have changed or will change during your move abroad. Then try to make a new list for your new environment. Think especially of ways that you might be able to "be the kind of person you want to be" in your new country. You may even find ways to do so even more effectively than at home—for instance, expressing a creative talent or helping others through volunteering.

If you would like to explore this issue further, we recommend an excellent specialized workbook on the topic: *A Portable Identity: A Woman's*

---

*"Many Women Many Voices" Study of Accompanying Spouses Around the World, conducted by Dr. Anne P. Copeland at The Interchange Institute (*www.interchangeinstitute.org*) and commissioned by Prudential Financial, p, 8.

Guide to Maintaining a Sense of Self While Moving Overseas by Debra Bryson and Charise Hoge (Transition Press, 2005). Don't be put off by the title if you are a man, especially a male accompanying partner.

The importance of social networks

Unlike employees at the office and children at school, accompanying spouses can find themselves completely isolated during the day—or perhaps chasing a transition-shocked toddler around an empty apartment. If you're an accompanying spouse, it's especially important for you to heed our advice from chapter 7 and start making friends and developing your own social networks in the new environment. It can be tempting to avoid the strange new environment outside as much as possible and just stay home (especially if you have a high-speed Internet connection and satellite TV). But the study mentioned in the previous section also found that "making friends" is one of the most important contributors to successful adjustment among accompanying spouses. Fortunately, you will likely find that other spouses have been there before you and have set up networks you can easily join. If not, go back to our suggestions and start creating your own—you'll be glad you did.

An Austrian-American spouse in Taiwan notes:

> *The support network of TAS (Taipei American School) is excellent and includes parents with time on their hands (the unemployed spouses) in their outreach and makes them feel welcome. The Community Services Center offers counseling, various classes, coffee mornings, and networking opportunities. I have met many wonderful women in these two places, and dealing with challenges together with other people in the same situation makes it a lot easier.*

Employment and other meaningful activities

What you choose to do with your time abroad will depend on your situation, the available options, and your personal choices. The important thing, however, is that you find something to do that *you* consider worthwhile, something that gives you a reason for being there, a reason to get up in the morning. This is the answer to the annoying party-guest question, "What do you do?" as well as to the middle-of-the-night question, "What the heck am I doing?"

Comment made to an American husband accompanying his wife to Eastern Europe:

> *What are you going to do with all your time over there—teach the [football] zone defense to the Women's Club?*

Three general categories of activities constitute the options for spouses overseas: traditional jobs, nontraditional work opportunities, and unpaid work or self-enrichment. Many spouses switch off among the three or do some of each. Often, one type of activity leads to another type; for example, a volunteer job may evolve into an opportunity for paid work. In the following sections, we take a brief look at each type of activity and then offer some suggestions to help you decide which one is right for you.

Traditional jobs

Typical traditional job opportunities to consider may include the following:

- Continuing with your current employer abroad, either by teleworking as an employee or consultant, or working in a branch office in your host country
- Finding a job within your partner's organization; some groups make special efforts to find or create positions for accompanying spouses
- Working for an international company or nonprofit organization active in your host country
- Teaching or taking another position at an international school, local university, adult education center, or language school
- Working in your field for a local company

Nontraditional work opportunities

Increasing numbers of twenty-first-century expatriate spouses are carving out their own niches overseas by discovering (or creating) nontraditional work opportunities: starting their own businesses, working as consultants or on a freelance basis, or providing personal services. Using the Internet, they can work for clients around the world, no matter where they are located.

Many spouses say that working independently gives them "the best of both worlds": the satisfaction, pay, and respect that come from paid work combined with the flexibility to be available for their families and to travel and explore their new environment. Independent work may not give you the largest possible paycheck, but it can provide lots of room for creativity and the chance to try something new.

Some areas to consider:

- Consulting, teaching, or developing training materials in your current field
- Becoming a cross-cultural consultant or trainer
- Becoming a freelance writer: consider creative writing, journalism, travel writing, editing, technical writing, educational writing, and translating (caution: if you choose to go into investigative journalism, find out what risks you are taking; in some places, organized criminal groups or even government agents may take action against journalists who write about corruption or repression)
- Providing services (usually to other expatriates but not always), such as tutoring, hairdressing, personal coaching, personal organizing, decorating, catering, and so forth
- Teaching special skills (cooking, art, flower arranging, self-defense, music, etc.)
- Conducting seminars in your field
- Teaching or tutoring English
- Working as a website designer, web editor, or computer consultant
- Working as an online "virtual assistant," doing administrative work for a company located elsewhere
- Obtaining a grant to conduct an academic research project

The possibilities are nearly endless. A nurse we know who accompanied her husband to India does contract work there for an international health organization as well as technical writing over the Internet for a company in Switzerland. A British man accompanying his wife to Spain started his own magazine. A spouse in Prague started a web-design business and has clients in three countries. An expatriate in Chile wrote a popular and successful booklet called *The Gringo's Guide to Chilean Wine*.

A spouse in the Dominican Republic states:

> *I played the violin with the National Symphony Orchestra, helped start a school (the country's first) for children with cerebral palsy, worked as a music therapist in private practice, and wrote for the weekly English-language newspaper.*

One group of spouses solved several problems at once when they organized a catering service. Their employee partners had often held dinner parties to entertain contacts in their homes, which put a burden on the spouses. With their catering service, however, they were able to turn this unpaid duty into a business opportunity. While the host and hostess relaxed and enjoyed their own party, the caterers earned money and developed marketable skills.

A word about working online

Teleworking abroad—whether as an employee or independently—can offer tremendous benefits. It generally does not require a work permit (if your employer or clients are in another country), and you may be able to continue working in your field and earn higher pay than is possible locally.

However, working at home on a computer in a foreign environment can be extremely isolating. One spouse we know worked full-time for six months in Prague as a telecommuter for her previous employer, but found the lack of social engagement "unfulfilling." She was happier after she found a job with a branch of an international company in her host city.

If you plan to work online, we recommend putting extra energy into building and maintaining social networks in the host country. Perhaps you might work part-time at home and spend the rest of your day on volunteer work that involves contact with interesting people. Or simply be sure to get out several times a week to pursue activities you enjoy with friends and social groups. Recent research has shown that regular social contact is important for mental and even physical health. As we advised full-time online workers in chapter 7, don't think of your time away from the computer as lost income, but as an essential part of your overseas routine.

Unpaid work and self-enrichment

Your stay overseas can provide a great opportunity to take time for your-self, help others, do something you've always wanted to do, or, as expat coach Margarita Gokun Silver puts it, to figure out "What is your reason for living on this planet?" For example, you might

- take time for your family and enjoy the adventure of raising inter-nationally mobile kids,
- help others through volunteer work,
- organize a community group in an area that interests you or where you see a need,
- continue your education—or study something completely new—at a local university or adult education center, over the Internet, or through independent study,
- gain in-depth knowledge of your host country: travel, learn the lan-guage, and get to know the culture and local history better than any tourist or short-term visitor possibly could,
- become an expert on aspects of your host country that interest you or that are relevant to your professional field,
- pursue your favorite sport or hobby—golf, tennis, bird-watching, scuba diving, sailing, gourmet cooking—or take up a new one,
- develop your creative talents: painting, sculpture, music, crafts, dance, photography, and so forth, or
- write your memoirs, your family history, poetry, or a novel—for your own satisfaction, without worrying about making money.

Volunteer work abroad can be particularly satisfying. As a volunteer, you can choose work that interests you and set your own schedule. As you help others, you may learn new skills, meet interesting local people, and "gain perspective on life," as one long-time volunteer notes. Be sure to keep records of the skills and experience you gain as a volunteer and add them to your résumé—they may be useful for future employment.

Melissa reports:

> Any foreigner living in Kiev could see that Ukrainians from every walk of life needed help. Orphans, widows, the sick, the elderly, the homeless— you name it, if you wanted to help, you could make a difference. While I was there, I decided to start a charity group. We identified Ukrainian charities in need, and then held a variety of events among expatriates to raise funds. There were arts and crafts festivals where local vendors sold their wares. We organized ethnic food dinners, such as Egyptian Night, for which we even found a belly dancer and had one of our colleagues dress up like a mummy. Lots of hours went into making events happen. Although I never received a salary for any of it, I made lots of friends, helped boost morale in my community, and assisted Ukrainians in need. I know my work made a difference, and you can't put a price on that.

Raising young children abroad can also provide a great deal of satisfaction. Children are the ultimate portable career in a sense—they move with you wherever you go, and they certainly provide a reason to get up in the morning and something worthwhile to focus on every day. You have an instant link with other expatriate parents, who tend to get together for play groups, outings, school projects, and so forth. Furthermore, inexpensive household help in many countries can free you to play, learn, and explore with your children without worrying about endless household chores.

Finding your niche

With so many options, it may not be easy to decide what you want to do with your time abroad. You may also face unexpected limitations and barriers to your activities.

A career consultant or personal coach specializing in working with expatriates can be extremely helpful as you plan your activities. Many offer consulting by e-mail. If your partner's organization does not provide this kind of assistance, consider investing in it yourself; it can make a huge difference in your satisfaction—and even your potential earning power—abroad. If your budget is limited, consider attending a group seminar or networking more intensively with expatriates already in your host country.

The following suggestions can help you in your search for a new role for yourself abroad.

Take stock of your skills and achievements. Assess your accomplishments and qualifications, perhaps with the help of a career development workbook. Include your work experience, education, career goals, family responsibilities, hobbies, volunteer activities, and so forth. What are your main talents and interests?

Set priorities. How would you like to spend your time overseas: Earning money? Enjoying what you do? Meeting interesting people? Getting to know the country? Being available for your children? Developing your skills? Use these priorities to guide you as you plan your course of action. They may lead you in directions you might not have considered.

Consider making a fresh start. Going abroad may give you a chance to break away from a tiresome routine and start over with something new and more satisfying—and even to find your "true calling" in life. Take some time to think about the things that you really enjoy doing. In the United States, some people express their fondest desires on stickers on the back bumper of their cars: "I'd rather be fishing" or "I'd rather be sailing." What would your slogan say? Whatever your ideal activity is, you may be able to pursue it overseas—or even turn it into a career.

Identify barriers. When looking for work abroad, you may face a surprising number of barriers that did not exist at home.

- The host country may refuse to grant work permits to accompanying spouses, or work permits may be expensive or difficult to obtain.
- Your language skills may be insufficient for the local job you would like.
- The prevailing pay scale may be so low that it doesn't seem worthwhile to take a local job.

- Your professional credentials may not be accepted in your host country.
- You may be limited in your commitment to a local job because your stay in the country will be short or your partner may be transferred at short notice.
- There may be a lack of opportunities in your field.
- Starting your own business overseas may be difficult because of local restrictions.
- Slow Internet connections and an unreliable mail system may hinder telecommuting or freelancing.

It is important to identify these barriers before you make a commitment to go abroad, so you can make an informed decision. However, don't rely only on information from your partner's organization. It may emphasize the positive in an attempt to encourage you and your spouse to accept the position. On the other hand, the organizational view may be overly discouraging in order to avoid raising your hopes inadvisably.

Consider factors other than money. Taking a local job at a low salary may offer rewards other than financial. Similarly, if a high-paying job (or a work permit) seems unattainable, consider volunteering in your field.

The same spouse in the Dominican Republic notes:

> *Some other foreigners there thought that writing for the local English-language newspaper was beneath them in terms of money. I went ahead . . . and got free press trips to neat resorts at times, became coauthor of a book, was hired to do freelance assignments for a nonprofit that took me to obscure parts of the country, and made some very interesting acquaintances. Since leaving the country, I've gotten e-mails offering me work over the Internet. Was the money beneath me? I don't think so!*

Network before you go. Seek out people with a connection to your new country and phone or e-mail them. Let people know what you hope to do, and ask if they have any relevant information or contacts. If possible, find people who are already doing something similar to the activity you hope to pursue in order to get a realistic view of the barriers and rewards. Networking is still important, even if you are not looking for a paying job; your satisfaction and self-confidence are at least as important as money.

Decide whether to set up a job in advance. Having a job lined up when you arrive has advantages. Some organizations (such as international schools) offer higher salaries to people hired from abroad than they do to local hires. You are immediately "plugged in" and can avoid many of the transition shock symptoms experienced by nonemployed spouses. If you really need a second income or if you feel you would be lost without a job, this may be the best choice for you.

However, arriving without a job in place can have advantages as well. For example, one young wife accompanying her husband on his first overseas job admitted to having no idea how she really wanted to spend her time overseas. She wasn't sure how to begin, so she started by making friends with other expatriate spouses and getting involved in various community events. Her first year was spent getting out and about with other women, traveling around the country with her husband whenever his work required him to do so, volunteering within the community, and becoming the editor of her husband's office newsletter.

She then decided to go back to work and took a full-time job within her husband's organization. A few months later she remarked, "I'm really glad that I didn't immediately go to work when I first arrived. Had I done so, I would not have as many friends or know the city as well as I do now. Having that first year to experience this place really helped me a lot. It was a valuable way to spend my time."

Continue to network after you arrive. To find opportunities to use your skills or to find friends with similar interests, you must take the initiative to tell people about yourself. Prepare a few lines you will feel comfortable saying to new people you meet. Including a couple of questions helps make it clear that you are networking rather than simply bragging about yourself; for example, "I taught Thai cooking classes at home. Do you know of an Asian food market anywhere around here?"

Practice saying no. What happens if, when you arrive, you have too many opportunities rather than too few? Volunteer groups may be clamoring for your help as soon as you arrive, especially if you are moving to a less-developed country. In your impatience to "do something," you may be tempted to plunge in and get involved right away. You may also feel pressure from your spouse's colleagues to get involved in local groups.

If the opportunity interests you, by all means give it a try. However, at least consider postponing a long-term commitment (such as becoming a club officer) until you get to know the group a little better, until you have explored other alternatives, and until you can assess more objectively what fits into your overall plans abroad. Prepare a polite refusal to be used when people try to press you into volunteering, such as, "I'm sorry, but I've promised myself not to get overcommitted until I've had a chance to settle in." A good compromise is to offer your help on a limited committee or with a one-time project.

Define yourself on your own terms. What should you say when people ask questions like, "What do you do?" A party guest asked a spouse we know, "Are you in the same line of work as your husband?" "No, I'm just baggage," she answered with a rueful smile.

Our friend's answer was funny, but not exactly calculated to win respect or build self-esteem. If you don't have a paying job, at least do yourself the favor of having an answer ready for "the question." One Canadian man we knew who enjoyed playing golf and raising his two small children happily announced that he was "retired." The wife of a Fulbright scholar, a busy teacher back home, told people she was "on sabbatical." Need more ideas? Here are some other possibilities:

"I'm raising multicultural kids."
"I'm getting serious about photography."
"I'm exploring and learning about the country."
"I'm writing a family history."
"I'm building up a freelance business."
"I'm studying the language intensively."
"I'm taking a scuba diving course."

Mentioning your specific activities and interests can also spark conversation and help you network; if the person asking you doesn't share your interest, he or she may know someone who does.

Melissa reports:

When people ask me, "What do you do?" I usually answer by discussing activities I'm involved in: "I'm writing a book," "I teach English to

*Ukrainian university students," "I started a charity group," or
"I volunteer at the animal shelter." My answer gives the person some
information to go on and the conversation usually continues from there.*

No matter how interestingly you describe your activities as an accompanying spouse, you may still find some people you meet, especially at a work-related function, looking distractedly over your shoulder in search of someone more "important" to talk to. But as one male spouse puts it, "Don't feel bad if you're treated as a 'nobody' if you don't bring home the bacon. Just assume that the other person is only interested in seeking out professional counterparts."

Focus on your own values, not external prestige. Try not to judge your own worth (or let others judge it) by the size of your paycheck. Ask yourself instead, "What is the value of my activities to myself, my family, and my community?" Expatriate spouses tend to have their "midlife crises" early (asking themselves, "What am I doing with my life? What do I really want to accomplish?"), and they often discover that living according to their own values is more important to them than rocketing up the career ladder.

Go easy on yourself. If you don't already have a job when you arrive, it may seem like months before you accomplish anything on your list of goals. Settling in and getting to know a foreign environment takes a huge amount of time and effort. It's not true that you are doing "nothing"—you are learning intensively about a foreign country (some people go to graduate school for that!), maintaining a home under challenging conditions, and supporting your family. If you find yourself supporting everyone else but neglecting your own needs, then it's time to take stock of the situation and make changes. This is your life, too. And besides, if you are frustrated and depressed, your spouse and family will suffer along with you.

A mother of two in Zimbabwe reports:

*A very wise person is recommending that I do something good for myself
every day. So I go to exercise, have a lunch out, get a massage, go for a
swim, read a book, see a movie—just for me. I know it is very hard to do
this with younger children, but then you need this even more. It is so easy
to forget who we are when we are in this nurturing mode. And we are the
ones who need nurturing the most.*

"Trailing males"

According to the Permits Foundation, a group advocating the liberalization of work permits for accompanying spouses, the companies they survey typically report that some 10 percent of accompanying partners abroad are male.

The growing numbers of men accompanying their partners overseas face all of the issues described in this chapter and need to find their own niches, just as female spouses do. The most satisfied "trailing males," like their female counterparts, are usually those who are less preoccupied with climbing an institutional career ladder and more interested in creative pursuits, family life, and self-fulfillment. We have known accompanying male spouses who were at-home dads, telecommuters via the Internet, novelists, journalists, consultants, avid sportsmen, and part-time or temporary workers in their partners' organizations. We've also known a master chef, an architect, a masseur, and a dedicated orphanage volunteer.

It takes a certain strength of character to thrive as a trailing male, just as it does in any case where people depart from traditional roles. Spouses abroad in general need to have a strong sense of identity and self-confidence to confront culture shock and their changing roles. This need may be even stronger for male spouses. Trailing males abroad confront two general differences.

A husband accompanying his wife to Kiev claims:

> *When people learn that you are an accompanying male spouse, you always get quizzical looks. People are curious. Why would a man be doing this? In a foreign culture where this concept is completely new, the reaction is even more intense.*

One long-term trailing male reports:

> *At our first post I worked via fax and modem with the U.S. while teaching computers locally. The second posting I worked long-distance, taught some, and shot goofy home videos all around the city and countryside. The third posting I became a serious dad and also teamed up with another guy to explore the city in detail each week. The next posting*

I was Mr. Stay-at-Home Dad, pursuing my hobby of writing, never to be seen outside the house. My self-image seemed to radically change from place to place, but that can be broadening rather than destructive. I have also tried to maintain some kind of professional continuity in my life— forget the term "career," however.

First, they have a smaller peer group. As noted earlier, accompanying husbands are no longer a rarity, but their numbers are still small. There may be only a few trailing males in the expatriate community in your new location, and support systems may be designed specifically or solely for women.

Second, men may encounter differing attitudes, depending on the country. Male spouses may feel greater social and self-imposed pressure to work. On the other hand, they may receive more help from their partner's organization in finding jobs (or even have a job created for them). If an accompanying husband decides to stay home with the children, some people, especially in traditional societies, may find the role confusing. However, others may admire the husband's progressive choice.

If you are an accompanying husband, the following suggestions might help.

- *Join the crowd.* Even if the local expatriate club or parents' group is entirely female, give it a try. We have known several men who were the only male members of spouses' groups, parents' circles, or even so-called "women's clubs" and found enthusiastic acceptance, support, and friendship there.
- *Seek out your peers.* In some large international cities, accompanying males are numerous enough that they are starting to form their own clubs. If no group exists, try starting one by networking among expatriates to find other trailing males. There are also online discussion groups where accompanying male spouses can share their concerns and find support.
- *Focus on your interests.* If you are home during the day, finding other men for companionship may be challenging. If the activities of the local expatriate groups don't particularly interest you, get creative about finding people who share your interests. Give a talk on your

favorite hobby to an expatriate club; you may get an enthusiastic response. Or consider starting your own interest group.

Retirees in your host country can be another good option in this case. Look for groups such as local history clubs, chess clubs, and sports interest groups. Retired people, with plenty of time on their hands and fascinating stories to tell, can also offer a unique window into your host country and culture.

It can be hard to adjust to life as a trailing husband at first. But many report feeling freed by their new role once they adjust. Taking a break from the career track and pursuing their interests or raising their children can give them a new perspective on life, just as it does for female spouses.

Keeping your marriage strong

Many expatriate couples report a "magnifying glass" effect on their relationships: moving overseas can make good relationships better and struggling ones worse. Thrust into a strange environment, you may have no one to depend on except each other. Some quarreling and stress during this difficult period is normal, but if you can communicate well, support each other, and face the challenges and adventures of your new environment as a team, you may (eventually) find yourselves growing closer than ever before.

However, if you have trouble communicating or feel that you cannot depend upon each other for support, the stresses of a move overseas can easily drive you further apart.

Robin Pascoe, author of *A Moveable Marriage: Relocate Your Relationship without Breaking It* (Expatriate Press, 2003), gave us this advice for couples:

> It helps to be knowledgeable about the emotional part of the relocation— all the ups and downs. Otherwise, the moving boxes may be emptied and the household goods put away, but a couple's feelings for each other may be left out in the cold.

Moving abroad will definitely not solve preexisting problems in a relationship. If you believe there are unresolved conflicts in your marriage, work on them long before your move. There are several specific challenges to expatriate marriages.

- *Different experiences during the transition.* As we have discussed, accompanying spouses usually have a harder struggle with culture shock than their employed partners do. This can easily lead to a cycle of resentment and blame: nonemployed spouses blame their partners for putting them in this situation and providing insufficient support, and employed partners feel defensive and resentful about their partners' complaints and sour moods.
- *A changing balance in your relationship.* If the accompanying spouse has given up work and a source of income, he or she may feel uncomfortably dependent.
- *New routines and distractions.* In a new environment, spouses may find themselves caught up in new, separate activities and spend less time together.
- *Flattering attention from local people.* Let's face it: especially if you are moving from a wealthy country to a developing one, your social status and desirability may increase considerably. You and your spouse may appear as attractive as celebrities or millionaires to the local people.
- *Periods of separation.* Many couples find themselves separated for months during the transition. (See the next section for further discussion of this challenge.) Many overseas jobs also require extensive travel and overtime hours.

Here are a few suggestions for facing these challenges—and perhaps emerging stronger than before.

Practice constructive communication. Tell your partner what is bothering you and how he or she can help. Some anger and resentment during the transition are normal; it is what you do with these feelings that matters. Don't turn them against your partner for getting you into this situation (see the section "Making your own decision to go" earlier in this chapter). If you feel your needs are not being met, work with your spouse to figure out solutions instead of falling into a cycle of blame—especially the kind in which the employee works longer and longer hours to avoid problems at home. Some couples find that they can communicate better about subjects that raise negative emotions by e-mail.

Stand together as a team. Face frustrations and setbacks together. If you are the employee, it is especially important for you to represent your partner's as well as your own interests when dealing with your employer or with local officials. Make sure that neither of you feels "dumped on" with an unfair burden, especially during the moving and settling-in process.

Build a support network quickly and establish ongoing links with people back home to reduce the pressure on your relationship (see chapters 1 and 7). At-home spouses, particularly, need to find friends and outside activities quickly to avoid the syndrome in which an employed spouse comes home exhausted and uncommunicative at the end of a draining workday to an at-home spouse who is starved for interaction and conversation.

Place a priority on togetherness in your new routines. Make time for meals together—or just a dessert or glass of wine if your spouse comes home late each night—with all electronic devices turned off. Work on finding new shared and enjoyable activities if previous ones are no longer possible. For example, if you used to bicycle together but now live in a crowded city, perhaps you can join an indoor tennis club.

Use the power of shared adventure. Recent research into brain chemistry supports the idea—long known by teenaged couples riding roller coasters—that the bond between people strengthens when they share exciting experiences. (This is true for memorably awful times as well, as when Patricia and her husband first arrived in Germany as students and spent their first days with a violent stomach illness in a cheap hotel room with bathrooms down the hall!) As you weather transition shock, learn about the new environment, and explore your host country together, you will strengthen your relationship and build lasting memories. Go on adventures together and laugh over the inevitable mishaps and difficulties.

If you find yourself having trouble in spite of measures like these, get help. Identify sources of support right away, and don't hesitate to turn to them if you sense a problem. If you face a crisis, such as substance abuse, physical abuse, infidelity, or the threatened breakup of your marriage, you will need help. Consult your religious community abroad, expatriate groups, and perhaps your country's embassy for referrals to appropriate counselors and other professionals.

Periods of separation

Late arrival of one spouse

Some expatriate couples delay the arrival of one spouse—perhaps the children are finishing the school year or a work project must be completed. This can have advantages and disadvantages.

A late-arriving spouse may be able to move straight into a permanent home, with the household shipment already in place, making adjustment easier. Tasks such as buying a car, having a phone line connected, and hiring household help may already be completed. Furthermore, the employee who arrived early may be able to devote more time to the family when they arrive, after putting in extra hours at the beginning to adapt to the new job.

On the other hand, missing the early period also means missing an opportunity for the bonding that comes from teamwork and shared challenges. Furthermore, the late-arriving spouse may not agree with his or her partner's choices of housing, car, or domestic help and may thus feel even more alienated in the overseas environment.

The late-arriving spouse, particularly, needs a knowledgeable sponsor (see chapter 1), preferably another accompanying spouse who has been in the country a while. Even if the employee partner already knows the country well, he or she will probably be unavailable during the day to help with such matters as shopping and enrolling children in school and may not be able to recommend expatriate groups, spouses' organizations, and so on.

Allow plenty of time to get to know each other again. The spouse who arrived first has had many new experiences and may feel that he or she has changed in some ways. Spend extra time as a couple to bring your relationship up to date and to reestablish a close connection.

Living apart

Sometimes it is impractical or impossible for a partner and/or children to accompany the employee abroad—as, of course, when a soldier, journalist, or diplomat is assigned to a war zone. For other couples, a job back home, children's schooling, medical problems, or other pressing personal issues may keep one spouse in the home country for the entire overseas assignment. Even though this may be the best solution for both of you, it can put a strain on the marriage (and parental relationships, if you have children). Special efforts such as the following are important in this case to keep your relationship strong.

- *View your situation as temporary.* Even if you will be living apart for several years, remind yourselves that it is an extraordinary situation and not a permanent state.
- *Consider a trial period.* Maintaining a long-distance relationship is a difficult challenge. Unless you have no choice in the matter (such as a military deployment), consider trying the separated arrangement for a set time, perhaps three or six months, and then evaluating the situation.
- *Keep each other current.* As Melissa and her husband found (see p. 241), e-mail allows you to share the little details that help you feel involved in each other's lives. Use it as often as you can. Also, find a time for regular, intimate phone calls—not an easy task when you are living in quite different time zones.
- *Clear up specific problems and disagreements as they come up*—by phone, e-mail, or letter, so that the "decks are clear" when you visit each other. Your time together will be far too precious to waste any of it arguing or discussing unpleasant issues.
- *Avoid the idealism trap.* Many partners idealize each other during a long separation, focusing only on positive memories. This can lead to disillusionment when you are reunited. Although it is tempting to "be on your best behavior" during visits and phone calls, try to relax and act naturally.
- *Build strong, overlapping support networks.* Make sure you have an effective support network in each country, and take time to get to know each other's friends and other contacts. If you have children, relatives and friends can be recruited to help fill the shoes of the absent parent in everyday life.
- *Maintain shared interests:* read the same book and discuss it, follow your spouse's favorite sport, or take up your child's favorite hobby.
- *Don't forget romantic gestures.* Flowers, love notes, and unexpected gifts are popular for a reason. There is a certain romance in being far away from each other. Put it to work in your favor.

- *Make each visit a celebration.* Invest your money in happy moments together rather than expensive gifts.
- *Enjoy the best of your host country.* Your overseas spouse can seek out interesting and enjoyable things to do and look forward to sharing them with you when you visit.
- *Relax; not every visit needs to be perfect.* Focus on enjoying each other and not on the little things that go wrong.

Melissa reports:

My husband spent two years on an assignment in Sinai, Egypt, where he lived on a military base in the middle of the desert. Very few women were there; only a few officers' wives. No employment opportunities for spouses were available, so I decided to stay in the United States, where I could continue to work. Two years was a long-time to be away from my husband, but thanks to e-mail, we were able to stay connected on a daily basis. Though we weren't together physically, we were able to stay up-to-date with what was going on in our temporarily separate lives. In addition, he was able to come home once a year, and I went to stay with him for the last three months of his tour of duty. Before we knew it, the two years had passed and we were back together, off to the next overseas assignment.

Measuring success: individually and as a team

After you have settled in abroad (perhaps after six months or so), ask yourselves the following questions. They may indicate areas that still need work.

- Does the accompanying partner feel satisfied and confident or frustrated and resentful?
- Have you found people (besides each other) to whom you can turn in case of a crisis?
- Do you both think you are dividing up the work of overseas life fairly and facing its challenges as a team?
- Do you spend time together enjoying the opportunities offered by your host country?

- Is your marriage at least as strong as it was before you left home?
- Are you both glad that you moved abroad?

If you are enjoying the adventure of living overseas together and finding satisfaction in your activities, whatever they are, then your overseas experience will be a success in the truest sense.

CHAPTER 10

Keeping in Touch . . . and Moving On

Establishing and maintaining a solid home base while you are abroad is more important and challenging than it may seem. While you are abroad, your life will change rapidly; you will travel, make new friends, and have unique new experiences. If your family members and friends receive regular updates on your adventures—and even better, if they visit you abroad—they will feel like participants in your overseas experience instead of excluded bystanders. If you remain available and interested in their lives, even though you are far away, you can stay close rather than growing apart.

Melissa reports:

> *When I look back on our first overseas assignment, 25 years ago in Kaduna, Nigeria, I realize how much life has changed for expatriates. When we lived in Nigeria, CNN and satellite TV did not exist. We didn't have e-mail or the Internet. Even making an international phone call—if you could get the phone to work—was a major success as well as a huge expense.*

"Out of sight, out of mind" can apply to your professional life as well. However, continuing to network with colleagues and keep up with your field while overseas can help keep your career on the right track, whether you are an employee sent overseas or a spouse planning to reenter the job market.

Similarly, maintaining ties to your own culture can help give you a sense of home in a foreign land, keep your cultural identity (and that of your children) strong, and reduce the feeling of alienation if and when you return home. This chapter focuses on ways to maintain personal relationships with family and friends, keep your professional networks active, and help reduce "reentry shock" if you plan to return to your home-country environment.

Ways to keep in touch

Twenty-first-century expatriates are using both high-tech and low-tech communication methods in creative ways to keep in touch with friends, family members, and colleagues back home. Before you depart, be sure to find out about the reliability and prices of different communication methods in your host country and consider the options available to you.

E-mail and instant messaging

E-mail and instant messaging have globalized the workplace as well as personal communications. You can stay in constant touch with colleagues around the world, serve as a consultant for someone in another country, exchange documents, and even participate on a committee or with a work team.

If you plan to return to work in your home country after your time abroad, maintaining e-mail contact with your colleagues and offering your ideas and assistance is an excellent way to remain an active member of the professional community—and reintegrate more easily on your return.

In their personal lives, besides individual communications, many expatriates send out a periodic e-newsletter to friends and family, reporting on their adventures and the odd and humorous phenomena they encounter abroad. Besides being an excellent way to keep your loved ones involved in your experiences, your letters will also help you preserve your own memories of your time abroad, so be sure to save copies! (Printing them out is a good idea, since electronic documents may be lost over time due to computer crashes and software changes.)

Some groups of colleagues, friends, or family members set up e-mail listservs (available from sites such as *www.yahoo.com*), in which each message sent to the group goes to every member. These groups are easy to set up and allow you to share news and discuss professional or family business in an ongoing "virtual conversation."

Laptops and PDAs

Coverage for wireless innovations such as BlackBerry devices varies greatly around the world. Some countries, such as Chile, have widespread data networks that will allow you to use your device nearly anywhere. Others may have little or no data coverage. Even if your host country does offer a data network, your device may not be compatible with the local system. Check with colleagues or other expatriates about the situation in your new location.

Even in less-wealthy countries, wireless Internet connections may be offered in airports, restaurants, coffee shops, malls, and universities. In some cases, you must pay for the service or be a registered customer of a local telecommunications company.

It's a liberating feeling to work on a freelance project at a café in Prague or to keep in touch with colleagues and friends while hiking and bird-watching in Costa Rica. However, depending on where you are going, security for your high-tech equipment can be a major concern. Carry your devices in a secure inner pocket of your clothing or an unobtrusive bag such as a backpack, and don't use them on crowded streets.

A well-traveled and long-time resident of South America advises:

> *Even while it may appear to be very attractive to haul your laptop to the local Starbucks for a free hookup, the risk of getting mugged on the street between the parking lot and the coffee place, and ergo losing the laptop, is very high. Thieves target foreigners carrying readily identifiable computer bags (those Dell, Apple, and HP logos are a dead giveaway, as is the structure of most carrying cases).*
>
> *Cell phone users are also advised not to talk on them while walking down the street: step into a shop if you absolutely must take that call.*

A similar warning is valid for BlackBerry and Palm Pilot users: wait until you get to your destination or stop for a coffee to answer your mail. If you try to walk and type, not only will you bump into people, you're highly likely to get the device swiped right out of your hand.

Blogs and personal websites

Increasing numbers of expatriates are maintaining weblogs, or blogs, to record and share their adventures abroad. Blogs are easy to create and update even for people without programming skills. If you do know a bit of programming—or are willing to pay a professional for help—a personal or family website provides more power and flexibility.

One expat family we know always e-mails a holiday greeting which includes their family website address. Their relatives and friends can easily access the site, view photos and personal holiday messages from each member of the family, and respond by e-mail.

Before posting your personal journal on a blog or website, remember that your comments are open to the world (unless you password-protect your site). In some parts of the world, negative comments about your host country may be taken very seriously by the authorities. Also, current and potential employers may take the time to read your blog, so keep your professional image in mind as you write.

Sharing photos and video

Digital photos and video clips can be e-mailed or uploaded to a personal website. Numerous photo processing websites offer a service that is especially useful to expatriates: after you upload your photos, friends and family can order prints in the sizes and quantities they want.

Telephone

If international calls are expensive in your host country, consider signing up for a service that allows you to call at lower rates. Voice over Internet Protocol (VoIP) is becoming increasingly popular as a method for placing free or inexpensive calls using the Internet. (A U.S. expat in Venezuela insists: "Not having it is not even an option!") Consider adding cameras for two-way viewing during your conversation. Other inexpensive telephone options may include calling cards or "call-back" services.

If phone calls are the best method for you to keep in touch with loved ones, consider setting a regular time for "getting together," when both of you, in your respective time zones, are awake and have time to talk. However, some people (especially elderly relatives) may become quite upset if you must miss a call at the accustomed time, so it may be better to call on a more random basis.

Between phone calls, make note of everything you would like to mention to the other person, and use your notes when you call. Too often, we've remembered something important we wanted to mention just after hanging up the phone!

Mail

Some organizations provide an internal mail service for their employees. In other cases, you may have to rely on an unreliable local mail system. In some places we've been, the best—or the only—way to send letters home was to find people who were traveling to our country and ask them to carry our letters and drop them in the mail when they arrived! A postal scale and a supply of home-country postage (which can sometimes be printed online) are helpful if you face a situation like this.

If you and your friends and family are not equipped to exchange voice recordings and digital video over the Internet, consider recording and exchanging cassettes and videotapes by mail. Share a narrated video of your host city, tell jokes on tape, record your child singing or playing the piano, or recite a bedtime story for a niece or nephew.

No matter what methods you use to communicate, keep these suggestions in mind.

- Keep the people close to you informed about smaller details of your life, not just the big events, to help them feel involved and included.
- If someone doesn't seem responsive to one form of communication, try another. Some people enjoy talking on the phone but not

e-mailing, or vice versa. In her book *GenXpat*, Margaret Malewski shares the story of a colleague who never responded to her e-mails. Remembering his love of gadgets, she sent a text message to his mobile phone—and had no trouble communicating with him from then on.

- Share photos (and video if possible) of your home and everyday activities overseas, not just tourist attractions, to help your loved ones visualize how you are living.
- Maintain shared interests with your loved ones to give you something in common and a ready topic to talk about. Order them a copy of a book you're reading, follow a favorite sport together, or report on your host country's birds to an avid bird-watcher.

Visits from family and friends

Having family members or friends visit you abroad can be demanding at times but also extremely rewarding. Instead of sitting around telling the same jokes and anecdotes, relatives who have visited Patricia's family overseas have ridden horses in the Andes mountains, watched sea turtles laying their eggs on a tropical beach, snorkeled on coral reefs, shopped at German Christmas markets, and spent the night in medieval castles.

To make the travel expense worthwhile, visitors abroad tend to stay for longer periods than they would in your home country. This gives you a chance to spend a lot of quality time together—perhaps even more than you would have at home—but it can also be exhausting for both guests and hosts. A bit of preliminary planning can help you both get the most out of the visit.

Avoid crowding your own schedule. Especially if you are living in an attractive tourist destination, you may have people lining up to visit you. It's great to take time off from your responsibilities to spend time with them and show them around, but your stamina may flag after the third visitor in a row. Don't be shy about asking visitors to postpone their trip if you are burned-out and exhausted; they wouldn't have a very good time anyway. Another alternative is to suggest that several groups of compatible guests visit you at the same time. You may need to rent a van and reserve some guest housing, but exploring the country in a group can be enjoyable, and your guests will have each other for company at times when you are not available.

Brief your guests in advance. Tour companies send out informational material to participants before a trip, so they know what to bring, what to wear, and what to expect. Consider doing the same thing for your guests in an e-mail or whatever format you choose. Be alert to unrealistic expectations; for example, if you live in the tropics, your visitors might imagine walking to the beach from your house—when in reality you live downtown in a large city, far from the beach.

Address health issues. Ask your guests about any specific health or dietary needs they may have, so you can plan ahead to accommodate them. Remind them to bring their own medications, special foods, and so forth. Ask them to make sure their health insurance will cover them on the trip. If not, suggest they purchase supplemental insurance, including medical evacuation benefits if high-quality emergency care is unavailable in your host country.

Plan your "tour package." Although some guests arrive with an agenda, most of them tend to wake up the first morning after arrival, yawn, stretch, and ask, "So, what are we going to do today?" Having a plan in advance can make the visit more enjoyable and less frustrating for both of you.

Before your guests arrive, scope out places and activities that may interest them, and make a note of things like hours of operation, directions, travel time, and the availability of food and restrooms. Then you can either plan the whole visit yourself, or, if your guests are more independent, present them with options to choose from. Beware of guests who have already "done their homework" and arrive with an impossibly full agenda. Don't be shy about trimming their schedule a bit.

Find some guest-friendly restaurants. Here's a pathetic sight: expatriates and their guests wandering around a foreign city well past lunchtime, saying, "Where do you think we should eat?" "I don't know; where would you like to eat?" "What about this place?" "I'm not sure; it looks expensive." "What do you think?" You can avoid this painful experience by checking out restaurants in advance in the areas you plan to visit with your guests. Consider your guests' tastes, dietary requirements, and budgets, of course, as well as their interest in getting to know the local cuisine. Look for a restaurant offering menus in English, if possible, to spare yourself the headache of translating each menu item (usually more than once) for everyone at the table.

Call in reinforcements. Being burdened with constant cooking, cleanup, and laundry chores on top of translation and tour-guide services will not help you enjoy your time with your guests. Consider hiring extra household help during the visit, or booking your guests into a nearby hotel or guest house instead of having them stay with you. Likewise, if your guests are uncomfortable about venturing out on their own, it is no disgrace to set them up with a bus tour, professional tour guide, and/or driver at times, especially to visit attractions you have seen many times before.

You might even feel that you can assign them a few chores. For example, Patricia's parents enjoy going grocery shopping alone in foreign countries—they may return with sour cream instead of yogurt, but it's all part of the adventure. Her mother-in-law loves to cook and even brings her own ingredients in her suitcase—now *that* is a welcome guest!

Build in downtime. Too much togetherness can turn an enjoyable visit into an ordeal. If you are not working outside the home, find a reason to get away for a few hours at times. Even something as mundane as a haircut can be a welcome break. One expatriate puts it this way: "I like elderly visitors best. They take naps!"

Make the visit enjoyable for you. Take your guests somewhere *you* want to go—not just the same tourist destinations you've already visited. If you have children, ask your guests to babysit one evening while you enjoy an evening out. Grandparents may even offer you the opportunity for a longer getaway without your kids, once they are accustomed to the country and if they have reliable support (perhaps from other expatriates) in case of an emergency.

Also, don't be shy about asking your guests to bring specific home-country treats with them—they'll probably be wondering what to bring you anyway and will appreciate the advice.

Keeping up with colleagues and your career

Working abroad can broaden your professional vision, fill you with new ideas, and help you advance in your field. On the other hand, many expatriates report feeling left behind when they return to their home countries. The colleagues they previously worked with may have moved on, and the technologies and even the important issues at work may have changed. Instead of viewing the expatriate's time overseas as valuable enrichment, colleagues at home may see it merely as time out from the career track. Returning expatriates often complain of being given lower positions and having to carve out a niche for themselves all over again. Statistics show that a large number actually leave their organizations within a few years. Luckily, there are numerous ways to prevent these problems, whether you work for a large organization, are going abroad to do something other than your regular career, or are accompanying your partner overseas.

Recruit a mentor. An experienced, helpful person in your field or within your organization can do wonders for your career continuity. He or she can keep you informed about changes in your field, speak up for your interests within your organization, look out for opportunities on your behalf, and give you advice about keeping current and competitive. If your organization does not have a formal mentoring program, try to recruit a mentor yourself, perhaps in exchange for reports on the situation in your host country.

Stay involved. Keep yourself informed about the current situation in your field with the help of a network of colleagues. As with your mentor, you can keep the e-mail flowing with interesting reports about the situation in your host country and other useful contributions. Consider offering your help to the home office as a consultant or project committee member via e-mail. Working with you on a regular basis helps remind colleagues at home that you are part of the team. Regular contact will also help you stay "in the loop" with events and issues in your field.

Broaden your knowledge and experience. You can stay active in your field while overseas by subscribing to professional journals, reading and contributing to relevant websites, and so forth. Consider attending conferences and workshops, if possible, or taking professional courses online to keep up with developments in your field and continue moving your career forward. If you are not working in your field abroad, consider volunteering in a related position. Remember to document any training and volunteer work on your résumé.

Network during home leave. In between visiting relatives, shopping for necessities, and vacationing, schedule some time to get together with your mentor and other colleagues at home. Face-to-face contact every year or so helps remind people about your specific strengths and interests. Your colleagues may also provide information in a relaxed, face-to-face setting that they might be reluctant to share in an e-mail.

Maintaining your own culture overseas

After the adjustment period of the first few months, an expatriate's level of cultural adaptation will fall somewhere along a sliding scale. On one end of the scale is a state of nearly complete isolation from the host culture, perhaps within a foreigners' compound. On the other end is what expatriates often call "going native"—living as the local people do, speaking their language and not your own, and dropping your accustomed cultural practices in favor of the host culture's.

Isolation from the host culture may be necessary at times (for instance, if you are assigned to a war zone), but it denies you the benefits of confronting and understanding new ways of thinking and living. On the other end of the scale, many expatriates who immerse themselves completely in a foreign culture experience a strong case of reverse culture shock when they return to their home countries or move to a third culture.

During your time overseas, you will have to strike your own balance between adopting local ways and maintaining your habits from home. This balance will depend on factors such as the degree of difference between the host culture and yours, your personal level of comfort with host-country practices, and the size of the community of expatriates available to help support your home-culture lifestyle. You may also consider it more important to maintain elements of your home culture if you have children.

Patricia reports:

My attitude toward cultural assimilation changed quite drastically after I had children. As a graduate student in Germany, I leaned far toward the "going native" end of the scale. In fact, my husband and I shared housing with Germans and spoke the language throughout our student

*year there. When we returned to the United States, we sounded funny at
first when we started speaking English! Nine years later, however, when
our first child was born abroad, we realized that he would need a more
stable cultural identity, not one that changed completely when we took
on a new overseas assignment every three or four years.*

Dual-culture couples, in which the partners are from two different
countries (a common phenomenon among expatriates), may also consider
it especially important to maintain their cultures within the home. For
example, we know a family with a Swiss mother and Brazilian father who
are living in Germany. The children speak both Swiss German and Por-
tuguese as well as standard German, enjoy Swiss and Brazilian traditional
foods at home, listen to Brazilian music, follow Brazilian soccer, and go skiing in Switzerland. Their home is a lively mixture of cultural influences, and
the children identify strongly with the countries of both of their parents.

Back in your home country, of course, your culture surrounded you—
you could not escape it. Overseas, however, following your own cultural
traditions requires some preparation and effort.

Keep current with your culture. Cultures are fluid; they change over time,
especially in the fast-paced wealthy countries of the world. Isolated overseas, you may find yourself caught in a time warp, unaware of new technology, current events, music, fashions, habits, and topics of conversation.
To keep up with events at home and make your eventual reentry much
easier, try to follow not only the top news stories but also the everyday
events unfolding in your home country. If you have access to the Internet,
keep up with a range of websites and blogs. You may be able to watch
home-country television programming over a satellite, cable, or online
service. If not, consider asking (or even paying) someone back home to
record a few shows on a regular basis. Magazines from your home country
are also an excellent way to keep current. If you can't subscribe from overseas, ask visitors to bring a few in their suitcases.

Create a cultural "oasis" in your home. Many expatriates feel most comfortable creating an "oasis" of familiar culture within their homes overseas. Before you move, think of cultural traditions from home you may
want to follow overseas—such as sports, crafts, or music—and take along
the necessary supplies. You may even want to take up a tradition you

neglected in your busy life at home, such as your grandmother's needle-work or the model airplanes your father built with you. There often seems to be more time for such things overseas.

Cultural traditions even include the foods you grew up eating. You may find yourself craving the typical tastes, even the junk food, of your home country. Melissa once paid $12 for a jar of Hellmann's mayonnaise in a Nigerian store—not because the mayonnaise itself was so wonderful, but because it was a reminder of home. Consider taking along a supply of nonperishable familiar foods or ingredients if they are not available in your host country (see chapter 3).

Celebrate holidays overseas. Celebrating holidays overseas may seem strange or even impossible at first. The host country may celebrate the holiday differently or not at all, the traditional supplies you expect may not be available, and even the weather may seem completely wrong. If your country's traditional holiday decorations and supplies are not available where you live, a few special items packed into your household shipment or sent by helpful relatives can seem like treasures. It can also be fun to improvise. One American we knew in Cuba made a jack-o-lantern for his front porch on Halloween, using a large grapefruit instead of a pumpkin! Having host-country or third-country guests at your holiday celebration can make it even more enjoyable, as they ask questions and enjoy getting into the spirit of the occasion.

Patricia reports:

> *In Chile, I found myself strangely unsettled by the reversal of seasons from the pattern I was used to: Halloween arrived in glorious springtime, while Easter came amid the spooky, swirling dead leaves of fall. I often felt like my heart wasn't in it when I set out to celebrate a holiday overseas. But somehow my heart always seemed to take the cue and get into the spirit anyway.*

A British expatriate makes a point of celebrating Pancake Day (Shrove Tuesday) in Spain:

> *We have friends around, both Spanish and British, and cook the traditional pancakes, rolled up and eaten with lemon and sugar.*

A Canadian woman in Japan reports:

In Japan, the women give the men chocolate on Valentine's Day. A man's popularity is indicated by the amount of chocolate he receives. I follow my own tradition and give everybody Valentine's cards.

We have been privileged overseas to be invited to other expatriates' celebrations as well, such as British bonfires for Guy Fawkes Day and a new-baby party among Saudi Arabian women in Washington, D.C. However, cross-cultural misunderstandings are always a possibility.

Melissa reports:

When we lived in France, a group of the Americans in our church decided to introduce our French friends to a real American Thanksgiving dinner. We prepared the traditional foods, including turkey and pumpkin pie. I am not a pumpkin pie fan, so I brought a lemon meringue pie instead. The Americans dug in with gusto, piling their plates high with all the delicious Thanksgiving foods. We sat down, chatted, and started to enjoy the feast. The French guests were puzzled. They were astounded that we would pile so much on our plates. They were unsure how to begin and asked which of the dishes was the first course. Someone had made a Jell-O salad, and they could not understand how we could eat it with meat. To them, it looked like it should be a dessert. The real dessert was a major disappointment. None of the French guests liked the pumpkin pie. When they saw my lemon meringue pie, several of them exclaimed, "Ah, une tarte aux citrons!" My pie disappeared immediately.

Practice your religion. Many expatriates report that they don't really feel settled abroad until they find a way to practice their religion. English-speaking churches and other expatriate religious communities are common in many large international cities. Alternatively, if your religion is practiced in your host country, it can be very rewarding to attend services with the local people. One Jewish expatriate assigned to Tunisia was surprised to find a small but ancient and "very spiritual" Jewish community there; she reports that her connection to her religion deepened during her time in the country.

If your religion is not represented in your host country, however, you may have to be creative in following your traditions. In numerous countries, we have known small groups of expatriates who organized their own in-home religious services and found them very satisfying. Even if you find yourself completely alone, you can probably find inspirational readings, communities, and services to follow online, or you can observe traditional rituals at home. Be sure to bring along any books and supplies you may need.

Home leave

Whether or not you plan to return to your home country at the end of your stay abroad, traveling there on a regular basis is another very important way of keeping in touch with your roots. It can be tempting to use all of your scarce vacation time to explore exotic places overseas, but home leave can serve a number of very useful purposes: it is a time to catch up with family and friends, see what has changed, enjoy your favorite foods, shop for a few familiar products to take back with you, check in with your doctor and dentist, and remind yourself how it feels *not* to be a foreigner for a while.

If you are planning to return home after your time overseas, we recommend visiting once a year or at least every two years if possible. The longer you stay away, the more you will feel like a stranger when you return—and the more you will seem like a stranger to the people back home. Here are some ideas to help you get the most out of home leave.

Set up a home base. Rushing around from place to place to visit relatives and friends wastes valuable time and can be extremely tiring. Consider reversing the situation: rent a temporary apartment in your hometown or a vacation home in an attractive and convenient destination, and invite everyone to come and see you. (As an added bonus, if someone doesn't find time to see you during your visit, *they* get to feel guilty, not you!)

Throw a party. If dozens of friends will be upset if they don't see you, but you'll only be in town for a week, having a big get-together might be a solution. (Another might be to avoid letting them know you are there in the first place!)

Minimize all those chores. When you're abroad and think of something that needs to be done in your home country, it's easy to tell yourself, "I'll take care of that during home leave." However, huge lists of chores can make home leave a nightmare. It's better in the long run to find ways to handle as many errands as possible from abroad—both for your sanity during home leave and your ability to take care of personal business overseas.

- Be sure to maintain good relationships with your accountant, broker, property manager, and so forth via e-mail, so you don't have to visit their offices during home leave.
- Order special home-country purchases online, if possible, instead of rushing around to shop while at home. Or ask a helpful friend or relative to shop for you in advance of your arrival, so you can simply carry the purchases back with you.
- Take care of routine medical and dental checkups and tests abroad, to lessen the time you spend running to doctors and dentists at home.

Find children something to do. If you are on an extended home leave with children, signing them up for some kind of structured activity—such as a summer day camp, swimming lessons, or sports camp—is an excellent idea. While you take care of chores and appointments, they will meet other home-country kids and naturally begin fitting back into their home culture. Having something challenging to do also helps kids avoid thinking of home leave as an endless parade of special attention and gifts from relatives.

Moving on to the next country

If you will be moving on to another foreign country after your current expat experience, start reading this book for the second time! In spite of all that you have learned abroad, you will need to begin all over again with your research and planning. Even if the two countries are culturally similar and you don't need to learn a new language, the living conditions in the new place and your own personal situation may differ in surprising ways.

You may hope that after one international move, you are accustomed to the experience and will have an easier time adjusting. It's true that you will be more familiar with the tasks of packing, moving, and getting set up. But as we have learned in our own mobile lives, the more personal aspects of moving—weathering transition shock, making a place for yourself in the new environment, and building a social network—remain nearly as challenging as they were the first time. A recent study of expatriate women showed that previous international experience did not significantly affect their current level of adjustment.*

In fact, some expats who have moved multiple times start to neglect important tasks such as making friends, since they know from experience how much work it is and how soon the next round of good-byes will come along. If you find your thoughts tending in this direction, make an effort to turn them around. Having friends and getting properly settled overseas takes work—the first time or the fifteenth—but it is essential to your well-being. We know that the good-byes are painful, but we also know from experience that international friendships can remain satisfying and enduring, through e-mails, phone calls, and visits, long after you've left the country.

Reentry issues

People naturally expect moving abroad to be challenging. However, many think that moving back to their home country will be easier, not requiring much preparation and adjustment. Ask nearly any returned expatriate, however, and you will find that this is not the case. Many, in fact, have found the reentry process even more stressful and challenging than their initial move overseas. There are a number of reasons why the transition back home is so difficult.

First, the same change overload, sadness at leaving, and self-doubt you faced when originally moving overseas revisits you in full force when you return home. As we mentioned in chapter 7, transition shock doesn't

---

*"Many Women Many Voices" Study of Accompanying Spouses Around the World, conducted by Dr. Anne P. Copeland at The Interchange Institute (*www.interchangeinstitute.org*) and commissioned by Prudential Financial.

only arise from the experience of confronting strange foreign customs. It is also caused by the stress of changing your habits and routines, finding your way in a different environment (perhaps a new job, home, and/or school), and missing the places and people you left behind. All of these apply to a move back home as well as a move abroad.

Second, you will have changed. After the initial shock of adjustment, you may have learned to feel at home overseas. When you return to your country, you may find that things "feel wrong"— just like someone who has gotten used to a low-salt diet or skim milk may suddenly be shocked by the taste of salted food or whole milk. Some of these changes may be permanent; being exposed to other ways of perceiving and thinking may have altered your perspective for good. The longer you have been away, the more likely you are to feel that you have changed and no longer belong where you once did. You may feel like an "invisible immigrant"— you look the same and people may expect you to be just as you were, but you're not; your experiences have changed you.

A returning expatriate notes:

> It's been much more difficult than the move to Germany. Maybe it's because I expected it to be difficult in Germany. Maybe it was because it was a temporary adventure. The other surprising thing to me is how much I miss Germany. Home seems so sterile and strange now. Yesterday in the store I couldn't remember how to say "pea soup" in German, and I burst into tears.

Also, you may experience changes in your home environment and personal situation. Colleagues and neighbors may have moved on; businesses you frequented may have closed. You may be bewildered by new technology that others around you take for granted. At work, far from being appreciated and respected for your experiences abroad, you may feel that you have been forgotten while you were away and that your new skills are considered irrelevant. You may have gotten used to being a "big fish" overseas and must now confront a radical change in your social and work status. Or instead of coming home, you may find yourself adjusting to an unfamiliar part of your own country.

A returned expatriate recalls:

We had been so impressed by our son's adjustment abroad. He went to a local school and was thrown into the language and culture. He never complained. For work reasons, though, we returned to a new state instead of our native one after our assignment. Our adaptable son suddenly became an emotional wreck. He had assumed we would return to the same house, and to his old friends, after a few years abroad. That had been the bargain, in his mind, and when it fell through, everything crashed to the ground.

This may sound strange, but expatriates become used to the feeling of being different, of being noticed, and of living in an exotic place. Back home, these feelings evaporate. You are no longer a special person in a special place—and if you have trouble with the details of everyday life at first, the excuse of being a foreigner is gone.

During the settling-in process, you may find you have more work and less support. Organizations rarely provide the same level of support for a move back home that they do for an overseas move. When you arrived overseas, you probably had access to a community of expatriates who understood your difficulties and helped you through the rough spots. At home, however, everyone may seem too busy to help. You may have to find your own housing, buy a car, handle work problems, get the kids in school, unpack the household, and much more, with no special support from your organization. And let's not forget household chores! You may have gotten used to having household help abroad, and the sudden realities of cooking, food shopping, and laundry can be a rude awakening.

Last, and possibly the most painful to deal with, is the lack of understanding from others. As we have mentioned elsewhere, people gravitate toward others with whom they have something in common. This phenomenon, which was so helpful when you were making friends with other expatriates overseas, is turned against you now. Most people at home will have trouble relating to your experiences overseas. To many, your stories and offhand remarks about visiting the pyramids in Egypt or shopping in Italy may sound like bragging—as if you were talking about riding in your limousine or sailing on your private yacht. You may even find them reacting defensively, as if your tales of worldly adventures are somehow intended as a criticism of your home country or their own "boring" lives.

A British expatriate who lived in Washington and Warsaw states:

People don't want to hear about your great adventures in another country. And they really don't want to hear about the things you thought were better over there. The hardest time comes after a month or so, when you're still having trouble, and everyone says, "You're home; what's your problem?"

We close this chapter with one final list, one we hope will help you minimize the stresses of reentry if and when you return home.

- Maintain strong family ties and friendships, cultivate good relationships with colleagues, and keep up-to-date with cultural information while you are abroad. They can all ease your readjustment.
- Prepare for reentry and readjustment as much as you prepared for going overseas.
- Say a proper good-bye when leaving your host country, as we recommended when leaving your original home (see chapter 3).
- Be prepared for transition shock. Expect to have trouble readjusting at first, and recognize that this is normal and you are not alone.
- Prepare for conversations with friends and family. People at home may ask politely about your experiences overseas, but their eyes may soon glaze over if you launch into long stories or explanations. A good solution is to be prepared with a funny anecdote, a little-known fact about a famous place, or an interesting prediction about your host country's future development. Then quickly change the subject to a topic of interest to people at home.
- Be sure to listen and ask questions of the people at home, rather than monopolizing the conversation, even if they continue to ask about your experiences abroad.
- Seek out people with international experience. Just as you did overseas, look for people who will understand what you are going

through. People who have lived in other countries, no matter which ones, are likely to understand your dilemmas—and be interested in your stories! If you don't have colleagues who have worked abroad, seek out contacts through international clubs, expatriate websites, or an international school in your area. Consider immigrant groups, language schools, and international students in university programs as well.

- Maintain your ties to the country you have just left. Although it may seem pointless or make you sad at first, keep in touch with the friends you left behind.
- If you have family members with you, try to maintain the spirit of teamwork that you probably developed overseas.
- Keep the lines of communication open among family members, and make sure everyone's concerns are taken seriously and addressed.
- Take time to remember your experiences overseas together, too. Look at photos, laugh over mishaps, and reminisce about your travels together.
- Seek out opportunities for fun and adventure, just as you did when you arrived abroad. You may think of your home country as familiar territory compared with your life overseas, but look for new things to discover.
- If you find your work and your daily routine dull and even depressing after the challenges of overseas life, look for ways to enrich them. Volunteer for a special project at work or in the community, take a professional development or continuing education course, or consider striking out in a new direction.
- Get involved. The feeling of belonging to a community may be the best remedy for reentry shock. Choose some old or new interests and follow them. As you did overseas, make an effort to meet your new neighbors and make new friends. You'll soon be feeling at home again.

Conclusion

In this book, we have tried to give you most of the tools to prepare for a successful and enjoyable experience overseas and transition home. We say "most," because there is one more essential tool we would like to mention, as unnecessary as it may seem: your own personal attitude. How you choose to face the inevitable ups and downs of expatriate life can either help or hinder your adjustment abroad.

As we have described, moving abroad (even to an "easy" country) is an enormous challenge. You may have to come to terms with unfamiliar rules and customs, a new language, uncooperative local authorities, new colleagues with their own ideas about how things should be done, family members' difficulties, and a thousand little frustrations in daily life, from leaky pipes in your new housing to the unavailability of your favorite breakfast cereal.

Especially when you first arrive overseas, you may feel as if you have little control over what happens to you. One thing you *can* control, however, is your own attitude and the way you choose to react to your circumstances. Although the natural reaction may be to become angry, resentful, or even depressed, in the long run these feelings can negatively affect your overseas experience as well as your health.

It is never easy to get a grip on emotions, especially when we feel unjustly hurt or wronged in some way. However, making the effort—however difficult—to maintain a balanced attitude and emotional state is a constructive step that steers you in a positive direction. You will have better health *and* be a happier person. Ultimately, your life overseas will be richer for it.

Your sense of humor can be one of the most effective tools to help you maintain your emotional balance. Consider sharing the stories of your mishaps abroad with family and friends. Many expatriates write up hilarious accounts of their misadventures, which they e-mail home, post on a blog, or even publish in their hometown newspapers.

Staying active and involved is another excellent way to keep your attitude positive while overseas. If you are feeling overwhelmed by events overseas—your shipments still haven't arrived, you dislike the apartment the company has chosen for you, and the bus driver yelled at you today for having the wrong ticket—get moving; take control of your life in whatever way you can. Enroll in a language class, go sightseeing with a friend, join a volunteer group, or take up a new sport.

Finally, and perhaps most important of all, open yourself to all of the benefits of living abroad. Expatriates have the privilege of getting to know another country more thoroughly than any tourist. The challenges of overseas life are undeniable, but the advantages you will gain overseas are greater: travel opportunities, new friendships, language skills, increased flexibility, intercultural awareness, a broader worldview, and even stronger family ties as you experience trials and adventures together.

When you hike to a waterfall deep in a rain forest, bargain for a carpet in a Middle Eastern market, see the smile on the face of a sick child you have helped through volunteer work, explore centuries-old ruins, talk with new friends at a sidewalk café in the local language, swim at a deserted beach, watch traditional craftspeople at work, or discover gourmet cuisine in one of the world's leading cities, you'll remember why you agreed to move abroad. It's a fascinating world out here—welcome to it!

For further research

Because resources become obsolete so quickly these days, especially online, we offer an updated list of the resources relevant to this book on our website, *www.expatguide.info*. We hope you'll visit our site for more information about organizations, websites, and books that may help support you before, during, and even after your international adventure.

About the authors

Melissa Brayer Hess is the creator of Foreign Service Lifelines, the website of the Associates of the American Foreign Service Worldwide, located at *www.aafsw.org*. She has an M.A. in education and has taught English as a second language in Europe, Africa, and the U.S. She has also worked as a newsletter editor, cross-cultural trainer, and educational writer. In addition, Melissa is a licensed Registered Nurse and her medical background includes experience in medical-surgical, operating room, and hospice nursing. Melissa and her husband have lived and worked in Paris, France; Kaduna, Nigeria; Leningrad, U.S.S.R.; Oran, Algeria; Sinai, Egypt; and Kiev, Ukraine.

Patricia Linderman has an M.A. in German and works as a freelance writer, editor, and translator from Spanish and German into English. She is Editor in Chief of the nonprofit expatriate website Tales from a Small Planet (*www.talesmag.com*). She has also worked as a language teacher, foreign student program director, and U.S. embassy community liaison office coordinator, among other positions. Patricia first lived abroad as a graduate student in Erlangen, Germany, with her husband in the position of accompanying spouse. When he joined the U.S. Foreign Service, she was happy to reverse the roles, raising two multilingual, globally aware sons while living and working in Port of Spain, Trinidad; Santiago, Chile; Havana, Cuba; Leipzig, Germany; and Falls Church, Virginia.

Appendix: A Sample Moving Plan

The following is a general moving plan that covers the typical preparations involved in an overseas move. This plan assumes that you have at least six months to prepare for your international move, which is ideal. Of course, if you have less time than this, you will need to speed up the process. Take your timetable into account when drawing up your own plan. We suggest that you prepare your own version of this plan with the specific tasks and timetables that apply to your particular case. Divide the chores with your spouse if you are married, and decide where older children, friends, relatives, or hired professionals may be able to help. Post the list in a prominent place in your home to remind you to stay on track when the inevitable distractions of everyday life get in the way.

As soon as you make the decision to go

- Obtain passports for everyone in the family, including young children.
- Check on visa and work permit requirements, and make applications as necessary.
- Read through this entire book to get an idea of the challenges and issues you will face abroad.
- Negotiate benefits with your employer according to your needs and/or make plans to obtain needed support from relocation agencies, moving companies, etc.

- Identify and start reading books, websites, and blogs with information about your host country (e.g., expat life, culture, current events, history, the natural environment, etc.).
- Begin studying the language and culture of your host country, independently or in a formal training program.
- Begin making contacts in the host country (with colleagues and/or other expatriates).
- Choose a relocation consultant and local real estate agent if you do not have full support from your employer.
- Check out housing, living conditions, schools and schooling requirements, work permit requirements and spouse employment opportunities, and requirements for bringing pets, if applicable.
- Find out about medical requirements; for example, a series of vaccinations may be necessary.
- Get tax, financial, and insurance advice (including health, property, and auto insurance) from professionals who work with expats.
- If you own a home, decide what you will do with it—rent it, sell it, or leave it empty. Choose a real estate agent as soon as possible if you plan to sell.
- If you are a renter, review the terms of your lease.
- Plan an exploratory trip to your host country, if possible.
- Request sufficient time off from work to handle moving chores.

Five months before departure

- Choose a moving company.
- Based on your research, select insurance plans (health, property, auto, etc.).
- Get detailed information about shipping your belongings, pets, and car (if applicable).
- Purge children's belongings, if necessary.
- If you have both children and pets and cannot take a family pet abroad, find a home for it now, so that your children's sadness over the loss of the pet does not coincide with your departure.
- Begin working with a property manager if you intend to rent out your home.

Four months before departure

- Start preparing lists of what goes into storage, what will be shipped by airfreight and seafreight, and what you will take with you in your luggage.
- Decide what to do with high-value or irreplaceable objects.
- Arrange a premove survey with your moving company.
- Organize your important documents (as described in chapter 3) and identify a secure place to store the ones you leave behind (such as a lawyer's office or a bank safe-deposit box).
- Prepare a power of attorney for your spouse and/or a trusted relative.
- Arrange ways to handle your bank accounts, credit cards, and mail while abroad.
- Get advice from people with experience in your host country about appliances and supplies you might need abroad (see chapter 3) and begin purchasing these.
- Have medical and dental checkups, including vaccinations, and ask for health records you can take with you. Also obtain advice about maintaining your health abroad, and ask if you can e-mail questions to your doctor and dentist. Figure out how you will obtain needed prescription medicines abroad.

Three months before departure

- Start actually sorting your belongings and selling or giving away things you don't need.
- Renew your driver's license or find out how to do it online or by mail if it will expire during your time abroad.
- Maintain regular e-mail correspondence with contacts in your new host country. Find out if there is anything you can bring for them. Identify and correspond with a sponsor, if at all possible (see chapter 1).
- Make schooling decisions, if necessary (if schools have waiting lists or you must apply early); notify your children's schools of their departure and ask for records to be sent to the new schools or issued to you to be hand carried.

Two months before departure

- Buy consumables to be shipped with your household effects, if possible.
- Make arrangements to "unlock" your mobile phone, if necessary, and to terminate your contract or transfer it to the new country.
- Prepare your final inventories for shipping and insurance purposes.
- Make travel and hotel or temporary housing reservations; plan a stopover trip, if you decide to take one.
- If you are a renter, give notice to your landlord of your departure date.
- Schedule your packout (at least a week before your actual departure, if possible).

The final month before departure

- Find homes for your houseplants and pets such as tropical fish that you are not taking with you.
- Notify banks and credit card companies that you will be accessing your account from another country.
- Prepare to leave your home; notify utility services (electricity, cable, water, telephone, etc.), newspaper services, post office, and so forth.
- Pack your suitcases and carry-on bags before the movers arrive, and get them out of the house. If you have children, let them choose some treasured belongings to carry with them.
- Ship your belongings (see chapter 3).
- Prepare and send out change-of-address notices, including a Web-based e-mail address.
- Notify your sponsor, relocation consultant, or colleagues in the new country of your arrival information and any specific requests.
- Arrange farewell parties, take pictures, and begin saying your good-byes.

Index